Running Through the Gears

the Gears

by

Harry McPherson Fenton

Disclaimer

I have related my stories as well as I can remember them. I know they are true because I was there and witnessed them. For the one or two tales that were told to me, I am positive they happened the way I tell them. Otherwise, the book would be pointless. I have, however, changed one or two names to protect people`s identities. If there are any mistakes with dates, names, or places it is down to me.

Acknowledgements

Without the help of my old school friends and work colleagues this book could not have been written. Their comradeship and sense of humour kept me going in the hard times and helped me enjoy the good times.

ISBN: 9798464982741

To Phil and Clive, my two great friends.
Died too young and missed every day.

Contents

Introduction

Clipper, Maid of the Seas.

"Ok lads, listen in," I barked "We have an exercise planned for tonight, nothing too serious as it's nearly Christmas. End of exercise and back to the station about nine o'clock for clearing up and stand-down. A nice easy night." That was my brief to the watch after the roll call at 6pm. How wrong I turned out to be!

On the night of 21st December 1988 there were a total of thirteen firemen on duty at Dumfries fire station. We were crewing two fire engines and an emergency tender loaded with cutting equipment and specialist rescue gear. A 100ft turntable-ladder was also available but was only deployed if hi-rise buildings were involved.

The station officer on Red Watch was a reliable, unflappable type, experienced and very able to cope with most emergency situations. The watch was also managed by two leading firemen and myself, the temporary sub officer, responsible for training the men and in charge of a fire engine. The remainder were a pretty typical bunch of firemen, guys like them sat on fire engines across the land. On most watches there was a practical joker, a couple of moaners who took the fun out of everything, several skilled old hands, the sportsmen and a new lad desperate to be accepted by the others. Dumfries and Galloway fire brigade has only one full-time station. Emergency cover across most of the Region was provided by retained firemen. These tradesmen, all volunteers who lived within 5 minutes of their local fire stations, were capable firefighters and skilled at dealing with RTAs. They had to be, the incidents they attended were in their own communities and assistance was often at least 20 minutes away.

That evening, after the 6pm shift change and parade, I took the emergency tender to a derelict care home in Dumfries.The evening was cold and still. Stars were shining brightly in the night sky above us as we set up our equipment. The home was due to be knocked down and I had obtained permission to hold a training exercise in the building before the demolition. Deep inside, I had rigged up a couple of smoke generators to make searching the building as realistic as possible. My driver helped me drag heavy canvas dummies into the building. The crews would search the premises and attempt to locate and rescue the person-sized dummies. The last one to be positioned and always the hardest one to find was the child-sized dummy. Usually it was hidden in a cupboard or under a sofa.

We had just finished our task when I received a message from the control room operator, "Come in Harry, exercise aborted, please return to Dumfries fire station, a military aeroplane has crashed into a garage in Lockerbie." This sounds like it could be interesting, I thought, as we quickly turned off the smoke machines and drove rapidly back to base wondering what the night had in store for us.

I pulled into the appliance bay to find the two fire engines had been dispatched to the incident and the retained crew for Dumfries were gathering together in the station. They had been summoned from their homes by pager and once a full complement of six arrived, they too headed to Lockerbie, blue lights flashing and horns blaring. The journey took about eighteen minutes. The crews would all have seen the red glow in the sky over Lockerbie as they approached but nothing could have prepared them for the sights that met them on arrival in the town. Realising that we may have a major incident in progress I made two quick decisions. I told the next four retained firemen that arrived, to load a truck with all of our twenty five litre containers of fire-fighting foam and then head for the incident. I reasoned that if a garage with fuel tanks underneath had been crashed into by any type of jet it would very quickly be an inferno. We would need all the foam we could get our hands on to put it out before it spread to the surrounding premises.

I then grabbed hold of a full-time fireman who had turned up in response to the newsflash on the television. He was on sick leave, unable to work, but wanted to make himself useful anyway. I gave him a pen and sheet of paper, sat him in the watch room and told him to take the names of any other firemen reporting for duty and the time that they did so. Unforgivably, when the next few men turned up he joined them and drove to Lockerbie in a private car, going against my order. This left us with no way of knowing who was attending the incident and how long they had been there. During the evening many more off-duty firemen arrived at Dumfries station to help out. They organised themselves into teams, picked up their gear and made their way to the scene in their own cars.

I decided to check the control room to see if the two staff working there needed a hand. In 1988 the female controllers were still doing everything manually, before computerisation of the brigade's communications system. Messages, by now, had come back from the fireground that started to reflect the full size of the incident and the scene was quickly labelled a major disaster. Retained crews from across the region were mobilised, the ones nearest the incident were sent directly to it and crews from further west were moved towards Dumfries to provide fire cover in their absence.

The hard-pressed controllers were working flat out under severe pressure. I was handed an index file and told to telephone the utilities and the council offices to inform them of the on-going incident. I gave whoever answered my calls a rough outline of what I knew about the situation, then impressed on them all that it was indeed a major disaster and that they needed to respond quickly and with significant resources.

The firemaster, who lived close by, strode into the control room looking very serious. Following a quick briefing by the senior controller he took command of the incident. At this stage it was still thought that the aeroplane involved was a military jet. No mention had been made of a passenger airliner.

He ordered me to take the turntable ladder to the incident in case it was needed to carry out rescues from rooftops. I was delighted to be given the chance to get across to Lockerbie. I gathered up my firegear and slung it into a locker on the huge vehicle. I hadn't driven the turntable ladder since my promotion a year or so before but was a confident driver. An officer jumped in alongside me and started dressing himself as we pulled out of the appliance bay, bells ringing and blues flashing.

A few hundred yards from the fire station I tried to negotiate a difficult corner controlled by traffic lights and cut it a bit short. As I turned, in my rear-view mirror I could see the front of a Ford Orion being lifted off the ground by the back end of the huge vehicle. I was only moving at walking pace and decided the driver of the car probably hadn't been injured. The officer sat next to me was oblivious to the collision. I said nothing and instantly decided to press on to Lockerbie, hoping the occupant of the car would understand why I didn't stop. (He did understand. He finally reported the accident several days later).

We could see a glow in the sky above the town as we approached and as we crossed the bridge over the M74 we were met by a truly amazing spectacle. A huge fire was burning to our right-hand side almost on the motorway itself. Smoke was billowing from this and many smaller fires around it. I parked the TTL down a side road and made my way towards the fire. The devastation in that part of the town was incredible. Twelve or fourteen of the houses were ablaze in one road. Aviation fuel had fallen onto their roofs and caught alight. Many of these fires had then spread down into the rooms below. Debris from the 500mph impact of the wings and part of the fuselage had been blown up into the air, then landed in the streets around about, along with the contents of a house that had been hit by the wreckage. Many of the passengers will probably have been inside the fuselage when it hit the ground. I remember seeing half a radiator sticking out of a flowerbed, the remainder having embedded itself underground. The surrounding area was about nine inches deep in soft soil, thrown up by the massive impact, mixed in with thousands of small pieces of aluminium, all tiny parts of the aeroplane. The unmistakable smell of avgas, reminiscent of airport runways, was all pervading, mixed with huge plumes of billowing smoke. I was reminded of urban war scenes where two sides had fought an action then pulled out, leaving carnage behind them but not totally destroying the battleground.

Small groups of firemen, in their old-style yellow legs and donkey jackets were moving in and out of clouds of smoke, dragging fire hoses behind them. Even though it was a dark, mid-winter evening, the whole fireground was illuminated by the many fires. Further down the road the biggest fire raged. I was tasked to chaperone a police video cameraman, who was filming the scene for evidential purposes. We walked carefully towards the major conflagration and crept ever closer, bending low as we did so. We could feel the searing heat through our uniforms and were shocked by the intense wall of flames coming out of the gaping hole in the ground. It was the size of two tennis courts end to end and at least twelve feet deep. We were the first to make our way to the crater and seeing the magnitude of it realised that a military fighter jet couldn't have caused such devastation.

I left the cameraman to his own devices when we moved away from the inferno. I wanted to help organise the search and rescue operations going on in the surrounding premises. Water supplies were almost non-existent as the main supply pipe to Lockerbie had been damaged by a jet engine falling onto it. One of the many heroes that night was the fireman that stayed with a lightweight fire pump all night, away from the action, ensuring that the firemen were supplied throughout the incident with a constant supply of water.

Because the devastation covered so many different parts of the town and surrounding hillsides there was very little overall command on the ground in the early stages. Crews relied on using their own initiative to search houses and put out the fires raging inside them and on the rooftops. More and more firemen arrived during the evening, some from Dumfries and Galloway and others from Cumbria and Lothian and Borders. Dumfries and Galloway's mobile control unit was eventually set up near the fireground which made communications easier with the men doing the firefighting.

I stayed in the vicinity of the crater most of the evening whereas most of Red Watch were deployed elsewhere in the town. Gradually we dealt with the fires and a semblance of order was established. Whilst liaising with the control room staff, I made my way through an undamaged part of the town to let them know the situation on the fireground. As I passed some shops I came across a body lying face up on the pavement. There were no signs of injury though the young man was obviously deceased. He was the first intact dead person I saw that night and I was struck by the walking boots he was wearing. He was dressed similarly to, and looked like, many of my friends. The chap was probably going home to his family for Christmas. As I walked on, a policeman arrived and covered him with a blanket.

Hard work from the fire crews gradually turned the tide against the flames. Eventually we were summoned to a briefing that took place about 11pm. The drained firemen were spoken to by a senior officer from Cumbria Fire Brigade who stood on top of a fire engine so that he could be seen. The lads grumbled that one of our own officers hadn't turned up to brief us. That is the problem with an organisation stuffed with yes men, when the chips are down nobody has the

leadership qualities to take charge. Our own brigade officers were tucked safely away in the control unit, which had now moved away from the fireground. They were located with the other command vehicles from different agencies. Unfortunately, they didn't let us know that they had moved, which caused much confusion. At the briefing held outside under the stars, there were about two hundred of us milling around with blackened faces, all talking loudly and full of adrenaline, pleased to see that our colleagues were ok.

The Salvation Army had arrived on the scene fairly early on to provide sustenance. During the briefing I drank the best mug of tea ever and smoked my first cigarette for years, compliments of the Sally Army. Those men and women worked wonders through the night keeping us all hydrated and fed.

Most of the firemen were ordered to go home to get some rest. They needed to be fresh the next morning and there wasn't much they could do now that almost all of the fires had been extinguished. The next phase of the operation would be locating bodies and human remains so they could be sensitively taken to a central point. A makeshift morgue was set up at the town hall for this purpose. At least forty-seven bodies were found to be still strapped into their seats in one part of the fuselage that fell onto the town. Many other bodies were found on the local golf course. One man's body was found on the roof of a house in Sherwood Crescent, lying against a chimney breast. We desperately hoped that one passenger, just one, would be found to have survived. Sadly, it wasn't to be.

Those of us that stayed overnight at the incident carried out various tasks. We damped down the remaining fires and continued the search for bodies and body parts. The police warned us that potential looters were roaming around the site, something we found quite shocking. If we had come across any they would have received some fairly heavy retribution from us. Young soldiers and airmen, I think from training regiments, began to be organised into search teams to scour the hillsides for human remains. We felt sorry for them as their task was a horrible one and, unlike most of us, they hadn't any previous experience of that sort of thing.

At first light we began to take in the sheer enormity of the devastation. I walked around the streets and saw that the partly intact fuselage had come down between two rows of houses, a very near miss for so many town dwellers. The amount of aeroplane wreckage was quite astounding. Scattered everywhere were pieces of broken and twisted aluminium, some pieces as big as cars, with wires wrapped around them, while rags of clothing hung on the sharp edges. Evidence of travellers' baggage lay in the mud. Suitcases, rucksacks and books were mixed in with the aircraft debris. It was quite horrific to view the possessions of the poor passengers and think of what they had been through a few hours previously.

We were given up to date information that Pan Am flight 103, a jumbo jet called Clipper, Maid of the Seas, had left Heathrow airport during the early evening of 21st December, with two hundred and fifty-nine passengers and crew on board. Approximately forty minutes later the plane exploded whilst flying at a height of about 35,000 feet over the town. Everyone onboard perished, along with eleven Scots who lived in the town.

Soon after 8am the day shift from Dumfries arrived to relieve us. We climbed exhausted and hungry into our transport and travelled back to base in virtual silence, alone with our thoughts.

After putting away my firegear I drove home listening to the rolling news coverage about the disaster. Stopping at my local newsagents for a paper I realised my face was still black from the night's exertions. "Some night," said the man behind the counter. I nodded but said nothing.

Part One 1959-1976

Early days in Oxford.

How did a boy who grew up in a different country, many miles from Lockerbie, end up driving a turntable ladder to the UK's biggest ever terrorist incident, in a small Scottish market town that nobody had heard of? My tale is one of good and bad times, humour and tragedy. High drama and periods of intense boredom. On my travels I have worked with kind, funny, interesting people and with some dreadful types who are best forgotten. I may not have climbed Everest or served in the special forces, but I have done and seen many things that few people have the opportunity or the desire to witness. My story is unique but also unremarkable, many others of my generation have similar tales to tell but rarely do so.

I noticed two overriding themes from my younger days that have long gone: the amount of freedom we all enjoyed and the disregard for personal safety that most of us displayed. Yet we nearly all survived into adulthood.

I finished editing this autobiography in July 2021, having begun writing in the Spring of the previous year. Those hard-won freedoms that we enjoyed in our youth are now rapidly disappearing. Over the years, countless millions of servicemen, parliamentarians, civil rights leaders, workers, early trade unionists, suffragettes, feminists and others suffered and died for those rights for common people, so they could live freely and in peace. It appears to me today, that the world's politicians and money men are rapidly taking those rights away. Worse than that, many enfeebled people are gladly giving them up for the illusion of safety. A life without a bit of risk and adventure is no life.

Born in the dying weeks of the 1950s at my parents' home in Headington, Oxford, I was the second son of Judy and Gordon, a big happy baby. It became apparent at my Christening that I was a member of a rather odd family. Uncle Ian was the godparent who named me Clifford John McPherson Fenton. Mum was furious, she didn't like the old Scottish family name, so McPherson was left off my birth certificate. Why they chose the name Clifford I do not know. I never liked it.

My earliest memory is of lying in a hospital bed on my third birthday. My party had ended abruptly when I slid on a rug over a polished floor in my grandmother's house, which resulted in me headbutting a sideboard and badly breaking my nose. For years after I would wake in the night with frighteningly gruesome nosebleeds.

I can also just about recall the bad winter of 1963, there was a foot of snow on our road and the single-glazed windows of our house were frozen for weeks on end. Mum used to transport me to nursery school on the back of her bike. I cried terribly when we arrived but once I was in the building I loved it. We would have a nap at half time, when we were tired, which became a lifelong habit, whenever possible. As small kids, we were able to roam in our small, safe part of Oxford without parental oversight or trouble from older boys. We had the freedom of three roads and a patch of waste ground leading to our favourite playground, a golf course. Like all small boys of that era, we made dens, played war and generally mucked about outside all day. My brother, as ever, deciding the agenda.

Dean, my brother was two years older than me. One of life's natural leaders, wherever and whoever he was with, he called the tune. Very sharp, quick witted and full of ideas, he led us into many scrapes, adventures, and boyhood expeditions. When he was around, you could guarantee boredom was off the agenda. A small guy with a very big personality.

Fireworks night was a major event in our calendar. Building a bonfire was done on the waste ground nearby, for weeks beforehand. All the local boys with their little gangs joined forces to make it a good one. As my birthday was the day before bonfire night I often received boxes of fireworks as presents. I became increasingly miffed about that. Everyone else had toys that lasted more than twenty-four hours. One Bonfire Night we had a party at home where I ate potatoes in their jackets with butter and salt on, for the first time. I can still taste them now. Wonderful simple food on a freezing cold night.

As a family we would travel to the New Forest every summer in a Dormobile camper van. The type with sliding doors and an elevating tarpaulin roof. Harold and Clarice, Mum's parents, would follow us in their Morris Minor. The forest was still undiscovered, and it was possible to just drive onto a Common and camp there. This was probably when Dean and I began our love of nature and the outdoors. We would spend sunny days on Highcliffe beach and walk to Mudeford to see the sailing boats.

At Mudeford beach, one sunny evening in June 1966, we sat outside the Lobster Pot pub and watched England beat Portugal in the World Cup semi-final, whilst eating fish and chips. That was our last ever family holiday. A few days later, back home, the three males of the family watched the final. I think Mum was in the bath, keeping away from the racket in the lounge.

Dad lived for his sport, nothing else ever seemed to interest him. A very talented cricketer, he opened the batting for his school's first eleven when still very young. He excelled at rugby, playing scrum-half for Morris Garages where he worked. He also trained to a good standard in judo and knew how to box. Motorbikes were a permanent fixture during his upbringing, he rode large Nortons and Triumphs, once riding to Cornwall from Oxford with Mum asleep on the pillion.

One Friday, during his National Service with the RAF, Dad was ordered to drive a coach to Paris, loaded with high ranking American and British officers. A dream job for most young men. On dropping them at a hotel he was told to "enjoy the weekend, pick us up on Monday morning."

Rather than sampling the delights of 1950s Paris, Dad turned the coach around, drove back to Oxford, played rugby on the Saturday, football on the Sunday, then headed back to his rendezvous with the officers.

On finishing his national service, Dad worked as an experimental engineer for Morris Garages. His job was, as part of a small team, to turn the blueprints and sketches of concept cars into prototypes. He worked on the new Mini, then test drove it many thousands of miles before it went into production. It's first fuel tank was a five-gallon jerry can strapped into the boot. When he married Mum and they moved into their own house with a garage, he fixed other people's cars, often late into the night. Most of the cars had been built in Oxford and replacement bits were not, ahem, always bought from a parts department. Many years later he admitted to having dug a storage hideaway under the kitchen floor with a trapdoor above it. This was where the half-inched parts were hidden until they were needed to mend somebody's car. The stolen parts were smuggled out of Morris's under an old rain cape, worn when cycling past the security gate. Dad would tie a piece of string around his neck, tie it to the car battery, radiator, or whatever, then balance it on the crossbar.

Cars didn't have rear seatbelts in those days, so if Dad thought we were about to have an accident he would shout loudly "crash drill" to us boys in the back. Our reaction was to quickly dive onto the floor behind the front seats, the safest place if we had a collision. It certainly kept us alert when we were in the car, as he would occasionally have a practise alert and we would race to be first in position.

Going to primary school in Oxford only presented one problem for me, for me, being pressed into itchy long trousers in the winter. Apart from that misery, life seemed very settled and peaceful. My brother and I shared a comfortable bedroom. We had pals, an adventurous time outside, all was good.

Padua Guest House.

My next vivid memory is of sitting in a car in Bournemouth with my brother, wondering what Mum and Dad were up to. They had disappeared into a High Street office and seemed to have been away for an age. We had no idea this was the meeting with an estate agent that was going to turn our lives upside down. My parents were fed up with living in Oxford and because of their love of the sea and the forest, decided to move to Bournemouth. The plan, which was a sound one, was to buy a garage and Dad would make a living doing what he knew best, fixing cars. Unfortunately, the estate agent explained, there was nothing suitable on the market at the time, however, had they ever thought about running a guest house? We have plenty of those to choose from, he said. Mum had never cooked for more than six people and Dad wasn't particularly gregarious, so it seemed to be a ridiculous idea. My parents certainly hadn't given that idea a thought until that moment. But, in the one big brave decision of their entire lives, they took the plunge and very soon owned Padua Guest House. In actual fact, the bank owned most of it and it took years of hard work to pay off the mortgage. Things were financially very difficult for many years.

The move itself was drama free. Past the villages with funny names, Stoke Poges and Sutton Scotney, under the Spitfire Bridge then through the beautiful New Forest and finally down Southern Road, Southbourne, Bournemouth. Our Canary hung in its cage in the cab of the lorry Dad had hired. Padua was a beautifully built brick house of three stories with eight bedrooms. The top floor bedrooms had dormer windows and sloping ceilings. The first floor bedrooms had the benefit of a balcony, which was supported by pillars guarding the front door. It was a substantial house in a road of similar properties. Most of the guest houses had car parks rather than gardens and the road was lined with mature trees. At the northern end of the road was a grove of shops but at the other end, no more than four hundred yards from our new home was the clifftop.

We arrived in April 1967. There was no time to lose, a few weeks later we had twenty-six guests booked in by the previous owners, one of whom died very shortly after they moved out. They had run the accommodation as a Catholic guest house and their old regulars had been coming to stay for the same fortnight for many years. They were in for a surprise. My parents didn't have a religious bone in their bodies, thank god. Job number one was to hire a skip or two and get rid of all the statues and crosses. Most of them were flung off the balcony into the skips, followed by the dreary old curtains and old people's furniture. There wasn't the time or money to alter much else, and anyway, the regulars liked things how they were and had been for many years. There was only one bath and two toilets for the guests, none of this showering every day modern lark. We also had an outside loo for our use that was full of cobwebs.

My brother and I certainly weren't kept in the background. We were given jobs to do from day one and our responsibilities increased as we grew bigger and older. We started by laying the tables and doing a bit of clearing up but soon we became invaluable members of staff. In the summer we started at 8am, I would fill the guests cereal bowls and fruit juice glasses then, when older, help Mum cook the breakfasts. At 9`o`clock I rang the breakfast bell then took orders when the guests sat down to eat. Breakfast was always a fry-up with white toast, tea or coffee. If you were late you missed out. No one ever did. Once the guests had finished their food they all headed for the beach. We would clear the tables, help wash and dry up, lay the tables for dinner then set to on spud peeling. Dad was chief washer-up. He must have stood at that sink for thousands of hours. Not what he had intended but at least he was by the sea. On Saturdays, us boys would have to help clean the bedrooms once the guests had vacated them. My main job was cleaning the sinks and mirrors. As the guests packed up and left, my brother and I would hover around in the hope of receiving tips which we often did. Two bob here and there helped buy fishing gear and bike tyres. Once we had finished our jobs, we were free to do whatever we had planned until 5pm, when we had to be back

in the kitchen ready to go for the evening meal. This took a couple of hours to prepare, serve and clear up. On a hot summer's day it was sweltering in there and if we were a bit salty and sunburnt after a day on the beach it was awful. Those were the times I hated putting on smart formal clothes to do the waiting.

We all seemed to get on pretty well doing the work. There was plenty of laughter at some of the guests, the fatty, the quick eater, the guy that went round the tables when they were empty and pinched all the cold toast. There were times when Mum and I had the giggles in the kitchen and could hardly go back into the dining room to face the guest we were laughing at. One of the redeeming things that kept us all well-behaved was that Mum employed some lovely girls to help out. Linda and Charlotte, who were both bright, funny and very pretty, were around for many years. They lifted the atmosphere by just being around. Clarice also busied herself putting the hoover round and helping with other jobs.

The guests loved their holidays and kept coming back, many re-booked for the same fortnight the following year, before they went back home on the Saturday morning. Quite a few of them became friends with each other and with us. All they wanted was the sea, the sun and good food. Mum's cooking was excellent. There was a two week menu that stayed much the same with fish on a Friday. Good British cooking every day, braised steak, chops, steak and kidney pud. All the usuals with filling puddings. Spotted dick, steam pudding, lemon meringue pie and cherry pie with custard. Dean and I would stand in the kitchen and finish off what the guests hadn't eaten. After a long day adventuring and working we could eat tons of leftovers whilst managing to stay as thin as whippets.

Because Mum and Dad had stretched themselves financially, they had to take as many guests as possible during the summer. Sleeping arrangements from Easter until September for our family were, therefore, pretty grim. Us boys found ourselves relegated to an old garden shed with two small beds to sleep on for the first season. I clearly remember lying there looking up at a gap in the ceiling and seeing the sky. In Bournemouth in those days there used to be terrible thunderstorms. One night, during a particularly violent one my nerve broke and I ran across the garden to the house. In pouring rain I tried to open the back door but to my horror found it locked and I couldn't escape the storm. Lightning streaked across the sky above me, followed a few seconds later by the deafening crash of thunder overhead. I was terrified and still occasionally feel nervous when thunder threatens.

Once the holiday season was over we moved back indoors into bedrooms on the top floor. Mum and Dad bedded down on a z-bed in our back room. I hated the top floor bedrooms when I was a child. Some of our guests felt there was a spooky presence up there and one morning one of our girl helpers came flying down the stairs, white as a sheet as if she had seen a ghost. She thought she had! A little old man in a grey suit, much like the previous owner, in fact. I slept up there with one eye open every winter. Not nice. My brother couldn't care less. After a few years we had a purpose-built chalet put up for us which was much better, but there was still nowhere to do homework or keep stuff permanently.

It was a funny old life. Much different to many of my school friends but we became used to it after a while. There were good and bad sides to it. We met many people and learnt how to be polite and friendly with them. We certainly learnt the value of money and most of all, we got used to hard work and time-keeping which stood us in good stead for the future. The only real downside for me was the lack of a bedroom of our own and somewhere to study peacefully. There was never a choice about how much work we did in the guest house. One look from Dad was enough to quell
any momentary protest.

Primary School.

Pokesdown County Primary School was a lovely little brick school with big tarmac playgrounds, about a fifteen minute walk from our new home. Because there was a surfeit of pupils in my age group, I was put in the class above for a few months when I began there, until the summer holidays. Of course, on the first day of the autumn term I moved down a class into my correct age group and it was like starting again. Very upsetting for an eight year old. The new class teacher held my hand at the front of the room and addressed the class.

"Who will be Clifford's friend," she asked?

One little boy, Philip Metcalfe, raised his hand and agreed to befriend me. He was the best friend a guy could ever wish for. We remained great friends for years until regrettably, time and distance loosened our ties somewhat.

Primary school was great fun once I had settled in with my new class. The schooling was easy, I never found difficulty with any of it but I realised that some poor kids just couldn't understand what seemed to be the simplest sums or English grammar. During lunch-time the boys played war and the girls chalked hopscotch lines on the ground with chalk, or did weird skipping games whilst calling out numbers or rhythms. Lunch was eaten in a long prefabricated building at the bottom of the playground. We sat eight kids at a table. Food was traditional fare, stodge and more stodge but I loved it. We drank water from little aluminium coloured mugs. I was a well-behaved boy but one meal time I was sat in the canteen having filled myself up with a big helping of pie and custard. There was a big dollop of custard on my spoon. For some unfathomable reason I thought it would be funny to launch it, trebuchet style, down the room. To my horror I saw it land, splat, on the cheek of a boy about four tables away. Thankfully, he was so shocked that he never said a word and I got away with it.

There was only one blot on the horizon during my first happy year with my new schoolmates. The dreaded Mr Hooper. He was the teacher in class four and was to be our form teacher the following year. The only male member of staff except for the Head, he was an old guy, probably a war veteran who cycled to work on an old, rod-braked, pushbike and wore the same brown tweed suit every day. Every child that ever went to school knows the type. Some of my young pals were

absolutely terrified. To prepare us for what was coming, we began spending a couple of periods a week being taught by him.

The lesson was always the same. He would draw a simple diagram of a boat or something similar on the blackboard, including its dimensions. Our task was to carefully copy it onto a sheet of A4 paper using a ruler, protractor and a pencil. It sounds easy but if your knees were knocking under your desk it made it all a bit tricky. As we desperately tried to copy the diagram onto paper the old devil would stalk around the classroom reducing the more feeble kids to jelly. On one memorable occasion a rather dim-witted boy was stood next to Hooper at the front of the class being angrily told off. Hooper suddenly leapt back off his chair in astonishment. The poor boy was so scared that he starting weeing out of his little grey shorts onto Hoopers leg. Served him right, the old sod. We thought it was hilarious.

Schooldays saw us learning to write longhand neatly, performing mental arithmetic and reciting times tables. We spent many hours copying the flowing longhand that was popular at the time. Hundreds of F's all across and down a page, then hundreds of G's. Being a leftie made it a bit awkward for me but, as we used pencils, I managed. All of our times tables up to twelve times were written on posters on the classroom walls. We chanted them as a class until they became fixed in our brains. It must have been hell for the teachers listening to us, slowly repeating four fours are sixteen, and the rest, over and over again. We spent ages learning long multiplication and division. Once again, some pupils just couldn't get it. I found that level of work simple and hardly needed to try. Being at the top of the class was a lovely feeling that wasn't to last for much longer!

After surviving a year with Mr. Hooper, whom most of us coped with quite well when we got used to him, we had the joy of being taught by Miss Marks. Young, modern and artistic. We all had a great year and blossomed in her class. By then most of us boys were beginning to notice the girls in the class were different to us in interesting ways. One daft kid let the rest of us know he had feelings for Miss Marks, so we dragged him across the playground to tell her himself.

Our final year at Pokesdown saw us being taught by an old dragon. By this time most of us felt ready to move onto secondary school having spent several years together. Things like fashion were beginning to become apparent in the way some kids dressed. The usual suspects were the ones that always had the new pushbike, or the smart haircut. One lad had a pair of George Best football boots. Wow! They actually had laces up the side. It didn't make him a better player though.

One or two of my friends came from particularly poor homes and it showed. They were always scruffy, with worn out shoes and had an air of poverty about them. We were a pretty classless bunch though and there was no bullying and rarely any fighting. Only one lad in the class of thirty kids was a bit tubby, the rest of us were slim and fit. We played a couple of football matches against other schools but were hopeless even though we all played football every day. But the annual school sports day was looked forward to and ultra-competitive. I won the obstacle course race and was delighted. The sack race was another hotly contested event, as was the three-legged race.

One of the highlights of the week was country dancing in the school hall. It was a terrible time for the less popular girls and boys though. For any dance where you had to partner up, there was a stampede for the pretty girls, whilst the rest were left standing until the slower off the mark boys gradually moved over to them and paired up begrudgingly. Not good for their feelings but we were just young kids, we didn't understand the hurt we caused. An hour of Dashing White Sergeant and other traditional dances was our first chance for us boys to hold hands with a member of the opposite sex that we liked and we wanted to make the most of it.

Since day two at Pokesdown, my brother and I had always walked to school together. It was only about a mile and a half from home. For my last two years there, once he had moved up to the Grammar school, I walked alone in the morning but had the company of friends most of the way home. One afternoon I was mucking about with a friend and a girl with long brown hair. For some daft reason the three of us thought it would be amusing to squeeze our chewing gum into her shiny locks. After we had truly gummed up her hair we said our goodbyes and separated at her front gate. At registration the next morning all hell broke loose. The Headmaster flew into the classroom in a rage. My pal was hauled out of the room for interrogation and I had a feeling in the pit of my stomach of impending doom. Our female friend was also absent, I noticed. About ten minutes later the door was thrown open and the Head was back even angrier than before with a cane in his hand. We had never set eyes on it before and it looked horribly whippy. Nobody was ever caned at Pokesdown. His eyes cast around the room until he saw me. I was terrified.

"You" he cried out, red faced, "I thought better of you. Get out here now."

In his office we both admitted to the offence. Apparently the girl's mother had spent half the night cutting her hair and getting crosser and crosser. She was quite right to be mad, it was a ridiculous thing to do. The Head was a good man and realised we were incredibly sorry and scared stiff so the cane was put away unused, I'm relieved to say. Our female friend was back in the class later and we were all smiles again. She thought it was all highly amusing.

Two incidents in the playground remained with me. There was a boy who was a bit mentally challenged, in the class above mine. One day, he threw a wobbly and ended up climbing up into a large Privet hedge which ran along the back of the schoolground. He was yelling and swearing at everyone. Whilst we crowded round to see what was going on, Mr Hooper, of the wet trouser leg incident, had to follow the lad up into the bristling canopy and pull him down. Much to our amusement of course.

The other time was a bit more serious. Two big hefty lads had a bit of an ongoing disagreement. During a game of footy in the playground one of them snapped and threw a punch whilst shouting loudly at his opponent. He then moved in close and grabbed hold of his adversary's tie which he pulled horribly tight around the boy's throat. The kid was instantly gasping for breath, going white, quite obviously in desperate trouble. I was the nearest person and saw what was going on. I realised I had to act rapidly. I ran up to the struggling boy who hadn't breathed for a minute or so and managed to get my fingers around the ligature and loosened it. He recovered quickly and we just carried on with the game. Nothing more was said about it.

In the Spring term the class went on a wonderful field trip to the Isle of Purbeck. We stayed in a study centre called Leeson House, in Worth Matravers. For me, it was an introduction into the beautiful world of nature and planted a seed in my mind, about the direction I wanted my life to take. Outdoors was much better than indoors. We collected wild flowers and found out their names from the guide books. We watched sea birds in their native habitat, flying over the cliffs and the waves. After dinner, back at the centre, we drew pictures of hawks and owls. Best of all, some of us went badger watching one evening. We lay for ages in a row on a bank, overlooking the sett. At twilight, a couple of stripey heads appeared for a few seconds, sniffed the air, then disappeared back inside. They must have smelt us so we picked ourselves up and left. I was so proud that only the Ranger and I had been awake to catch a glimpse of them. The rest of the kids had fallen asleep in the grass and missed it!

One June morning after assembly we sat at our desks when the Head marched in with a sheaf of

exam papers. He implored us to do our best and to think before we wrote our answers. This, we found out later, was our Eleven Plus exam. There was no fuss, no prepping, no tears or hysterics. The exam was fairly easy, I thought. One or two of the maths questions stretched me a bit but the English writing part was pretty simple.

A couple of months later the results were posted to our homes. I, along with two friends, had been selected to go to Bournemouth School in the autumn, following in my brother's footsteps. I would have been very disappointed if I hadn't been sent to the same school as him. Happily, my old friend Philip Metcalfe who had gone to a local private school for the past couple of years, passed and was going to be there too. The rest of the class were going to the local secondary moderns. There didn't seem to be any problems with the system. No parents complained or demanded a re-test, it was just accepted that some passed and some didn't. Most of the pupils couldn't care less as long as some of their friends were going to the same secondary school as them. The last day of primary school came and went, we left with hardly a goodbye or a look back. Most of the other kids lived nearby anyway. We would stay loosely in touch and, as we grew older, begin meeting up on the beach. I would never be top of the form again, or even near it. I was about to be plunged into an academic nightmare.

In Southbourne Grove there was a clothes shop that supplied school uniforms. One summer morning, in I went with a very proud Mum, to be kitted out. The grammar school uniform was a grey or black suit, worn with a blue and brown tie and cap. Previously, I had worn shorts and a hand knitted jumper over a flannel shirt. Lovely and comfortable even in hot weather. Now I had to look like a young office worker. I was too young and obedient to refuse the cheapest and most uncomfortable trousers in the shop. There didn't appear to be the money available to buy anything soft and comfortable. Mum never realised that I have unusually sensitive skin and am unable to wear anything that is even mildly prickly without suffering.

Years later I was diagnosed with a sensitive skin condition which causes a rash and itching if I wear polyester, wool or rough cotton close to my body. Even denim causes me grief. My entire school uniform including the nylon football shorts felt very uncomfortable every single day. Even my briefcase was plastic and a horrible muddy brown colour. Not very inspiring.

Fishing, The Cubs and Sea Scouts.

Our world was expanding fairly quickly. Southbourne was a very peaceful area of guest houses and retirement homes. There was a useful row of shops that supplied the locals with most of their needs. Many old favourites were there. Woolies, MacFisheries, International Stores, now all gone, of course. The hotel trade also had a cash and carry warehouse some miles away where bulk supplies were loaded up at a small discount. We bought huge square boxes of cornflakes and giant tins of

Knorr soups. Dean and I were often sent up to the grove to shop for meat, fish and vegetables or to buy a newspaper.

Two minutes walk from home was a wonderful boys playground called Fisherman's Walk. Situated between the shops and the clifftop, it was a wide area of Scots Pine and Rhododendron with a path through the middle, about a quarter of a mile long. Halfway along stood a Victorian bandstand in a circle of tarmac. At the far end was a large ornamental fish pond surrounded by benches. It was all very middle-class, polite, clean, Edwardian England. Where you came to holiday or to die. Or both. If you carried on walking along the grove following the bus routes, you would eventually get to Boscombe then Bournemouth centre itself, about three miles away.

As we grew bigger we walked further and further away from home. By the age of ten we were all allowed to get the bus into Bournemouth town centre and go swimming at the Pier Approach pool. Half of my primary school class would meet there on a Saturday morning in the winter. Swim, muck about, hot chocolate, then the bus home. One time some fool pushed one of the boys in and he fell awkwardly, hitting his chin on the poolside and cutting it badly. Cue a scene in the classroom on the Monday with the Head going bananas at the offending idiot.

There were two memorable shops locally. Steptoes, as the name implies, was a junk shop that sold all sorts of interesting stuff from house clearances. Old bikes, books, fridges, mouldy old taxidermy figures of bears and owls. There was probably a German helmet in there somewhere, if you looked hard enough. The shop was full to the ceiling and spilled out onto the road.

Our favourite, though, was George Courage's bike repair and fishing tackle shop. Painted yellow, the shop was a relic from the past even in 1970. The first room was for cycle repairs and spares. Old black rusty bikes, with punctured tyres and rod brakes, leant against each other awaiting new tyres and a drop of oil. Bikes with three speeds, dynamos and chain guards were the norm. Five speed racers were just coming onto the market for the general public. Front lights were heavy affairs with two large batteries that lasted a matter of weeks, before spewing acid over the copper connections, rendering the lamp inoperative. At least they stayed lit up at junctions unlike dynamos, which left you in the middle of the road in the dark! Behind George's pile of broken bikes, was a worktop usually surrounded by old fishermen, dressed in cable knit jumpers with worn elbows and cord trousers. Weather beaten and tobacco stained, these guys all had massive hands and wrists from years of hard manual labour and fresh air. They probably all served with the Navy during the war. George sold bait which he stored under the counter. Rag, Lug or Limpet. They were sold by the dozen, wrapped in newspaper like a bag of chips. The worms were coated in tiny little bits of wood chip that they were stored in before sale. The smell of bait, fish and tobacco in the shop was quite something, especially on a warm day when the worms heated up a bit.

The other room in the shop was devoted to fishing tackle. Wooden shelving was divided into small sections which held the fishing weights. Half ounce, one ounce, up to huge bombs of about six ounces with stiff wire spikes coming out of them. Miles of nylon filament fishing line from 4lbs up to 30lbs breaking strain. Fibreglass rods stood in rows in a rack, 12ft beachcasters for the sea fishermen, 8ft pier rods and thin, whippy rods for the softer river fishers. Reels were on display in a cabinet. Intrepid made cheaper reels for us kids, ABU the quality reels for proper fishermen. We looked at the reels that came with a level-wind mechanism with awe. Fly reels were nowhere in sight. That type of fishing was for the toffs, not George Courage's clientele. Although we pinched the odd bit of fishing tackle from other shops we wouldn't have dreamed of nicking from George. We had a natural respect for him and his generation.

At about nine years of age I, like most of my friends, joined the local cub pack. We wore green jumpers with badges on the sleeves, a neckerchief with a toggle and little caps. The female pack leader carefully introduced a little military style discipline into our lives. We were taught simple skills like making a camp fire, pitching a tent and very usefully, map reading. Some knowledgeable cub's mums willingly gave their time to teach us about the great outdoors and to take us on weekend trips to the New Forest. On one such trip, one poor lad had a sudden and very noisy night time asthma attack which terrified us all. It was probably brought on by his being away from home for the first time. Mucking in with the cooking, washing up and cleaning were second nature to me. I loved the camp fires, sausages and beans and the singing that we enjoyed every evening before crawling, exhausted, into our sleeping bags. (They weren't really sleeping bags as you see today, they were usually old worn out eiderdowns folded over and sewn down the side and across the bottom).

This, of course, was just preparation for the next step up, the sea scouts. And a very big step up it was, too. The sea scout's leader was an old weather-beaten chap who owned a very lovely but ancient wooden sailing boat. The older lads were keen sailors who also did the things lads did in those days. They smoked, drank, swore profusely, and made kayaks from fibreglass moulds. One of the boys who was probably about seventeen but looked to me about forty, specialized in folding my pinky over on itself and squeezing hard to see how much pain I could endure. There was little sign of any discipline or indeed uniforms in the 23rd Bournemouth Sea Scouts. Adventure was the name of the game. Our scout hut was in the basement of the local church hall which added a little spooky excitement on dark evenings. The scouts were funded by newspaper collections for recycling, so the basement, as well as being soaked in resin and petrol, was packed to the roof with dusty old newspapers awaiting collection.

Our scout troop owned a most beautiful 1950s vintage coach which was used for annual camps. In August 1971, my brother and I climbed aboard the coach, heading for a wonderful two week camp in the Lake District. The campsite was in a wood just behind Lake Windermere and was owned by the Scouts Association. Troops from all over the UK camped there amongst the trees, and firepits abounded. We pitched our heavy canvas eight man tents, with the damp musty smell which I would become very accustomed to over the next ten years. Days were spent kayaking on the lake and hiking in the wonderful fells. At night we mucked about, sang by the bonfire and began our relationships with alcohol. Phil Metcalfe's elder brother nearly killed himself due to alcoholic poisoning. For some unknown reason, he filled his white and blue enamel mug with Teachers Whiskey and downed it in about ten minutes. He had never drunk anything before and had no idea of its strength. He quickly passed out and remained comatose in his sleeping bag for forty eight hours. The older boys kept a bit of an eye on him. Thankfully, he finally woke up, seemingly unharmed, gaining the new nickname Whiskey Met. Another highlight of the holiday was invading neighbouring scout troops camps and running up the side of their canvas tents, over the top, sliding down the other side and running off into the night whilst they were lying inside wondering what the hell was going on. All good stuff.

The following year the Troop spent the summer holiday on the Isle of Wight. How nobody was killed on the trip is still a mystery to me. We sailed from Tuckton in Dave Abbott's trusty old yacht.

All of us young lads were onboard enjoying the big waves as we steered for the Isle of Wight about twenty miles distant. After a few minutes the big waves became a bit less exciting as the first of many turned green, then spewed up his cornflakes. Incredibly, the older lads were sailing our fleet of 14ft open dinghies across to the island. Even to me, it looked like a foolhardy thing to be attempting in such big seas. They probably thought it was a good laugh. After a long, sicky passage we eventually made it to the Newtown River estuary but without any of the smaller boats. It transpired that they were all washed up on the beaches along the Solent. They finally joined us the next afternoon with tales of raging seas and capsized boats, which I could well believe.

Our group, led by my brother, spent most days mucking about in kayaks. One fine day we found ourselves in the Solent and we decided to head across to the other side, to Lymington. So seven of us, aged twelve and fourteen, without even spray decks paddled across one of the world's busiest seaways amongst oil tankers, ferries, ocean liners and many yachts. We had a quick look up and down the estuary then paddled back to our camp. Dave Abbott, the boss, never even knew.

I threw a wobbly during the holiday. It happened after capsizing my kayak, which resulted in some nasty abuse from Dean. The rest of our group joined in and I felt horribly upset and alone. I ended up lying in our tent crying my eyes out for hours, totally inconsolable. Not that anyone tried to console me. The comment was "chuck that kid out of the tent, someone, if he doesn't shut up." Eventually I stopped crying because nobody gave a toss, and got on with the adventuring.

One evening, a lad was sitting in the big eight man tent, telling stories with the rest of us. An old-fashioned and very heavy Tilly Lamp was hanging from the roof beam above his head, casting some light amongst us. Just before bedtime, the string holding it gave up the ghost, causing the lamp to come crashing down on his bonce. He was instantly knocked out cold. Luckily, the lamp hit him square on, so didn't cut his head open.

On a trip to Newport we all bought sheaf knives and I bought a packet of cigarettes from a machine. I also sent Mum a postcard which said that I was having a great time but can you please send fifty pence.

As we sailed home in calmer waters back to Christchurch having all survived our two weeks away, we didn't realise that was the last time the 23rd Sea Scouts would be together as a group. Not long afterwards, our base under the church hall caught fire and the whole building was burnt to the ground. Not surprisingly, two large homes were soon erected on the cleared site, sold for a fortune, and the sea scouts were no more. The end of an era.

About this time I lost my temper for the only time in my life. My brother and one of our friends were taking the mick out of me, god knows what about, but I saw red. Unfortunately for them, I was holding a thick bamboo cane and they were standing in our garden against a six feet high fence. When I snapped, I beat them with the cane quite uncontrollably. When they tried to go left I hit them from the left, then from the right when they moved to the right. The pair of them took a hell of a beating about their bodies. I eventually stopped and let them escape. I was traumatised by my actions. I could have seriously injured one of them due to my lack of control. I think that single realisation stopped me losing my temper ever again, despite some huge provocations over the years.

By this time, summer 1971, aged eleven, I was allowed to go to the beach with my brother and friends. We could roam as far as we could get by bike in half a day. We took up fishing as a hobby and spent many happy days casting out and mucking about. Often we would go to Hengistbury

Head groyne by bike and fish there all day. The groyne was about three metres wide by eighty metres long and marked the far eastern end of Bournemouth beach. Very often strong tides would often be tearing past the end of the groyne. Sometimes on a rough, windy day, the waves would be crashing down on it, then washing across and down the sides. On a good day there might be twenty young lads casting their spinners into the swell, hoping to catch mackerel or the spectacular garfish, that seemed to run upright on the water if you hooked one. Few of us ever did. The great thing was just being there, independent and free, in the fresh air and salt spray.

Bournemouth School

On the first day of term, the school bus picked my brother and I up about half a mile from home. We had to walk past our friends who were catching the bus to the Secondary Modern school. I felt ridiculous and very uncomfortable in my grey suit and tie, carrying a brown plastic briefcase. My cap was hidden well away. The kids going to the other school were all dressed in smart black trousers and v neck jumpers. They jeered across the street at us with just a touch of malice, even though we were all mates.

Bournemouth School was a very proud institution with nine hundred pupils going there from across the town. Roughly the top ten percent of eleven plus results each year attended the school. About four miles from my home, it was an impressive brick building with an array of prefabs that housed most of the science classes. A large Oak copse surrounded it on three sides. Behind the copse were huge playing fields that finished where the girls' grammar school playing fields began.

Just before 9am on the first day, I found myself in the junior playground with the two Simons who came with me from Pokesdown. I quickly realised that I was the third smallest in the year. This came as quite a shock, as size had never been a consideration before in my small pond. Now I was swimming with some very big fish indeed! We were herded into our classroom, where we sat in alphabetical order, at old wooden desks with lifting lids and inkwells. I was positioned halfway down a row which I didn't like very much. The lads at the back looked much happier.

We were then given timetables for the week. I had little idea how awful some of the lessons were going to be when I first studied it. Double maths, double French, chemistry, physics, English and history. What a nightmare!

My first big problem came on the second day. The Latin teacher charged into the room, an old balding chap with tiny wire glasses, in a mouse coloured threadbare suit. He had an air of menace that I hadn't noticed in a teacher before. He made old Mr. Hooper look positively kindly. I put my hand up straight away and stated innocently that I was meant to be studying German, not Latin. He became instantly furious, went purple in the face and denied that could be the case. Thankfully, four other boys raised their hands and said the same thing as me. Safety in numbers, hopefully! At this affront to his authority, the teacher left the room and marched off to fetch the Deputy Head. It seemed that somebody had messed up the timetable. The five of us were sent into the German class next door. I don't know why I bothered because I didn't learn a word of German in three years of lessons, sitting in that room. What an idiot.

It was obvious early on that some of the boys were tremendously bright and quite a few others were not. Many went on in later life to be doctors, solicitors, businessmen, bankers and the like. One lad in my class became a Knight of the Realm and an Ambassador to the EU. Some of us became firemen, sailors, carpenters, musicians and one worked as a thatcher. A real mixed bag of fairly smart cookies, most of whom had a thirst for knowledge. A few of us were not yet mature enough to benefit from the education, even if we had the brains.

I found the view out of the window more interesting than most of the lessons. I saw Concorde on a test flight from Hurn airport one day. It made a wide sweep across the sky only a mile or so away from us, looking so elegant and full of power. The council crematorium was situated just across the road which caused many a joke when the chimney was lit. Trapped in the hot classroom, I just longed to be out on my bike, playing football, or down by the beach.

Geography, English and history I could relate too. The rest of the subjects I struggled with from day one. I had been good at maths at primary school but it was an enormous step up to the Schools Maths Project. In the first term we came to binary, base * and #. That was the end for me as regards learning anything at that school. It was just too hard intellectually and because most of the boys understood the concepts straight away the work moved on quickly. I became one of the lost and uncared for. I think we should have been put together into a duffers class, taught less subjects and encouraged to pass any five O levels. As it was, we were punished for not keeping up, put in regular detention and frankly, sometimes scared witless by one or two unhinged teachers.

Many of the staff were of the right age to have served in World War Two. Certainly there were plenty of rumours that many had done so. One was said to have been captured and tortured by the gestapo. (There was possibly a grain of truth in this rumour). It was said that the highest ranking man in the school was an art teacher who was an ex-admiral. If that was true, he must have been through some tough days. PTSD was not acknowledged at the time, but it would have forgiven those that did serve, their erratic and sometimes crazy behaviour.

My first French teacher was a very tall chap in his sixties. He specialised in asking a question, whilst we would sit there thinking, please not me, please not me. Whoever was picked would either answer correctly, or, if the boy made a mistake and was one of the less bright, the teacher would slowly stalk down the aisle towards the stricken individual who was by now completely unable to think, especially in French. A very painful bonehead often ensued. (A bonehead was a rap on the top of the head with a bony closed fist, administered from a great height). He once made a friend of mine, who conjugated a verb wrongly, kneel at the front of the class whilst he emptied the classroom waste bin over his head. The poor kid was covered in crisp packets and pencil shavings. Our suppressed laughter was mixed with thoughts of who will be next? He also threw a pair of compasses at my brother, luckily they missed but they became embedded in a wooden window frame next to his head. You certainly had to be on your toes in his class, which I never was.

For those of us that were lost, it was a bit of a nightmare. For the lucky kids that learnt easily and put the work in, there was no problem, school was a breeze. Home life also had a bearing on how well a pupil progressed. Some boys had supportive parents who could help with homework, making sure the pupil had the right conditions at home for working. Others had little encouragement and assistance. Partly because my elder brother found it all quite easy, it wasn't ever thought that I might struggle. I didn't have a bedroom for most of the year, nowhere to study, no bookshelf or desk and no support. Mum and Dad had enough on their plate just getting by and would have understood the work even less than I did.

The school gymnasium was a relic from the past. A wooden floor, heavily varnished wall bars to about twenty feet high and, wow, climbing ropes to the ceiling. There were also long heavy horizontal beams that could be fixed in position at different heights across the gym as part of an obstacle course. An array of heavy wood and leather vaulting and pommel horses like something from Stalag 13, were kept in a store to be brought out if the physical training teacher was feeling sufficiently vindictive. Sometimes the weekly PT session included circuit training on this equipment, other times it was games of British bulldog or basketball. Of course, after working up a good sweat we had time for a two minute shower and towel flicking competition, then into those damned itchy trousers and off to the next class dripping wet.

The PT teachers seemed like giants to me. Huge hairy bodies and legs like tree trunks. In one lesson, the teacher was propelling himself from one end of the gym to the other, with a ball under his arm, at least twenty small boys were hanging off his legs, arms and back, vainly trying to bring him down or stop him. I felt an affinity with those guys as they weren't academics and sometimes gave the smart kids a bit of grief.

The school was proud of its sporting reputation. The playing fields were constantly busy with games of football, rugby and some hockey in the winter. Cricket, volleyball and athletics were the usual summer sports with tennis for the wealthiest who could afford the equipment. One particular horror that we endured was cross-country running. It is difficult to imagine anything more likely to put youths off exercising. We would change in a freezing cold pavilion then head outside into an icy wind and stand around waiting for the off, our thighs a mass of purple goose pimples. Then we ran a lap of the entire playing fields to thin us out a bit, then up through the woods and away into the surrounding roads. Most of us hated it but a few nut cases were there at the front racing each other for glory.

Possessing good timing, sharp reflexes and good dexterity, I was pretty handy at all ball sports but being small and lacking determination, I never made much impression. All of my pals favoured rugby over football so I went with them. This was an ego driven mistake because I was hopeless and scared of tackling the big lads. On a cold frozen pitch, wearing nylon shorts, plastic boots and wearing a tee-shirt I would dive the wrong way every time to avoid the tackle. Most of my mates had rugby shorts and shirts and proper leather boots, how I envied them. I became an expert at seeing how play was progressing but, rather than get in position to affect the game, I would do the opposite and avoid the action as much as possible. When I did get the ball I would throw it away as soon as I could. Being tackled by a heavy boy running at speed on a hard pitch was incredibly painful. I was amazed that nobody else seemed to worry about it, they all got stuck in quite happily.

I enjoyed cricket more and was on the verge of the school team for a while. I could play the forward defensive reasonably well and would have made a good wicket keeper, given the chance. Facing fast bowlers in the nets could be nerve-wracking, the ball would fly up very quickly from the hard surface at your head at least once per session and you had to be very quick to duck away. Fortunately, my reactions were lightning fast, so I was never injured.

Volleyball was another summer sport. A funny old game for schoolboys as it didn't make us sweat or strengthen us up. We were mostly rubbish, especially the short-arses like me. One sunny afternoon we were playing a game when one poor lad punched the ball with a straight finger, which instantly dislocated. Ouch! We all gawped in fascination as the PT teacher held onto him and calmly put his finger back into its socket. The boy went as white as his shirt but kept manfully quiet during the manipulation. I had to do the same thing to someone about thirty years later and was glad to have witnessed it once, before I carried out the procedure myself.

So, I was a small lad, not helped by a rather bizarre home situation, not bright enough to stay afloat academically at the top flight and not very interested in the lessons anyway. And, I was always uncomfortable in my school clothes and felt I had the cheapest gear to use and wear on every occasion. Not good. On the other hand, I was proud of being, just, in the ten percent that made it to the best school in the town.

For me, the saving grace about the grammar school was the amount of good friendships I made. There were over one hundred boys in the year, all thrown in together and many with a common challenge (the teachers) which quickly bonded us. There was little or no bullying at the school. It would have been stopped by the group very quickly if anyone had tried it on. Whatever one's thing happened to be, academia, sport, pop music, the military, acting, chess or anything else, there was always someone else interested too, that you could team up with. And, because everyone was bright there were always entertaining schemes, jokes and amusing things going on.

There were two interesting school trips in my first year. One was when the school chartered a train up to London for the day and everybody spent the day milling around Soho and Carnaby St. To many of us, London was a far away and very exciting place. The other big trip was the annual day out in Cherbourg. Intended to help us all improve our French, it was really a jolly, a chance to see a bit of life. We travelled on the Portsmouth to Cherbourg ferry and arrived in the French port about 10am. I was struck by the small roads in the town, the slight smell of sewage and the bizarre vehicles. The cars were all ancient French marques, the vans were made of corrugated iron and many commuters buzzed around on little mopeds with an engine over the front wheel. Fascinating. I couldn't give a stuff about the language, it was beyond me. My friends and I sat in a small dingy cafe and bought coffee and some cakes. That was the only interaction we had with French people except for buying tons of bangers from a shop somewhere. I imagine quite a few of the boys will have taken the opportunity to practise the conjugations and vocabulary whilst on foreign soil but we just mucked about and did some sightseeing. *Fifty years later I have to study French as I am now happily settled in Normandy.* On the ferry back to Blighty hundreds of us sat on the rear deck and amused ourselves throwing bangers at seagulls. The coach trip from Pompey back to Bournemouth was fun too. As the driver made his way through the New Forest we sang endless chorus's of "Won't you roll away the stones, sha la la la, bush bush," by Mott the Hoople. We arrived back at the school exhausted and a little bit more aware of the big wide world waiting for us.

The school day had a routine to it. Leave home with my brother for the fast walk to the bus stop. Bus to school, then registration and assembly every morning. The entire school role except the non-Christians would be herded into the hall to stand together in their years, youngest at the front, oldest at the back. Classical music was played as we marched in, an attempt to give us an appreciation of Mozart and Beethoven. Once we settled in, the teachers would line the walls, ready to wade in and punish with detention any laughter or talking. Those of us who were nervous gigglers had problems keeping a straight face if anything even slightly amusing happened. Hot sweats often ensued whilst we struggled to hide our laughing from the eagle-eyed staff.

On one enormously riotous occasion, a lad farted so terribly that a gap appeared around him about five metres across. The teachers were apoplectic with rage because there was no noise or apparent cause for the disruption. Just a massive gap around one lad. (Incidentally, he was no intellectual but was the best footballer the school had ever seen. In any school match he was head and shoulders above anyone else on the pitch. He could keep hold of the ball all day. After leaving, he went on to play for several top teams and managed a first division club for a while. No doubt becoming wealthier than almost anyone else who went through the school).

As the music died down the Headmaster would step onto the stage and talk about the school news of the day. A sermon with a message about morals would follow. I remember vividly the parable of the hemp seeds sown on rough ground. A certain amount of harsh conditioning is needed to make a person tough, being the message. How right he was. The lesson was always followed by a couple of hymns. I enjoyed the singing, it gave us a chance to relax and make a noise. Onward Christian Soldiers and the like, sung dreadfully by nine hundred reprobates, is good for the soul. At this stage the Catholics and Jews would be allowed to join the rest of us. I'm not sure what they did during the first part of assembly. They were never treated any differently due to their religion by the nominally Christian boys. There was no religious bias by anyone, something very good about living in Bournemouth in the 1970s. The deputy head would then address the sea of faces, usually giving us a dire warning about our behaviour. This would be followed by a couple of swots being mentioned for winning a chess tournament or whatever. We then moved on to our first lesson of the day.

Visits to the Theatre

About this time I had my third visit to the hospital. Twice in the last year of primary school I had caught my winkie in my trouser zip. Terrifying and exceedingly painful. By stuck, I mean my zip was done up and my young chap was caught in the closed zip by a big piece of skin. The first time, Mum and Dad tried to hold me down and force the zip open. I fought like a screaming young primate being attacked, so after taking a few punches they gave up. I was taken to hospital and wheeled into a quiet room, down the corridor from A&E. A doctor and four helpers came in. The four tried to hold my arms and legs whilst the doctor attempted to do what Dad couldn't do, force the zip down. They too gave up after a few horrific seconds of flying little fists and I was whisked off to theatre. I went home with a bloody great bandage on my winkie making me look like a stallion. Two weeks later I only went and did the same thing again. This time it was straight to surgery without the fighting and all my trouser zips were removed and replaced with Velcro. I still occasionally shudder, just thinking about the terrible episode in my young life.

The third visit was more serious. I had been out all evening playing footy and went home to a huge plate of Mum's delicious curry. In the night I started to feel unwell and the next morning at getting up time, protested that I was ill and unable to attend school. Mum made me get up and get ready to go, thinking I was just making it up. By the time I had to leave home I was bent double in agony. The doctor was called and I had the horror of the probing finger diagnosis. If one howled when the digit hit the spot, then it must be appendicitis. I certainly did hit the roof, so off to hospital, this time in an ambulance. Into A&E where the diagnosis was repeated, Jesus Christ! Could they not have just asked my doctor? Then it was off to a ward to wait for surgery. I was in a great deal of pain all day, unable to move from the foetal position. Finally I was taken down for the operation at tea-time. My appendix had ruptured by this time, releasing poison into my bloodstream. I was awoken in a blurry state by a nurse speaking my name, "Clifford, Clifford, are you awake?" I realised I was and that I had a bandage stuck to me from one side of my body to the other and about six inches in depth.

I was made to get up the next morning and walk slowly around the ward. Ouch that hurt. On day four a rather gruff looking big nurse came to see me. She said it was time to remove the bandage. She had a little fiddle with one corner of it to get a handhold, then just ripped it off as quickly as she could. Ouch again. The scar was about five inches long and a bit raggedy. Some of my friends came to visit that day with their pockets stuffed full of johnnies. A huge supply of them had been found somewhere and every kid in town had pockets full of them to play with for a while. My pals played cards for the johnnies on my bed and blew up a couple of them. I was in agony from all the laughing. I went home on day seven and had a couple of further weeks off school. For many months afterwards I couldn't quite stand upright. This was in the days before keyhole surgery, or indeed, physiotherapy, it seemed.

Bikes, Footy and Fishing

Unless occupied with working in the guest house, my brother and I by this time were usually out and about exercising in some way. By now, aged twelve and fourteen, our train set and toy soldiers had been consigned to the loft. It was all about bikes, footy and fishing.

Kings Park, with it's twenty or so football pitches was the venue for much of our sport. As a gang, we often played on the one hockey pitch which had small goals. Sometimes, we could find ourselves in a game on a full size pitch with twenty a side. If a game was obviously just a match between whoever happened to turn up, players could just walk on and join in, as long as an equal amount joined each team. With a number of language schools in the town we could find ourselves playing alongside Italians or Spaniards, in matches that lasted several hours and could end with a score like 65-42. In the summer it might be skins against shirts, but if not you only knew who was in your team by seeing what way they were facing at kick off. I often walked home from such a game at dusk with aching thighs and grass ingrained into my knees.

Our bikes, or treaders as we called them, gave us mobility. The kid who lived next door had a Chopper, a dreadful showboat of a bike that had become very fashionable when it arrived in the UK. Another good friend had a very beautiful Sun racing bike with 23mm narrow tyres. I wanted a proper bike like that when I was about eleven years old. Dad had eventually taken me to a motorbike shop that sold a few second-hand bikes to see what was on offer. We came home with a reasonably tidy three-speed men's bike but it wasn't for me. It was the only bike in the shop and it fitted my brother, it was too big for me. I was devastated. But at least the purchase had been made and my first bike came along some time later.

These bikes were totally different to the bikes ridden by youngsters today. The three-speed system had a very dangerous idiosyncrasy. If you were peddling whilst standing up and chan̶g̶ gear from second to third, the gears could go into neutral, causing the pedals to freewheel, your legs to spin round wildly and your nuts to crash down onto the crossbar. Bad enough in itself but this could cause you to steer uncontrollably under passing cars in your agony. Of course, if you or any of your friends had the misfortune of this happening everyone else would nearly die laughing.

Bikes in those days had one similarity with cars. They fell apart very quickly. The wheels had a tiny veneer of chrome, as did the handlebars and the pedals. The chrome began to spot rust and peel off almost as the bike left the shop it was bought from. Polish and Turtle Wax made no difference. We started making our own bikes from old frames and wheels. My brother realised that the best place to find these valuable parts was the local council tip. So we organised several trips to Christchurch dump where we foraged for parts. We spent some very smelly and dangerous hours dodging the bin lorries unloading their refuse in our quest for a slightly worn twenty four inch wheel or a not too damaged frame. Dean famously built a tip bike that only cost him threepence to get on the road, the price of a cottar pin.

All of our bikes sported cow horns. These were wide handlebars that mimicked scrambling motor bikes bars. The wider your handlebars, the better a cyclist you must be, obviously! We knew of one lad who actually had a car steering wheel as his handlebars. A few boys used old mopeds as their bikes, with the engine removed for lightness. We also fitted the smallest front chainring that we could find, sometimes unbolted from a kiddies tricycle. The smaller the ring the lower the gear, so steeper hills could be climbed. Of course, these bikes were all deadly as they could fall apart just being cycled down the road, let alone racing up and down stony and muddy hills. Kids in Bournemouth called the sport of off-road cycling, tracking.

A popular area for tracking was an area of hilly woodland, about two miles from our home, called The Camel Humps. We would cycle over there on this collection of girls, boys and men's bikes with

s and wheels, and tiny chain rings with little pedals. We
ach other round a well-worn circuit, up and down the
ugh the mud and leaves, pretending to be Sammy Miller,
the top trials motorcyclist of the day. Clashes of the ridiculously wide
handlebars were common and blood was often spilt. The only bad
injury any of us received occurred when my brother attempted
immortality by descending a huge hill in a local gravel pit. As we all
peered down from the summit, he gained a ridiculous amount of
speed whilst losing control of his steering and veered off into some
gorse bushes, somersaulting along the way. The teeth on his
chainring bit deep into his leg, causing a nasty, deep wound and a
life-long scar. As ever, we all fell about laughing.

One summer's day we decided to cycle to Corfe Castle in the
Purbeck hills. To get to Corfe village we began with a long flat ride
along the promenade, to the famous chain driven ferry at Sandbanks.
This was new territory. We crossed by ferry and made good progress
past the even more famous nudist beach. Fascinating viewing for a
gang of teenage boys. When we reached the bottom of the first hill
we stopped to have a rest and a pee. Our sandwich bags were
opened, they were always filled with fish paste or cheese and tomato.
We were well used to cycling for hours, but our tracking bikes had
ultra low gears so just making progress on the flat took a huge
number of pedal revolutions. On any downhill piece of road,
pedalling to keep up with the speed of the cranks was nearly
impossible. So cycling twenty miles on our bikes, was like at least
three times that distance on a racer. But at least we didn't have to get
off and push on the uphills. After a very long morning, we finally
made it to our destination and climbed up the castle ruins with
wobbly legs. How on earth we made it home I don't know but we
never went so far again by tracking bike.

Between the age of eleven and fourteen I spent many hours
fishing. Sometimes we would cycle down to the river at Tuckton and
fish off the jetties for perch. On one bitterly cold Boxing Day, we

took part in the annual pike fishing competition at Throop. If one of us had hooked a pike we would all have died of excitement.

Mostly we fished from Hengistbury Head groyne, or just from the promenade at the bottom of the cliffs near home. The best fun was to be had when we fished in the evening as it became dark. We stayed until late at night, before wearily plodding home up the long cliff zigzag paths. If there were six or seven of us we would cast out our lines then muck about playing footy or climbing the cliffs, or maybe lighting a small fire and cooking mussels. We kept warm with flasks of cocoa and we all carried little charcoal hand warmers in the winter. Standing on the prom late at night listening to the sea rolling in and breaking on the sea wall, then hearing the ssshhhh of the small stones being pulled back out to sea was quite magical. The promenade was lit up by a row of white circular lights that stretched all the way to Sandbanks seven miles away. On a peaceful evening the view was breathtaking. It never occurred to us not to feel safe. Maybe because there were usually one or two adult fishermen somewhere about, or probably because there just weren't any threats around. The biggest risk was slipping down the slope into the sea. That would have been curtains at night with a big swell, so we were careful. We rarely caught any fish, but the point of being there was to have fun and be outdoors hunting and gathering with our mates.

We became very handy at the skills required to fish competently. Making sure we carried all the right tackle, knot tying, casting a weight, hooking a worm, killing and gutting a fish. All good skills to learn at a young age. We toughened up by being outdoors in bad weather and regularly being wet, cold and hungry. We gained an appreciation of nature, the tides, the night sky, how to have enough food, to weigh up risks and how to look after each other. Nobody would ever have been left behind if their bike fell apart. We would have given them a 'backy' to their house, on the crossbar or rack of one of our bikes.

Lead weights were expensive and regularly lost when a hook tangled with seaweed. Pulling the line tight in frustration often caused it to snap before the hook freed itself. Sometimes, and highly amusing for the onlookers, a big cast would snap the line and the weight would fly, unattached, for hundreds of yards before plopping into the waves. Another hard earned fifty pence gone.

Dean decided we should source lead from workmen's trenches, where gas pipe repairs were being carried out. A small roll of lead could be melted down to make twenty or so weights. It was just scrap anyway. Our mould consisted of a little box of sand with a triangular hole in it, the size of a fishing weight. We would melt a piece of lead in a spoon over the gas hob, then carefully pour it into the mould. The assistant held a small bend of wire in a pair of pliers. His task was to insert that into the top of the molten lead in the mould and hold it still until the lead set slightly. The risks were enormous of course: lead poisoning for starters, and I remember the smell of molten lead, so I must have breathed in some brain cell destroying fumes. Also, if the sand had some moisture in it the lead almost exploded as it was poured in. My brother once burnt his eye with a small rocket of molten lead which had blown back at him. Thirdly, it was very easy to pour some running molten lead on your or your partner's hands, or burn yourself with the hot spoon or the gas. Great fun, though and very satisfying to end the evening with a pile of new weights ready to go.

Having Bournemouth beach at the end of our road was a great privilege and we made the most of it. The clifftop and the cliffs themselves were a huge green playground. The slopes, steps and resting places for the holiday makers were fun places to muck about. Our gang developed a type of football to play in and around one such shelter on the cliff edge. The idea of the game was to kick the football against each other, painful enough if a good hit was scored but, more than that, the last person it touched had to fetch the ball from wherever it flew. If it glanced off your desperately swerving body, then bounced down to cliff face to the beach, off you went for a long jog to the sand and back, whilst the rest jeered at you from above. One hugely entertaining day, a lad was hit by the ball which bobbled along the top edge of the cliff for a few seconds. He quickly leapt the fence and dived for the ball which he just missed as it bobbled over the edge. He then rolled and somersaulted down the cliff, then at the bottom fell five feet onto the slope by the promenade. We all dashed down the path to see what the damage was and, of course, to fetch the ball. He was taken to Boscombe Hospital with a broken collarbone by some holiday makers whilst we played on without him, a little more carefully I suspect.

In the summer months we became part of a vibrant group of young beach goers and sunbathers. All of the kids from our part of Southbourne would congregate at the same place on sunny days and lay our towels out on the prom. On a warm day in August there might be thirty of us, boys and girls together. We would swim, listen to the Radio One Roadshow with Smiley Miley, run up and down the beach, and have a wonderful time. By the end of the school holidays we were all nut brown.

I was standing by a postcard kiosk looking at the silly postcards, on a hot July day, when an old chap nearby collapsed in pain. He died right there and then in front of me about two minutes later of a heart attack. I noted how grey his complexion went and realised that I was not concerned or upset by seeing my first dead person.

One sunny afternoon I was sitting mucking about with our huge group of pals when my uncle Ian walked by. He was holding hands with a tiny black boy. I couldn't believe my eyes. He walked on, without seeing me. Later in the day we found out that Angus, his son, had arrived with him from Sierra Leone.

Ian was Dad's eldest and domineering brother. Born in Edinburgh, he joined the RAF Regiment in the last month of WW2. Continuing his father's sport of shooting, Ian represented the RAF in pistol competitions for several years. He was proudly selected with two others from his regiment, to take part in the World Championships in Sweden in 1952.

Ian once visited me during his retirement in his old camper van, known as The Blunderbus. There were twelve very expensive pistols hidden in an old ammo box under the front seat. When the handgun ban came into force in the UK, he moved back to Sierra Leone, where he had enjoyed a career after his RAF days, as a diamond miner.

In his late 1980s Ian worked for a while mining in Angola. Whilst there, the camp he was living on was overrun by Unita rebel fighters and he, along with eleven other miners and security staff, were taken hostage. They endured a long arduous march of many weeks duration with little sustenance, undertaken at night-time to avoid detection from the air, back to the rebels headquarters deep in the jungle. After successful negotiations were concluded they were released and flown to Heathrow airport to be met by families and the Press. A slightly trimmer Ian announced it had all been a very interesting time and a lovely safari.

He loved to smoke large cigars and developed the somewhat disgusting habit of taking snuff from one jacket pocket, sniffing it up a nostril loudly, then producing a dirty old hanky from the other pocket and wiping it under his nose. All done with a big grin and a tale of his adventurous past.

By about 1974 the guest house was running really well. Mum's cooking was exceptional and the same guests just kept coming back, year after year. Dean and I returned home daily by 5pm to help out after a long day in the sun. I was on waiting duties, ringing the dinner bell and meeting the guests as they came downstairs. Dad always made the soup which I then carried in for the ravenous guests. One horrendous evening Dean was dashing through the kitchen door in his swimming cozzy when Mum, going the other way, hit him with eight bowls of soup on a tray and sloshed them down his exposed back. Much howling and crying ensued and splashing of cold water onto the quickly emerging blisters. The soup had stuck to him like Napalm, poor kid.

The guests were fed and watered by 7pm, within half an hour we had finished the washing up and laid the tables for breakfast. The drinkers amongst the guests headed for the local pubs, whilst the oldies moved into our lounge to watch the telly. Before bed one of us made them a cup of tea as there were no kettles in bedrooms in those days in a guest house. Due to the lack of a bedroom, I sometimes slept on the dining room or the lounge floor at night in a sleeping bag. The night clubbers amongst the guests were told to climb in an open front room window if they were going to return after the front door was locked. So it transpired that, one night, a half drunk giggling guest trod on my back as he crept through the unlocked window. I don't know who was the more shocked.

My brother and I had a variety of other unconnected jobs to earn us some precious pocket money. We both did morning and evening paper rounds at different times and the dreaded heavy Sunday round, when you earnt a couple of bob extra for dragging round the papers with supplements and magazines in. We struck lucky when we began football pools rounds as they were much better earners. We pocketed twelve per cent of the takings each week, good money. My round lasted about three hours, cycling from house to house every Thursday evening, come rain or shine. The customers were a friendly bunch, the weather was usually fine and the route from home down to Hengistbury Head, where my last customer lived, was lovely. No wonder, though, homework was often put off until the last minute, by which time I was too tired to bother.

Combined Cadet Force

By the time I was fourteen and beginning the third year at school the die was set. Unable, like most of the lads in my streamed class, to cope with the syllabus and therefore deemed a failure. The teachers only appeared to show any interest in the boys that would be going off to university. In reality, we didn't help ourselves either. Boredom caused us to misbehave which meant a good few of us found ourselves in detention most weeks. If I was in detention it meant coming out of school at 5pm, with three buses to catch to get home. The last thing I felt like getting done after a long day was my homework, so more trouble inevitably ensued. My classmates and I weren't generally a bad lot, we were just in the wrong learning establishment, being taught subjects we were not interested in.

For many in my group there was one saving grace on the horizon. We could join the Combined Cadet Force in the third year of school. The CCF was affiliated to the military, with good connections locally to regular units. The purpose of it was to give schoolboys a taste of military life, to see if they may be interested in joining up when they left school. It was also thought that, even if they didn't enter the services, they may still be well disposed to the forces if they became a captain of industry, politician, or in some other position of power, later in life.

I had wanted to be a soldier for as long as I could remember. What set me off? I don't know. I had sat in an armoured Ferret scout car as a small boy in Oxford, maybe that was the spark. I also owned a huge plastic army of little soldiers and Dinky toy tanks as a small boy. Like most gangs of grubby little boys, many of our games outdoors revolved around attacking each other, using sticks for guns and fir cones for hand grenades.

Dad had a keen interest in all things WW2, so war films and the documentary series `All our Yesterdays` were often on the TV. Whilst we washed and dried up in the evenings we discussed military campaigns from Dunkirk to D-Day. Dad was one of the many young chaps who had missed war service by just a few years, so would have been very affected by it. Most of his workmates will have seen military action. Dad served out his National Service as a coach driver which didn't really cut the mustard. He was very fortunate not to be shipped off to Korea, to fight the Chinese for two years. Many of his contemporaries were.

The early days of the Northern Ireland troubles, depicted on the telly every night when I was at a very impressionable age, possibly prompted some military romanticism in me. All those guns, armoured cars and Land Rovers, being crewed by tough looking guys in camouflaged uniforms. That type of life appealed hugely to a small boy with no interest in academia.

The school CCF had three branches, Army, Navy and RAF. My brother had signed up to the Navy section two years previously. He wore a most ridiculous uniform on a Friday, which was CCF day. His bell bottomed trousers were made of the thickest, itchiest serge imaginable which put me off straight away from joining him. The lads that joined the Navy section were a pretty good bunch though, whereas, the fly boys were a different breed. A few of them were the highly talented lads who would go on to be RAF or commercial pilots. The rest, it seemed to me, came from the can't walk and chew gum at the same time club. Their uniforms were pretty dreadful too, not at all cool. They wore old fashioned blue battledress and berets with a huge daft looking cap badge.

No question about it then. It was the green machine for me. And I loved every single minute of it. Friday was the only school day I looked forward to. On that day we finished our lessons at lunchtime and joined our respective units for training. I could also escape the dreaded school uniform once a week, because on cadet's day we wore our military uniform to school. I was issued with big boots, lightweight trousers, gaiters, a woolly jumper and a beret. After rummaging around in the quartermaster's store I eventually found a shirt small enough for me, made of lightweight khaki cotton. Fantastic. Due to the nearest Army unit being at Bovington we were attached to the Royal Armoured Corps. Our cap badge was, therefore, an iron fist. Even better.

The Brecon Beacons in Wales can be a bleak place, even on a good day. That's partly the reason why Special Air Service selection is held there. Big hills, heavy rain and strong winds combine to test the will and endurance of the strongest men. Sennybridge camp is on the edge of the Brecon training area, a collection of wooden huts built in the days of the Empire. Many national servicemen will have suffered deprivations in the hut that myself and twenty or so chums poured into with whoops of delight, at the start of our first annual camp. The accommodation harked back to a bygone age. Twelve metal framed beds each side of the room, each with a lumpy thin mattress and three grey blankets on top. The centrepiece of the long room was an ancient tall coal burning stove, with a rickety black chimney poking out of the top. Two or three trestle tables stood on each side of the unlit stove.

We each bagsied a wobbly old bed whilst laughing, joking and taking the mickey out of each other. Most of us had started a smoking habit recently so the air was soon thick with a blue fug. It transpired that the only cigarettes sold in the NAAFI were Senior Service. These were some seriously strong fags for hardened smokers, our schoolboy lungs were ill-prepared for them. By the end of the two weeks we all had smokers coughs and rasping throats.

Breakfast was always a giant fry-up with tea then it was into the Bedford lorries and off to the hills for map reading, long marches across the hills and signalling practise. During our training fortnight we were blessed with fine weather. We carried out ambushes, section attacks and overnight bivvying in little two man tents. I fell in love with the song of skylarks whilst lying in thick bracken waiting for the enemy to appear. When they hove into view we would unleash a hail of blanks from our worn out Lee-Enfield rifles, then charge through the tussock grass with screams and laughter, hats and webbing flying around and falling off. This soldiering game was a hoot.

To pass the time in the evenings we walked down to a little cafe in the village. Cups of tea, more Senior Service and a jukebox. Kissing in the Back Row, sung by the Drifters, was the song we played, time and time again.

We spent hours sitting around the wooden tables trying to bull our boots. This is a time-honoured ritual in the Army. We used hot spoons to flatten the leather then rubbed in polish and spit to try to raise a mirrored shine. All the while telling stories and mucking about. After lights out we would lay in our beds joking, smoking and resting our tired young limbs.

One or two of the more upper middle-class boys frowned upon our smutty humour and filth but even they cracked when the nightly `show` began. If a boy felt a fart beginning to arrive he would drop his trousers and rush to lie on one of the big wooden tables with his backside in the air. His accomplice, trembling with mirth, would light a match and hold it close to the bared arse. If the two timed it properly we would all hear a "parp" and see a bright sheet of flame shoot out in the darkness. To a man we laughed uncontrollably at this and cried until we ached. A failure to coordinate the gas and the spark would be met with a fanfare of boos and jeers. We were just a group of boys playing at being soldiers and what great fun it was.

Sgt. Major Bath of the Royal Welsh Fusiliers stood on the parade ground at Leek Camp, looking every inch the finest specimen the British Army had to offer. Over six foot tall, immaculately dressed, with his pace stick held tightly in his giant hand. He struck terror into each and every one of us. Leek was the venue for a week of rigorously hard training for some of us during the following year's annual camp. We were a cadre course, picked to see if we had the potential to make it in the Army. The Sgt. Major taught us drill as if we were young adult soldiers and the experience was very, very frightening. He then showed us how to prepare and deliver a lecture the military way. For our homework we had to write our own lecture to be presented the following day. Most of us struggled with this because we were so scared of him that we almost fell apart. We sat in the class the next morning praying that we would not be picked to deliver our lecture. Then it was off to the hills around Leek for section attacks where we took it in turns being in charge, under his eagle eyes and angry bark. The course did us the world of good. Soldiering could be very hard and brutal in the 1970s. He gave us a taste of it to see how we coped.

Sandy and Geoff from the Royal Armoured Corps depot at Bovington showed a more friendly side to Army life. Sandy was a Monty lookalike, Irish and as tough as old leather. He usually wore an old cut-down greatcoat showing the badges of his Regt, The Royal Anglians. He had been promoted to Lance-Corporal many times and bust back down to private almost as many. He and I got on famously from day one.

Geoff, his sidekick, was a Light Infantryman. Tall and powerful, he was rumoured to have attempted SAS Selection in his younger days. No doubt a good bloke when you were in a pickle. The pair of them were based at Bovington and helped our school teachers provide realistic and up to date training. They also had access to an armoury of modern weapons that we could use on range days.

The .303 Lee-Enfield Mk4 rifle is an important part of British history. Introduced before WW2, it was the rifle carried and used by millions of soldiers until the late 1960s. Capable of being fired at ranges up to thousand yards, it was very accurate in the hands of a reasonable shot at half that distance. When the famous old rifle became obsolete, it was passed on to the UK's cadet forces. Our school armoury was full of MK4 rifles and it's smaller cousin the .22 rifle, which we practised with on the school indoor range.

As a very excited member of the newly formed shooting team, I woke one fine Sunday morning, made some sandwiches and got on my old treader. A quick bracing four miles on the treader to school, where we met up with Sandy and Geoff. The teachers then issued our rifles, before we all piled into the Bedford lorry for the hour long trip to the ranges.

Salisbury Plain was only thirty miles away, with it's huge military training area, ranges and regimental barracks. I loved the wide open spaces, rolling hills and lack of people there. Travelling by Bedford was a great laugh for us. The canvas sides of the lorry offered no protection from the cold, the engine roared and the wind whipped in over the tailgate. As always, we laughed, joked and sang endless choruses of The Engineer and Hey Jude. If we had been professional soldiers we would all have been asleep before we left Bournemouth. As boys, it was all new and ace fun.

On these trips we were training for an annual cadets shooting competition. We went to the ranges on many consecutive Sundays before the event. Great credit must go to our teachers for putting in the hours to allow this. The .303 had a mighty kick when it was fired and made a hell of a noise too. I held the wooden stock tight into my shoulder and fired the first round at the target. Bang. Wow, that was huge! The top half of my little body was almost lifted off the ground by the recoil. Geoff stood behind me giving encouragement. After firing our first magazine we put down our weapons and walked up the range to view our targets. Not too bad at all, though I could already feel a growing lump in my left shoulder from the recoil. We usually fired at three hundred metres but once or twice attempted to hit targets at twice that range. At that range the target was little more than a tiny white speck, but we could all land rounds somewhere on it.

After lunch of sandwiches, tea and cigarettes those of us that had shot in the morning would swap over with the lads who had been operating and pasting up our targets. The targets were operated from a hidden concrete trench and gallery called the butts. Each target was held in an iron frame with pulleys that could be lowered into the trench or raised above ground, in view of the shooters. The butts and the firing point were connected by field telephone and a red flag was raised when firing was stopped. Two boys operated each target and were equipped with a pot of glue with a brush and a book of paper strips. These were used to paste up the bullet holes after each session. The command was given to raise the targets which we did by pulling down on a counter weight. The red flag was lowered and the shooting began. The bullets began to crack past the butt party, about four feet above their heads. The crack was followed by the thump of the round being fired. With practise we could estimate how far away the firing point was.

A terrible panic ensued one time when a lad called Hughie was asked to lower the flag. It must have been the first time he had been shooting with us because rather than simply use the piece of rope hanging beside him, he walked around the far end of the butts and climbed up the bank to the flagpole, exposing himself to the shooters lying three hundred metres away with their itchy fingers on their triggers. Hughie could easily have died from bullet wounds, the officer at the firing point almost died of apoplexy and we nearly died laughing.

One Sunday, Geoff was sitting quietly reading a newspaper at lunchtime. Sandy sidled up to him and sneakily set fire to it at the bottom with his lighter. We thought this was great fun. When the flames began licking up the page Geoff howled with great amusement. He had nicked Sandy's own paper from his bag and was now waving it around delightedly to burn it away quicker.

The 7.62 SLR was the semi-automatic rifle that superseded the .303. It was the weapon seen on the BBC nightly news from Belfast every night being carried in the `high port` by the British soldiers. How we longed to fire the weapon and it's larger cousin the General Purpose Machine gun. When Sandy produced one for us to drool over he told me I couldn't be allowed to fire it because I am left-handed. I was devastated by this news and nearly in tears. So much for the tough little soldier. The reason being that the ejected cartridge cases flew very close to the head of left-handed shooters when they pulled the trigger. Thankfully, it was eventually agreed I could fire it if I kept my head well over to the left and out of the way of the hot brass flying around. What a relief! I loved shooting with the SLR and became pretty useful with it. *When I joined my local shooting club In Normandy in 2019, I could not believe that an old French fella` was blasting away down the range with an SLR. It was a joy to be allowed to fire a few rounds with it.

The GPMG was a mighty weapon too. On one occasion the lads from Bovvy brought a `Gimpy` for us to try out. Sandy set it up on it's tripod at the three hundred metre firing point. A belt of two hundred rounds 7.62 ball were loaded ready to fire. Probably because I was the smallest I was allowed to go first. Maybe they sensed that I was the most likely to join up and use one in real life. Rather than firing short bursts as we were taught, I let rip with the whole belt, baba bada, two hundred rounds in one go. Take that! The Staff all fell about laughing as they watched the huge grin on my face as I blasted away.

The Ten Tors Expedition.

The Ten Tors expedition on Dartmoor was another highlight of our Combined Cadet Force days. Every May for many years the arduous walk has been attempted by teams from cadets, scouts and schools from all over the UK. Either the forty five mile or the gruelling fifty five mile walk can be chosen by the teams of six. We chose the longer distance. As the name implies the team's walk includes ten of the many high granite tors on Dartmoor as checkpoints on the route. Some years the moor is lashed with high winds and rain or even snow. We began our training early in 1975, our teams mainly comprising of the same faces that were in the shooting team. My friend Phil Metcalfe was ever present in these adventures. We hadn't yet gelled as best buddies, just as good mates who enjoyed the CCF.

So it was up early on Sunday mornings again and off on my treader with more jam sandwiches and a flask. Back into the trusty Bedford or, if we were fortunate, the luxury of the school minibus. We were dropped off by a teacher on the edge of the New Forest and simply walked all day. We averaged maybe sixteen or eighteen miles then were picked up, knackered but very happy after a good day out of rambling and mucking about. The New Forest was fairly flat, so, to prepare us for the hills of Dartmoor we were sometimes dropped off near Studland from where we walked over Nine Barrow Down towards Corfe Castle.

Our kit was abysmal. Youngsters nowadays are kitted out with lightweight boots, sleeping bags, tents and snazzy gear from camping suppliers. We got by with 1960s army surplus. Our boots were terrible, the same type that failed so badly in the Falklands. We were dressed in ancient baggy denim fatigues and wore woollen caps comforters on our heads. They were made of elasticated course wool, could be used as a scarf or a hat and boiled your head whilst itching you to death. Our two man canvas tents weighed a ton and came with wooden poles and rope guylines. Luckily, because I enjoyed backpacking with my brother I had an aluminium framed rucksack that was reasonably comfortable. Poor old Phil had an old canvas Bergan that bit deep into his shoulders when he walked.

A month before the event we planned to spend a weekend on the moor, practising walking on the tussocky terrain and through the notorious bogs. On a Friday afternoon we piled into a few teachers' cars and headed off for the sunny south-west. Phil, Muttley and I were crammed into a little Hillman Imp driven by 'Death Breath'. Six hours of cramp and winding down the windows ensued but we finally arrived in one piece, stiff and sore. We set up camp near Okehampton, ate our grub and settled down for a good night's sleep. We needed some decent rest before an early start the next morning. Not a chance. The teachers had a bit of a party and played Land of Hope and Glory and other patriotic songs on an old cassette player long into the night. We awoke at dawn after about three hours of light sleep and packed up our tents already feeling pretty exhausted. The effervescent singers from the night before kindly loaded us with bacon sandwiches and tea before we set off for the day's bog-trotting.

In case of accidents each team had to carry a certain amount of safety equipment and food and clothing during the actual event. Therefore, we prepared to do the same on the dry run. My share was the long rope which was carried in case a team member fell into one of Dartmoor's many bogs and needed pulling out. I found this highly amusing as it was usually me that fell into any water we crossed on our training marches.

Our food for the expedition was army compo tinned food which we had used many times during our annual camps. We cooked it up on little hexamine stoves. It didn't replenish the calories we used up and was lacking in starchy carbohydrates but we didn't know anything about sports nutrition at fifteen years of age. Nor did many other people at the time.

The terrain was certainly more difficult to cross than that which we were used to but the sun shone and we put in two good days walking with few problems. Roll on the main event.

A month later, in May 1975, we pitched our tents in roughly the same place although this time there were two thousand others doing the same. The weather was hot, with a clear blue sky. Thankfully, the teachers' chorus kept quiet this time and we managed to get some sleep. But, from the very beginning of the great trek, we had problems. Teams were given an envelope marking their route, shortly before the start. When the gun sounded all of them headed off to their first checkpoint. Many of the tors closest by had long trails of teams marching up them. For some daft reason we set off as the only team up a distant tor. A tor with no checkpoint on the top, as we had climbed the wrong one. So that made ten still to do and we were already hot and sweaty. Not good. We tried to make up some time but fairly early on I realised I was struggling. The smallest in the team and the weakest. My old primary school friend, Simon, also found it hard going. He was a powerfully built guy and carrying around an excess of muscle wasn't ideal across boggy ground and lumps of tussocky grass. Babies heads, as they are known in the military. He suffered terribly from a boot failure. One of his soles detached itself from the front half of his boot so every step he took it bent back, then schlopped down on the ground spraying muddy water up his leg. A cold and wet form of torture.

By mid-afternoon I began to think of packing it in. I did not think there was any way that I could keep struggling on for another forty odd miles over the unrelentingly difficult terrain in hot sunshine.

On the top of each tor that we had to climb, sat a group of soldiers ready to book us in. Once or twice we were checked that we still had all of our safety equipment. At any one of these checkpoints I could very easily have given up. A team was allowed to drop two members and keep going with four but not less than that. Twice I decided that I had the energy to push on for one more hilltop. The thought of retiring was horrible so I decided to push on as long as I could stand it. Finally, we made it to our fifth and last checkpoint of the day, booked in, then pitched our little canvas bivvies. Oh, my poor feet. They had been soaking wet since the early morning and looked decidedly wrinkly, white and fetid. One or two of the other lads had blisters, Simon still had dreadful boot problems and Phil's shoulders were cut to ribbons by his rotten old Bergen. We sat on tussocks eating our bacon burgers and processed cheese whilst we watched other teams staggering to the camping area looking just as shattered as us. Some even more so. The wet ground and the hot weather together made the going very tough indeed for everyone but the strongest. We had one of those in our team. A chap called Nigel who reminded me of Wilfred Thesiger the great adventurer and explorer. Nigel wore spectacles, was shy and retiring, didn't swear or smoke but was friendly and engaging when drawn into the conversation. He came from one of those families who went on long walking holidays in the hills and had been building up stamina ever since he could stand upright. He put us rougher lads to shame.

We woke at dawn on the Sunday and eased our tired muscles into action. It was going to be another scorcher. Oatmeal blocks and tea for brekky then we hoisted our rucksack straps over our tired and sore shoulders. Ouch! Especially Phil with his broken rucksack causing him all sorts of pains and trauma. Off we yomped with achy legs towards the first summit of the day, some five miles away.

Gradually, very gradually, we ate up the remaining miles and ticked off the summits. At one stage I sank waist deep into a hidden pool and had to be hauled out by the others, the rescue rope hanging uselessly from my partly submerged back. I just knew I was the wrong man to be carrying it. We struggled on through the heat of the day, heads down, once step after the other, talking very little. My thoughts about packing it in disappeared as finishing became a possibility. Occasionally we rested and munched a few hardtack biscuits with jam squeezed from a little green compo tube.

As we approached the last ridge before the final tor, a couple of miles from the end, we came upon Sandy and Geoff sunbathing. They were waiting to meet us and offer some encouragement. I was so pleased to sit with them for a few minutes and scoffed my last food, a can of peach slices, then smoked my only cigarette of the weekend. What a marvellous fag that was. We left them, feeling mighty refreshed and marched on with renewed enthusiasm. The hillside was covered with applauding parents and members of teams that had completed the walk before us. What a wonderful moment crossing the finishing line was. I felt very, very proud of myself. I had conquered the almost overwhelming desire to give up and for the first time, realised that I could call upon an inner strength in times of hardship.

The following Monday morning in assembly my name was called out with the other five team members to mount the stage and receive our medals from the Headmaster. When he shook my hand he wasn't the only member of staff that was surprised I had it in me to complete the walk.

Hills and Spills.

Just before the first Dartmoor trip I had persuaded a couple of my old gang to go on a brief, Easter time, walking holiday on the Isle of Wight. Things progressed well for us during the first day. We crossed the Solent by ferry in high spirits then set off along the road east out of the town. After strolling a few miles we found a quiet wood by Newtown river, where we pitched the tent and settled down for the night. My two pals were new to camping but spent their time outdoors on their bikes and swimming in the sea like everyone else. In fact, they thought of themselves as a good bit tougher than softy grammar school kids. That night, for the first time in many years, it snowed in the middle of April on the Isle of Wight. We woke the next morning to find the tent in a beautiful quiet, white world, with the snow about two inches deep. What a hoot. I was loving the challenge. I suggested that we should have breakfast in the tent then shake the snow off it the best we could and move on. However, to my sheer amazement and disappointment the two tough nuts decided they had experienced enough hardship for one weekend and just wanted to pack up and go straight back home. I had little choice but to go along with their request but, in my disappointment, was heartened by the realisation that they couldn't hack it, whereas I could.

The next time my faithful red rucksack came out was for a much more adventurous expedition. Mid-summer 1975, I was fifteen, my brother was seventeen and already an experienced hitch-hiker. One fine August morning before breakfast, Mum drove us down to the roundabout at the start of the Christchurch by-pass where she dropped us in the lay-by. We put out a hopeful thumb and within five minutes our first car stopped and asked where we wanted to go.

"North towards the M6 was our reply." He nodded, "righto, hop in then, lads," and we were off! During the day we received several good lifts and I learnt the etiquette for hitching on motorways. There was often a queue of desperate people at the slip road out of the Services, just where the cars started to build up speed. Some were backpackers like ourselves with camping gear. Others carried a car license plate and were always picked up quickly by their own tribe, the lorry drivers. Some were hippy types with sandals and long hair, the old camper vans took them off down the road. One or two were just sad, tired old blokes wearing threadbare suits and scuffed shoes, they had trouble getting lifts anywhere. A few carried a piece of cardboard with a town pencilled on it in big letters, `London` or `The north`. We spotted one or two doing a little jig or dancing for every car in the hope that the driver might think they would be amusing company on their tiresome drive. We relied on our youth and that we were obviously adventuring, not a threat to anyone.

It wasn't good form to start thumbing before the person in front was picked up and driven away. Neither was it good form to flick the V's to a vehicle that ignored you, as the next one coming might see your angry gesture and decide not to pick you up because of it. We made great progress that first day and were dropped off near Glenridding in the Lake District shortly after tea-time.

I had longed to return to the Lake District since my first visit a few years earlier with the Sea Scouts. The rocky peaks and crags make it, for me, the most beautiful National Park in Britain. Some areas of the far North-west of Scotland, where the majestic mountains reach down to meet sea lochs, equal it for scenery, but none surpass it.

We planned to walk for five or six hours a day, bag the famous tops, Helvellyn, Scafell, Coniston and Blencathra, then hitch home two weeks later. The campsite beside the lake at Glenridding was our pitch for the first night. Early the next morning, glad to be away from the sound of traffic from the previous day's travelling, we bought some milk in the campsite shop, brewed up, then left, full of beans and youthful vigour. I was as fit as a gazelle and Dean, no mean walker himself, was just as fast, with his huge thighs and lovely new leather walking boots. By lunchtime the heavens opened and we were caught out, walking along a high lonely lane, with beautiful stone walls on both sides, miles from anywhere. We took shelter in an old falling down garage and waited for it to calm a little. Our nylon walkers` coats stopped most of the wet from penetrating our top halves but the rain ran off the material mid-thigh and soaked our freezing legs. We didn't have waterproof trousers, just buying lightweight coats nearly broke the bank. So we searched around in the manky old garage, found some fertilizer sacks and set to with our trusty scouting sheaf knives. Ten minutes later, when the rain lessened slightly we moved on, wearing some rather natty leggings. We fashioned them from the cut up feed sacks that we held in place with bailer twine. A fine bodge!

The weather improved and we spent some wonderful days marvelling at the wonderful scenery and walking many miles. The low point of the fortnight was the massive blister Dean developed on one of his heels, caused by a new boot rubbing and then going septic. We visited a doctor in Ambleside who fixed him up with penicillin. Then we found a chemist for a bulk purchase of moleskin to stop the rubbing. Putting a few layers of that over the blister saved the holiday.

We were travelling light, with few clothes and Vesta dried meals for emergency dinners. We bought snacks for our lunches. Most nights we managed to camp rough near a pub, taking advantage of our tiny dark green tent's ability to almost disappear at dusk. We would wait until twilight, pitch our tent within walking distance of the pub then saunter in and order some food. The fashionable meal at the time was Chicken in the Basket with extra chips. We ate it most nights and managed to buy beer at the same time. Publicans could see we were under age but were quite happy to sell a few pints to the weary young hill walkers. We stumbled, a bit drunk, back to our tent, slept like logs but were careful to be packed up and away before the rangers were on the prowl for illegal tents just after first light. What problem the likes of us were to them I will never know.

One morning we were navigating down a scree slope near the Honister Pass when we realised that we had become trapped on a very crumbly little ledge. We couldn't go up, across or down, and we became very scared. Neither of us had a head for heights, we had no rope and nobody was anywhere near us to assist. We had a right to be scared because the drop beneath us was probably not survivable if one of us slipped. After a very anxious twenty minutes, it dawned on us that we had to either attempt to go back up or stay there forever. Dean very slowly began climbing and I slid him his bag, I passed mine up and joined him on the next tiny ledge, our knees knocking in fear. Somehow we inched our way out of trouble to safety. A frightening lesson learnt. Just because we knew how to walk, navigate, camp and live outdoors, we were not supermen, far from it.

We had our first visit to the famous Old Dungeon Ghyll Inn at Langdale. One of the best pubs in Britain and a haven for walkers, their Cumberland Sausage is legendary. We crossed the fells above Borrowdale and dropped down to see the Bowder Stone. Shortly after, we came across Borrowdale and I felt, and still feel, it must be the loveliest place in the whole world. The scenery everywhere was breathtaking, with the dry stone dykes the same shade as the beautiful grey Herdwick sheep which produce the world's itchiest wool, unfortunately.

After a demanding but exhilarating fortnight, we found ourselves walking from Keswick past Threlkeld, back to the M6 roundabout. Time had passed far too quickly. I promised myself I would be back again soon.

The hitch back home was long and tiring. The sound of cars and lorries hurtling past us became very wearing. However, we made reasonable progress except for one slightly dodgy lift. A swarthy middle-aged man in a Jaguar picked us up near Birmingham, just as it was getting dark. When he offered us a room for the night he set off our survival alarms. We bailed out rapidly on a quiet dual-carriageway, much to his surprise. This sharp exit was followed by a long walk, stiff and cold, back to a good place for the next lift. Such is the hitch-hikers lot. We joined the familiar queues of hopefuls at the motorway again and carried on our journey south. Finally, we found ourselves close enough to home to ring Mum to come and collect us.

Funnily enough, whilst I was away in the Lakes, my friend Phil's parents had been away too. Like all good teenagers he took the opportunity to hold a party during their absence. Beer and cider flowed and boys mucked about in the road outside his house. Someone stupidly mentioned that Ernie, our French teacher, lived two doors away. One lad thought it would be a good idea to lob half a brick through his window. Ernie, of course, came rushing out and when questioned, one snitch said "Fensome threw it," which was possibly correct. Unfortunately for me, Ernie heard "Fenton threw it." Brilliant. I was found guilty even though I was three hundred miles away behaving myself. After this idiotic event I was blackmarked by most of the teachers at school during my last year, without even being able to explain myself.

A bit of Bovver.

In the 1960s The Manor Ground was the home of Oxford United Football Club. The land that the stadium was built on was next door to my grandparents house. When Dad and his siblings were growing up, the ground was just a field with ponies grazing on it. When I was a six year old, Oxford United drew the mighty Liverpool in the third round of the F.A. Cup. Dad was given tickets to take Dean and I to our first football match. We sat on the edge of the pitch with all the other youngsters and were blown over by the atmosphere, the noise and the spectacle. I suspect Oxford were well beaten but we had both caught the footy bug by the time we arrived home.

Bournemouth and Boscombe Athletic Football Club (AFCB) became our local team when we moved south. At the age of about eleven we started going to watch home games. The ground was in Kings Park where we often played football ourselves, about a half-hour walk from home. Having paid our shilling we stood in the open part of the ground, not daring to go into the covered end where all the singing and shenanigans took place. The standard of footy didn't really matter, to us, the whole afternoon was an interesting spectacle. The adrenaline began to rise as we approached the stadium and picked up the noise of singing, chanting and banging on advertising hoardings. The cops were always in attendance. If the away team's followers had a reputation for trouble there would be a large police presence. On those occasions one could sense the potential for violence straight away. If the game was against a small town team from way up north there would be fewer police and a calmer atmosphere.

Bournemouth hovered between the third and fourth division, sometimes going down and often being promoted back up the following season. We all followed one of the big teams as well as our local one. I picked the mighty Leeds and my brother went for city slickers Chelsea. When they played a horribly nasty FA Cup final we sat in the lounge with Dad, willing our teams on. A 2-2 draw was battled out with Chelsea winning the replay a few evenings later. I cried. Manu and Liverpool were the teams our mates usually followed, they were just glory hunters.

Skinheads became a big thing in the early 1970s. They took over youth culture for nearly a decade before giving way to Punk. The uniform of Doc Marten boots, Levis, jean jacket, Harrington or Crombie, Ben Sherman shirt and almost shaven head could be seen all over England, both in town centres and at football grounds. Plenty of girls joined the gang too. Levels of violence between rival groups was incredibly high but an unwritten law of no knives prevailed in the early days. If you weren't in their uniform you were left alone. If you were watching the footy you were quite safe at the match if you were incognito. The skinheads just wanted to fight with each other, not beat up civilians.

At Dean Court, the home of Bournemouth, sometimes the only away supporters were a gang of skinheads who followed the opposition wherever they played. The police would escort them off their coaches, then into the open end of the ground. The Bournemouth yobs were at the far end, called the South End, under the roof. The chanting and jeering began before kick-off with both groups trying to out sing each other. Songs were often full of swear words and mocking the players or the part of the country they came from. Sheep shaggers, tractor boys, poor northern slums, etc. Sometimes it was very funny. We kept well out of it but kept one eye on the hooligan action, often it was more exhilarating than the footy. Occasionally some nut would run onto the pitch and dash towards the far end taunting the opposing fans. The cops would quickly catch them and march them off down the tunnel in an armlock, to a cacophony of jeers from everyone except their mates who would cheer them off.

Bournemouth could muster well over a thousand thugs for an important game and plenty of them were big, hard, manual labouring, bruisers. The dockers from Poole, just down the road, swelled their numbers. They loved their sing-song on a Saturday and if there was a bit of aggro, so much the better.

That is why we found it incredible that sometimes a couple of dozen away supporters would try to get into the South End and start trouble when hugely outnumbered. Once or twice I even saw a couple of kamikazes start chanting the away teams name from within the mass of Bournemouth skinheads. After a few incredulous seconds there would be an ominous rumble then silence before the idiots would be carried off to an ambulance. They became legends back at their home ground for such suicidal madness. The police seemed to enjoy most of the hooligan action. I never saw them fearful or intimidated at a game. They were a bunch of big lads too, in those days, and were earning plenty of overtime for working on a Saturday.

A few times we watched from a safe distance things become very unpleasant indeed. A top of the league match against Aston Villa was one such occasion. Villa brought thousands of fans with them and Bournemouth matched them for numbers, bolstered with every yob they could muster locally. The Villa hooligans forced their way into the South End and fought a long, hard and very ugly battle with the Bournemouth lads. If they had managed to occupy the end it would have been a disgrace for the local tribe. The cops had a pretty grim time of it that day with loads of casualties and their dogs taking retribution on every arse within reach. Most of the proper supporters just watched the match and let the fighting go on behind them as if it was normal Saturday behaviour at a football match. Which in those days, it was.

Brewing Up.

Football violence aside, Bournemouth wasn't a particularly dangerous or rough town and growing up there was fairly peaceful for us teenagers. However, the local discos were a honeypot for testosterone fuelled punch ups and ambushes. Being the boys from the grammar school made us targets at times but as I was a little shortarse I was generally under the radar. There was no kudos to be gained by sticking one on me. Some of my schoolmates were pretty badly beaten up though, usually in discotheque toilets where the bouncers couldn't see the trouble kicking off. Very often, as we left Tiffany's or La Maison Royale some poor sap would be receiving a shoeing from the toughs on the pavement outside. Poor old Phil was a bit of a mouthpiece when he was drinking and quite often received a fist in his gob for his troubles. Once, he and I were chased through the town centre by a gang who were pelting us with bottles having tried to mug us. We weren't going to hang about to reason with them, so made a sharp exit whilst laughing all the way down the road with the adrenalin rush.

I was an occasional smoker at the age of about fifteen but hadn't discovered the joys of drinking. Mum and Dad almost never drank, in fact, Dad was strictly tee-total, it seemed. If we ever found ourselves as a family in a pub beer garden he would sit with a half of lager and then not touch it. He just didn't like the taste of alcohol or the effects. So our limit as youngsters was a couple of cans of Heineken lager at Christmas, along with a glass of champagne and a cigarette with the turkey. Which we thoroughly enjoyed.

About this time a book came on the scene called `Making wines like those you buy`. We bought a copy and became little wine brewers, with demi-johns, corking machines and dozens of green wine bottles. We lifted them from the back of a restaurant in Christchurch and carried them home in a duffle bag on our treaders. Dean made a gallon of Carum-carvi wine as described in our book, which looked like muddy water and tasted worse. However, it was very alcoholic, which was the point of the whole thing.

I reckoned grapes had more promise and tried buying a kit from Boots of Beaujolais wine. That was pretty dreadful too but at least you could recognise it as a drink. Our next attempt was remarkable in that Mum and Dad didn't ask what the hell we were up to. We had cycled with the gang out to an abandoned orchard just outside Bournemouth and found the old trees laden with apples. We picked hundreds of apples but realised we had no way of transporting them back home. So we took off our Parka`s, tied the hoods very tightly, put the arms inside the body, then filled the coats with apples. We then held the bottom tightly shut, threw them over our shoulder and cycled home one handed.

When Dean and I arrived home we tipped the apples into the bath and smashed them to a pulp with two pieces of four by two wood. The mash was then scooped into a couple of buckets and the bath was cleaned up a bit. We fermented the apple wine for a few months then bottled it up and stored it in the attic. It was nicely out of the way up there and we could leave it for a year or so to mature.

Meanwhile, our friend Chris Summers had collected a giant bag of nettles, at some cost to his fingers and legs I imagine, and made nettle beer. As his house was down by the river Stour and ours was on the cliffs we could just about freewheel there on our treaders. On the day Chris decided the beer was ready we set off for a tasting session. It was a clear liquid, very strong and tasteless, not recognisably anything at all like beer. We had a small glassful each, felt pretty good and headed for home. We very soon found out that we couldn't pedal back up the big hill to Southbourne. Something seemed to be wrong with our legs which just wouldn't work properly and we ended up pushing our bikes most of the way home. Chris had, by chance, made a drink not dis-similar to potcheen or Norwegian moonshine in taste and strength.

To celebrate finishing their O' levels, my brother and his friends celebrated on the beach by Boscombe Pier one evening. They all took some booze, Dean's contribution was several bottles of the dreaded

Carum-Carvi. No expensive off license sales for him. He arrived home late that night in a dreadful state and spent the next two days in bed with his first ever hangover, a sick bucket by his side.

After a few similar horrific sessions followed by enormous hangovers and puking we realised that our wine wasn't very pleasant but it gave our friends a big alcoholic hit. We ended up selling it to them at our backdoor for thirty pence a bottle and spending that money in the offy on better tasting alcoholic drinks, usually Mead in those days.

Later on, during that beautiful hot summer, with a guest house full of guests, a loud bang came from the top of the house. The attic, in fact. Then another. On investigation it transpired that our hidden away bottles of apple wine had begun to ferment again with the high summer temperature. Bottles ended up blowing the corks out all over the place as we hurried to rescue them. Mum and Dad took it pretty well and the guests were highly amused but that was the beginning of the end for the young winemakers.

Our final attempt at making decent wine caused more amusement for the guests. We decided to try making Dandelion wine, another free ingredient, of course. Southbourne cliff top was a great place to pick them, we soon had several carrier bags full. That same evening, Mum and Dad had one of their rare evenings out so we began the process of brewing them up. Step one was to boil the dandelions for an hour, so out came a couple of big saucepans and on went the gas. Fairly quickly a foul stench became noticeable in our kitchen. We kept boiling the leaves and yellow flowers but I became a bit concerned at how awful the smell was. I nipped upstairs to check that it hadn't gone up there where I realised the entire house was full of a smell reminiscent of sun baked fish and hot dog's piss. Of course, the dandelions were probably all well soaked in dog's wee from the cliff top. I found the smell so bad that I had to stand outside whilst the hour long boiling was completed. All the windows were opened in every room and the fumes dissipated before our parents returned. How on earth such a stinking brew could ever make a pleasant drink never occurred to us.

The Long, Hot Summer.

This was 1976, in the early Spring I took my mock O levels. What an absolute disaster they were, too. I had been a disinterested pupil for three or four years by then. I didn't have many notes written up to study from, even if I had been inclined to do so. In the 1970s I don't think you could buy crib books from Smiths. So, even if I wanted to study, I was stuck. When the results came in I and many of my classmates were disqualified from taking some subjects as we stood no chance of passing them. It would have been a waste of time and money. The O levels proper were a few months away, a hindrance before we could get out of the hated classroom and get on with our lives.

My one and only careers interview with my first year form teacher was a complete waste of time. He wondered if I had ever thought about entering the hospitality trade, maybe a publican or hotelier? I suppose it was a step up from the chip shop I was told by another teacher that I would find myself working in. I was given a couple of leaflets about running a pub that I promptly threw away. He never mentioned my obvious keenness to join the military. I had long decided that the Army was the only career that I was interested in. I had carefully decorated my room with posters of tanks, rifles, regimental cap badges and other stuff that was far more interesting than pictures of pop bands. I eventually won a long battle with Mum to sign my joining papers for under eighteen year olds. Eventually she gave in, as she could see how keen I was and that I didn't really have any other good options. Dad showed little interest but warned me not to join the infantry. Stupidly, I would not even consider the other Services, even though uncle Ian with his interesting time in the RAF Regiment, had been an influence on me.

During the Easter holidays I visited the ACIO in Bournemouth and began the process of joining up. There was no prospect of me gaining the five O levels required for officer selection, so the lower ranks beckoned. Fine by me. Nothing in the recruiting process was a problem except that I was told that I suffered from colour blindness which would disallow me from learning certain trades. I knew about the colour thing as I had been checked at primary school years before. The rest was a formality and after a few weeks I received a letter from the army guaranteeing me a starting date a few days after my seventeenth birthday. No need to worry too much about the forthcoming exams then.

By this time I had become more pally with my school friends whilst becoming more distant from the local boys. We lived far and wide across Bournemouth but would meet up in the evenings at a disco or down on the beach. Some of my mates were fortunate enough to have been bought mopeds, Suzuki, Honda and the ubiquitous Yamaha FS1E. They were the top dogs and they knew it. I could only look on with a massive envy at these guys, with my rusty old five speed racer. It seemed very unfair that I worked what was basically split shifts every summer in a hot kitchen and had little to show for it. Most of the moped gang had never even been troubled by a paper round. Nobody said life was meant to be fair!

The Pinecliffe Hotel became a feature in our lives when we reached about sixteen years of age. Barely a mile from home, this huge pub hosted live music seven nights a week. Usually six nights of pretty decent bands and jazz on Sunday nights. In the early days we kept a low profile, playing darts in the back room whilst we very slowly sipped a pint of Devenish Bitter. Luckily, our beer of choice had a specific gravity of about three per cent, so we could glug a couple of pints without being too inebriated. Gradually the manageress got to know all our faces and we became part of the furniture on a Friday and Saturday evening.

One night my pal and I were enjoying a quiet game of darts when a large group of very noisy students came crashing into our games room. They were obviously Scandinavian and wanted to practise their English with us. We learnt that they had just arrived from

Finland and were staying for the summer at a language school. Within about twenty minutes my very happy friend and I were snogging with the two prettiest girls! We couldn't believe our luck and it was very enjoyable. God knows why they picked us out but we certainly didn't complain. The Finns were a lovely bunch and we all became friends over the next few months but, inevitably, the two beautiful young ladies very quickly moved on to older lads with cars and money, leaving us with our memories.

This was, of course, the long hot summer of 1976, when Bournemouth was such a fantastic place to be. Unfortunately, my O levels had to be sat, so I made an attempt at studying. Our neighbours kindly let Dean and I move into their guest house for a few months as they weren't letting rooms that year. We lived on the top floor and found we had more freedom than ever as we could come and go without Dad knowing. A few weeks before the first exam, our year at school finally finished and we all went home to revise. My friends and I actually went down the beach. Hot days, girls in bikinis everywhere, a beautiful warm sea, teenagers full of beans and testosterone, what else could anyone expect? Sitting at home trying to revise subjects I barely understood was an absolute nightmare and I did far less than the minimum required. Of course, my clever pals who put the work in performed well in the exams and still managed to have a good summer. We all mature at different ages, I suppose.

In the evenings, the local boys and girls all met up at the Pinecliffe, listened to the music, drank beer and then walked as a huge gang through Fisherman's Walk down to the beach where we sat around in twenty degrees warmth, or swam in the moonlight.

Some of the older lads had progressed to motorbikes, paid for with apprenticeships or hard hot work in the local pubs and restaurants. Scoop owned a Triumph Tiger Cub that we all envied whilst his pal Sid, from London, came down to visit on a Norton 750 with a purple fuel tank. Wow! That put the Suzuki 250s right back in their boxes.

I was expected to sit a total of seven O levels. At the end of May we were back in school to begin the month of exams. I gave the English, English literature, geography and history papers a pretty good go and felt that I had answered the questions reasonably well. Maths, physics and chemistry were still a complete mystery to me and I hardly answered a thing. Funny thing is, my mental arithmetic had always been fast and accurate but that was taught to me at primary school before we started the Schools Maths Project syllabus that was way above my head. I would have done much better academically if I had attended the secondary modern school near where I lived. I would have been top dog academically there, which would have kept me motivated to work hard to stay at the front.

By the end of June the nightmare was over. I was not alone, most of the boys from the duffers class who had endured five years of grammar school education, had been equally blank when they turned over their exam papers. We had a few days left in the classroom and I actually played truant one lovely hot day for the only time in my life. A bunch of us met by Boscombe Pier and spent the day by the sea. On 2nd July 1976 my classmates and I were dismissed for the final time. We all let out a huge cheer before charging out into the adult world. We didn't even say goodbye to each other, or shake hands before leaving. Many of the boys in that class had become good friends of mine over the years. That was the last time I saw most of them.

I carried on enjoying the summer, working at home and spending my days on the beach and the evenings at the Pinecliffe. Life was pretty good, girls became friendlier, beer was cheap and I was guaranteed a job in a few months time.

A few days before the O level results were due in the post, my pal and I came up with a cunning plan to have a laugh at one of our friends' expense. We typed up a set of official looking exam results, mostly fails, and posted them to his address. He was a bright boy and would have been horrified with those results. We thought it was hilarious but he had the last laugh as the results we sent him mirrored ours almost exactly, whereas he actually did very well when the real results came in. I passed two and had two near misses. On the same day Dean received three A levels to go with his ten O levels. Cheers brother.

The numbers of guests gradually eased off and the long hot summer finally broke early in September. The days of dozens of us boys and girls with our towels lined up along the prom, with radio 1 playing happy summer songs was finally over. Mum had no work for me, so I found myself cycling to a hotel about three miles away every morning to do some table waiting and washing up for twenty pounds a week. My schoolmates were either back at school starting their sixth form or, for many of my old classmates, re-doing their previous year. That seemed a bit odd to me and must have been an embarrassment for them and their parents who had to ask for them to be given another chance. The local crew were all starting apprenticeships, going to technical college or starting things like nursing training. Like us school friends, we all just drifted apart forever at the end of summer.

Early in October my brother left home for Aberystwyth University in Wales. It was no big deal. Mum and Dad drove him there with a suitcase of smelly clothes, a few LP's and a grant from Bournemouth Council. It was enough to live on if you were careful, which he certainly was.

A month later on 8th November came my turn. I asked Mum and Dad to drop me outside the railway station as I didn't want a fuss on the platform. We said our goodbyes and I walked inside with my ticket from the ACIO in my pocket along with all the money I had in the world, about a fiver. To my absolute delight a group of my friends were standing on the platform waiting for me. They had skived off school for an hour and ridden over on their mopeds to see me off. Bless them. What great pals. We laughed and smoked and shook hands and then I was off, next stop the Army selection centre at Sutton Coldfield. Seventeen years and four days old, I felt like an adult and embraced the fleeting freedom.

Part Two 1976-1979

Leaving Home.

In the 1970s the British Army was a massive military machine, with 56,000 soldiers based in Germany. At least twice that number also lived in mainly fairly dismal barracks in the UK. A further 20,000 or so patrolled on anti-terror duties in Ulster. There were smaller bases and training areas in places as exotic as Alberta, Cyprus, Singapore, Belize and a few others. The Royal Navy and RAF were also major players on the world stage with dozens of squadrons of aircraft and hundreds of ships.

Many bored teenagers opted for the forces rather than the pit or the dole queue. Some joined to get away from an awful life in their dreary home town. Plenty went into uniform from care homes or signed up when they realised they were at the early stages of a life of crime. They sensibly realised that borstal or prison was a poor option. Others, like myself, loved guns, tanks and read up on military history.

Some very bright lads took the King's shilling. Others that did so could hardly spell their names. It mattered not, there was a role for every type of young man. The guys being recruited reflected the culture of the day. A rough, tough, boisterous attitude dominated male life. Council parks echoed with the noise of football games during the evenings until dark and all weekend. Lads used bikes for transport, supported a football team, listened to music and chatted up every girl they met. Skinhead violence was a part of life. Most school playgrounds saw fist and boot fighting between rival boys on a regular basis. Fighting involved enthusiastic arm windmilling more than anything else. I only knew a couple of boys that went to boxing clubs and one who practised martial arts. Very few trained athletically and hardly anyone lifted weights. There was only one gym in Bournemouth. Because of all the time spent outdoors, most boys carried very little excess weight and were fit even though we all drank and most smoked. Our Dads mostly worked in manual labour and they encouraged their sons to play sport and be active.

On arrival at Sutton Coldfield for three days of ability tests I was allocated a room with seven other lads, given directions to the cookhouse for lunch and told to be on parade at 2pm. As people do, I chatted to one or two others, then we stuck together for meals and smoke breaks. Our first taste of Army Catering Corps food was excellent. The army didn't want anyone crying off on the first afternoon because the grub was not to their liking.

We spent the days sitting mental arithmetic tests, English language tests and a psychometric test. After five years of grammar school it was a breeze to me. Maybe the time there had been of use after all. Then came a day of physical tests where I did less well. I was one of the smaller recruits and not very strong or athletic, compared to some of the others. We had to complete sit-ups, press-ups, jump into the air with one arm raised and a host of other knackering things. My smoking probably went against me too. The last thing we had to do was to complete a long questionnaire about our likes and dislikes. Questions like: Do you prefer working indoors or outdoors? Do you enjoy working with your hands or your brain? Finally, it asked you to state which Regiment or Corps you would like to join. I filled it in quickly having given that last one plenty of thought over the previous few months. In the evenings we all sat in the bar, drinking a slow pint and tasting our first NAAFI pie. I began getting used to meeting and chatting with lads from other parts of the country with very different attitudes, accents and behaviour.

On the final morning we all had an interview with an officer who told us what role we had been selected for, and where we would be going to train to do it. My turn came to sit down for a chat with the officer. He was about to tell me in which direction the entire rest of my life was going to go in. My preference was to be a dog handler, a tankie or a member of the Intelligence Corps. He quietly explained to me that I had scored very good marks in the intelligence tests and would be wasted working with dogs or tanks. The Int. Corps. wasn't an option for recruits. I was then asked if I would like to be a Command Post Assistant in the Royal Artillery? As a naive seventeen year old boy I didn't have the bottle to say: "no, it's tanks or dogs for me or I go home."

So I said, "yes, that sounds fine, thank you very much," even though I knew nothing about the role. We shook hands and off I went, sending the next lad in after me.

Those of us who had been selected for the Gunners were driven down to the railway station with our tickets in our hands. With us was one other lad, a small Jock. He looked pretty miserable and we chatted for a few minutes. His ticket was to take him to a barracks outside Edinburgh where he was to become a member of the Black Watch. I didn't know a great deal about the military but enough to know that I had a better time ahead of me than he had. From his demeanour I could tell that he felt the same.

The train journey to Woolwich Arsenal was just long enough for us to swap names, towns of births and a few football team jokes before we arrived and were collected by a very smart bombardier. He drove us up Shooter's Hill to our new home for the next few months. Little did we realise that the direction our lives would take had been irrevocably changed in the past few days. Nothing would ever be the same again. We were soldiers now.

Woolwich Arsenal, the Fun Starts.

The Royal Artillery was one of the largest corps in the British Army with many regiments, most of them still with ties to the local communities where they recruited from. It helped create bonds between the soldiers in hard times if they had things in common with each other, like schools and football clubs. My local gunner regiment was the 27 Regiment, the Hampshire gunners. The Scots had a Lowland and a Highland regiment, and so on. All artillery recruits carried out their basic training at Woolwich, then were posted to one of the regiments. However, if the Welsh gunner regiment didn't need any surveyors, but another regiment did, then the Welsh lads who joined as surveyors never got to sing `Land of my Fathers` with their countrymen, as they ended up somewhere else completely. Singing `You`ll Never Walk Alone` or `Flower of Scotland`, perhaps. The system was too big to cater for individual needs and wants. We were just numbers, very small cogs in a huge machine. It couldn't be any other way.

The group of us leapt out of the tranny van and quickly fell into line. The bombardier welcomed us very pleasantly then directed us to our dormitory on the top floor the block behind us. Alamein was carved in stone above the imposing doorway and was to be the name of our troop for the duration. As I walked inside I could smell the thick layers of polish, paint and bullshine that had been imparted to the pristine old building. Soldiers had resided here for many decades and their sweat and elbow grease was palpable everywhere. The place positively sparkled with brasso, blanco and bootpolish.

I was shown my bed, one of twelve in the dormitory, with a tall locker for my clothes and a little bedside locker for bits and bobs.

The other lads took the others, then we followed orders to form up downstairs.

Those of us who had some CCF experience realised that we had a big advantage over the other recruits in the early days. We could march, salute, recognise rank markings and had many other useful skills that would keep us out of trouble. The CCF lads, on their annual camps, had also been subject to the delights of army cooking, so the grub and dark reddish brown strong tea came as no surprise to us.

We tried to march as a group to the cookhouse but we looked shambolic. Straight away it became evident to me who would struggle with learning how to drill. One or two walked doggy style, one changed step every five yards whilst desperately trying to fit in and we all felt ridiculous. As we neared the cookhouse, squads of lads who were several weeks into their training hooted their derision when they saw us. Those lads were marching fast with one arm behind their backs holding their mug and kfs. Their free arm was swinging rapidly back and forwards, propelling them to the cookhouse in front of our rabble.

We devoured the food which was nourishing and there was plenty of it. The cooks were a dour bunch of so and so's who looked hot and angry, typical ACC.

We had a couple of days of hanging around waiting for the full complement of recruits to arrive before we could begin our training course. Once we were up to thirty two in number our basic training kicked off with an introduction to our leader, teacher, drill pig and superb straight-faced actor: Sgt. Horwell.

Sgt. Horwell had been seconded from 50 Missile regiment for a couple of years to train the likes of us, before returning to his home regiment when another smart young Sgt. took over from him. The turnover of instructors ensured they didn't become stale. Sometimes it gave one of the older chaps a final posting in the UK before they left the Army. It also allowed some of the good young NCO's the chance to learn new skills. Only good quality guys were allowed to take charge of recruits though one or two of the skills instructors weren't of such a high standard, as I found out to my cost.

Sgt. Horwell was no Guards regiment drill pig, famous from the old films. He was a good guy, smart, decent, intelligent and patient. On many an occasion I could see him struggle to stop a smile crossing his face when one of us did something ridiculous or stupid. On these occasions, he had to deliver a two hundred decibel bollocking when he really wanted to crease up with mirth. It must have been hard for him and his sidekick, an old bombardier who did the running around for him. I bet they sat in their little office after work some days and roared with laughter at our antics on the square.

Our first major event was the issuing of our uniforms. This was one of the things that I had looked forward to over the past few years. Some decent new army kit, not the hand me downs I had worn in the CCF. We formed up in a slightly improved fashion and marched off to the quartermaster's stores where a couple of old timers smiled at us malevolently as we approached the counter.

"Name," they yelled?

"24446124 Gunner Fenton, Bombardier."

"Right then. Here you go, son."

They already knew our measurements so it was a case of piling up a huge mountain of clothing, boots, suitcase, kitbag, hats and other small items. We stuffed everything into our suitcase and kitbag whilst being hassled by Sgt. Horwell and his pal. Back in the dormitory we had a bit of time to sort it all out.

In the 1960s the Army had, thankfully, ditched the old battle dress of WW2 and national service fame. They modernised with an olive green cotton combat uniform. By the time I was issued my combats, this had morphed into DPM (disruptive pattern material) camouflage which was reasonably comfortable and easy to look after. The trousers came with a soft cotton inner layer which helped keep one warm when on exercise. Of course, there was bound to be a problem with me and the wearing of a uniform, my old weakness.

The day to day shirt that we wore was the Shirt KF. Whoever decided that it was a sensible choice for modern soldiers obviously never wore one. It was impossible to iron without using half a can of starch, it looked awful when worn in the summer without a jumper but worst of all, it felt as if it was made of 50% horse hair and 50% Brillo pad. The damn things were unbelievably uncomfortable, even worse when one began to sweat. I couldn't believe that some guys wore them next to their bare skin and thought they were fine. Many of us shaved them, washed them loads of times in softener, then learnt to wear long sleeved tee shirts underneath. (A couple of years later I bought a fabulous American army issue shirt to wear on exercise. I still wear it forty five years later and it looks as good as new). A soldier's life was difficult enough, giving us crap kit to wear was a stupid idea, just to a few bob from the military budget. Our kit was always provided by the lowest bidder. Just the thought of wearing that shirt next to my skin made me shiver and whenever I wore it for the next several years I felt uncomfortable.

Our two pairs of boots DMS (directly moulded sole) were the same type that I had been issued in the CCF. They were worn with putties, a strange old-fashioned piece of cloth bandage wrapped around the ankle. One pair of our boots were earmarked for best and had to be bulled to a glossy shine for our passing out parade in the Spring.

Our staff taught everyone how to wear the various uniforms, how to iron them and how to store them in our lockers. All basic stuff to me. Our civilian clothes found themselves being stored away for wearing at weekends and occasional evening trips to the NAAFI.

The squad of us were beginning to get to know each other by now, especially those that we shared a room with. I found the whole thing quite enjoyable, wasn't homesick and got on well enough with everyone else. I had noticed that I was the only SSG 1 (intelligence rating) soldier in the troop, as all our ratings were written large on a board in the troop office. After being bottom of school it was refreshing and motivating to be top of the tree for once. There were a few things I could assist some of the others with. One or two of the squad struggled with the more difficult drill movements which I could help with. Other lads did likewise with ironing and boot bulling.

For a week or so my muckers continued to call me Clifford. That was never going to last. No soldiers are called by such a mouthful of consonants. For a couple of awful days, it was Manuel, the waiter in Fawlty Towers, before they settled on my new and lasting nickname. At the time, there was a popular clothing company that had been in existence for some years. They had a shop in most towns in the UK. They sold reasonable quality suits, shirts, ties and the usual blokey wear for going out at night. Many of the lads sported clothes bought from the chain when we went out at the weekend. Harry Fenton was the name, so Harry I became! Clifford thankfully disappeared forever.

By week two, the routine was established and discipline standards had been set. Our kit had to be immaculate, our bearing soldier-like and everything done at double time. Sgt. Horwell was strict but fair, no favourites and no violence, just a very loud voice when something was amiss.

We started the day with a room inspection that eventually became a test of our composure. My bed was opposite the one slept in by a Scouse lad named Carson, a lovely bloke with a ready smile. He found it terribly difficult to take anything seriously except Liverpool FC which he worshipped. If there was sniggering to be done, he did it. Room inspection found me and him, standing to attention, facing each other about six feet apart. Sgt. Horwell would enter the room and begin looking for faults.

Our lockers would be wide open with our various uniforms smartly hanging or squared away on shelves. Everything had to be just perfect. He would begin his inspection of the lockers and of us. We made bed blocks with our sheets and blankets. A bed block was the name for the sheets and blankets being folded up together at the end of the bed, wrapped in a blanket with the pillows on top. There was plenty of room for error with a saggy pillow or badly folded blanket. If there was the slightest dip in the blanket left covering the mattress, or a fault with the bedblock there was a good chance it would find itself flying out of an open window. Boots sometimes followed onto the concrete walkway three floors below. Whilst this was going on somewhere in the room Scouse and I were standing to attention looking each other in the eye. Beads of sweat would appear, lips would quiver and shoulders would start to bob up and down. Sgt. Horwell knew what was going on and played it well. At just the right moment he would pace up to Scouse and glare at him, with his grimacing face about six inches from Scouse's trembling top lip. We were all dying with the tension and desperate to howl with suppressed laughter. Then, in the nick of time, Sgt. Horwell would stride out of the room just before we all cracked up, slamming the door and letting us relieve the tensions by sobbing with mirth. Meanwhile, some poor sod would be dashing down the stairs to retrieve his bedblock or boots from the concrete outside.

Two or three times during our training, the rooms were inspected by an officer, which meant an even higher level of bullshit than normal was required. We would have to polish the dormitory floors with heavy wooden bumpers to remove all of the footprints and to give the floor a glassy sheen. There wasn't time to do all the preparation on the morning of the inspection so we worked long into the night sorting everything out, then grabbed a few hours kip before making an early start. Some lads even slept on the floor in sleeping bags so they didn't disturb their immaculate bed blocks.

After morning inspection we would continue most days with a couple of hours learning drill. Beginning with simple stuff like left turn, right turn, marching and halting. Then moving onto changing step, open order march, eyes front and saluting. It not only taught us discipline it also helped the smaller guys like me build strength and gain confidence. Gradually we came together as a unit of men. Once again, there were times of great hilarity. When, as a body we turned left, for example, and one duffer turned right to be facing his mate, it was priceless fun for the rest of us. Sgt. Horwell would go mad, cursing and shouting at the idiot whilst we thanked god it was somebody else. The language was wonderfully colourful. I was called a c**t bastard for the first time in my life. The circumstance being a drill manoeuvre when, for some reason, I ended up standing to attention with one thigh parallel to the ground as if frozen half-way through a left turn.

"Fenton, you c**t bastard," he hollered at me as he dashed up, all fume, spittle and red cheeked,

"What do you think you are, a feckin' Stork?"

I very quickly decided, as he glowered at me from a couple of inches away, that it probably wasn't a good time to explain that those two profanities don't really go together.

I usually managed to play the grey man quite well. Small, not gobby, fairly well-behaved and ok at the ironing stuff and drill. I rarely stood out from the crowd. However, this was a double-edged sword because when I did mess up it really surprised the staff who came down hard on me. One or two of the lads just never got the hang of drill and ended up being hidden away in the middle of the formation. Others, looked like a bag of shite however much they washed, shaved, ironed their kit and bulled their boots. One or two others sparkled like guardsmen with hardly any effort.

We were given an allowance of ten pounds per week. The rest of our pay was held back until we passed out of Woolwich. They didn't want us going out on the razz at night-time, so they kept us all poor whilst we were there. Almost nobody had any money that they had brought with them to spend. The fortnightly pay parade was a time of much amusement for those of us who could march but an absolute nightmare for those with two left feet. It began with the entire Alamein Troop lined up outside the accommodation block in alphabetical order. I was one of the first to be paid every week so had plenty of time to go upstairs with my cash, then watch the hijinks from a safe third floor window. To receive your pay, you had to come smartly to attention when your name was called. You quickly marched up to the front entrance, navigated up the steps then marched a few paces to a desk specially set up in the foyer. On it lay a pile of little envelopes, one for each of us. Once you arrived at the desk you had to halt, salute the officer sitting behind the desk, say your name, rank and number, take your pay, salute again, about turn and march away back outside. What could go wrong? Some guys found the whole thing terribly stressful, so were doomed before they set off. Others couldn't walk up four stairs without nearly falling over when the pressure was on. Some halted about five yards from the desk and had to lean forwards but the funniest ones crashed into it because they couldn't judge their stopping distance correctly. Anyone that made one of these errors was chased outside to the back of the queue by the attendant staff with bellows of "fucking idiot c**t" and suchlike. That, of course, just made them more nervous and more likely to mess up the next time they tried. We watched from our windows and nearly died laughing. Some guys were in and out several times before the officer just gave up and gave them their cash before darkness fell.

Christmas was fast approaching and the two week break marked the end of the first stage in our training. A test of our progress, and of the competence of our instructors, was the formality known as passing off the square. This was bigged up as a hurdle to cross, before we could go on leave or resume our training after Christmas. To pass off the square we had to march as a squad on the huge parade ground, show we could drill as a unit, then, one at a time, march out to an officer, halt in front of him, salute twice, about turn and march back to our place in the squad. It should have been a doddle for me. Sgt. Horwell practised this last tricky part with us all many times, his reputation depended on us not messing up. The first time I marched out, full of confidence, halted and saluted. He instantly blew up at me whilst chasing me back to the squad, telling me what terrible things he was going to do to my testicles and calling me all sorts of bastards. I had only gone and saluted him with my left hand! Dear oh dear. Pride comes before a fall, as they say.

Someone else received similar treatment for concentrating so hard that he saluted with his tongue sticking out to one side. The parade ground at Woolwich Arsenal was the longest in Europe and, with the imposing pillars, archway and old military brickwork facing onto it was a very impressive place to be drilling. As we improved our timing as a group, we actually began to enjoy marching up and down there with the wind howling across the playing fields in front of us. The passing off the square progressed without a hitch and we congratulated each other as we walked down to Woolwich railway station on our journeys home.

The walk to the station always struck me as a bit of a risk. The IRA had targeted our barracks a few years previously, having planted a bomb in the soldiers pub near the front gate. How very brave of them. We were obviously young soldiers walking up and down from the station to our base carrying our army suitcases and sporting very short haircuts. An easy target. I marched up the hill as quickly as I could and kept my eyes peeled for dodgy looking cars.

The barracks had to be guarded over the Christmas holidays and all the recruits took their turn, it was part of their training. Those that lived closest to London carried out the guard duties nearest to Christmas Day. Coming from Bournemouth, which was only about a two hour drive away in those days, I ended up back in my room preparing my kit on the 23rd December. I reported for my duties at 9am on Christmas Eve and began a very, very long day.

We were buddied up and issued with our weapons. The Army has always held great faith in a soldier wielding a pick axe handle painted green. It is a fearsome tool in the right hands. As we hadn't yet done any small arms training, it was all there was. Our job was to patrol the barracks for two hours looking for intruders, fires, open doors or anything suspicious. At the end of the patrol we put our feet up for the same time whilst two other lads went off patrolling. We also had to man a couple of stationary guard posts which made a change from walking round and round. December 1976 was a very cold month and Woolwich was exposed to icy winds blowing off the North Sea.

After a tiring day, where I found it nearly impossible to nod off during my two hours off duty, I was sent for a stag under the main arch, opposite the parade square. I took over from the previous guy who was pretty much frozen to the spot and began pacing up and down under the arch. Midnight struck from a distant church, blimey, it was Christmas Day!

The wind blew but I was cosy inside my combats and two greatcoats, one small one large. I couldn't lift my pickaxe handle if had I wanted to with all those layers on. I thought about the last few weeks and how much I was enjoying the whole thing. Being away from school and in the adult world where I had responsibilities and a future gave me a big buzz. The stars shone brightly, the frost came down and I gradually became colder and more sleepy. Across the square and the grassy field was just a low fence, anybody could climb over it and get in. I had to stay watchful. I'm good at this stuff, I thought, I can stay awake all night. My brain disagreed and started to close down. My eyes wearied and half closed. I jerked back to full consciousness and spotted a figure approaching me from about twenty yards away. My sixth sense had saved me. I turned to face him and felt nervous and befuddled, still half asleep. The garrison RSM was briskly walking towards me, wanting to check if I was alert or dozing.

"Evening Sir," I squeaked as he arrived. He peered suspiciously at my tired face and accepted that I had been awake and had seen him just in time.

"Keep your wits about you son," he growled as he continued his prowl around the buildings. I had just learnt that if you are tired enough you can pretty much fall asleep while standing upright.

The sun came up on a lovely, cold and crisp Christmas morning as my mate and I were back walking around the camp. Its first warming rays slowly thawed out the frost on the ground. We reckoned we must have covered over forty miles in the twenty four hours and were completely done in by the time the London born lads took over from us at 9am. Dad picked me up at the front gate in his Austin 1800 and we sped off round the south circular and down the M3 to home just in time for our Christmas dinner. The après-lunch glass of champagne and cigarette tasted particularly good before I crept off to bed for a well earned snooze.

A week later we all found ourselves back in our billet and about to start weapons training. The rifle we trained with was my old friend the SLR. I had fired it with the cadets many times and looked forward eagerly to the skills sessions. My small group were in the hands of a huge Rhodesian bombardier from 19 Regiment. After learning to strip and assemble the weapon we began practising the drills for live firing. To do this we lay on the ground in the prone position and had to open various pouches on our belts and operate the weapon in the prescribed order. I made one small mistake with this and he spotted it, to my lifelong regret. The idiot stood in the small of my back and bounced up and down whilst telling me very slowly what I had done wrong. One word per bounce, just above the top of my pelvis. Shit, I was in a lot of discomfort after this stupidity.

I ended up spending several days in bed with back pains but was never sent to visit the camp doctor. I recovered after a while and carried on but my back has never been quite as good since. Years later when I had some x-rays taken there was evidence of a cracked facet joint in the area he hurt, which I believe he caused. This was the only time in my service I received physical bullying.

Training continued and we learnt to drill with our SLRs. This carried the risk of dropping the weapon during a drill movement, which would have been a terrible crime but none of us ever did.

We only ventured out of our barracks on Saturdays. Usually we headed to the laundry but on one occasion, a few of us went to watch Charlton Athletic play at the Valley. It was by far the biggest ground I had been to and only a couple of miles away. We hadn't have the money to do much else and kit cleaning filled most of our weekends anyway. The best we could manage was a cup of tea in the

NAAFI in the evenings. Us smokers even had trouble affording to buy enough fags to keep us going. Most of our cash went on boot polish, dusters and phone calls home.

Physical prowess wasn't as big a deal in the artillery as it was in some more well known units, such as the Paras and the Royal Marines. The gunner regiments didn't generally take the pick of the crop, so fitness wise, we were very much a mixed bag. We did, however, spend plenty of time running round the Dell, a muddy copse, carrying heavy logs in teams, whilst being yelled at. We did a bit in the gym too but it took second place to drilling and weapons training.

Once we had mastered the SLR we moved on to trade training. No matter what role we had been allocated in our prospective regiments, we had to be gunners first and foremost. So we began a few weeks of proper artillery training with the famous Pack Howitzer. I, with five other lads, came under the watchful eye of Bombardier Wally Hart, a wizened old Dundonian, also from 19 Regiment. We worked hard to learn the mechanics of deploying the gun and the skills required load, aim and fire. I wasn't a born gun bunny, you need to be built like a prop forward to enjoy the physicality of the work. It was hard going and there were many opportunities to hurt yourself, break fingers and pull muscles.

During one session we were working as a crew to bring the gun into action, when I fucked up dangerously, endangering the others by dropping a piece of heavy equipment. Wally delivered a sting rebuke with his open palm across my cheek. It stung like hell, the shock brought a tear to my eyes and I choked up. Wally put his arm around me, slightly shocked by his own reaction, and said, "It's ok wee man, just learn from it."

And I did. *Wally and I joked about this at a 25 Battery reunion in 2010.*

The course finished with a couple of days down on Salisbury Plain where we live fired the guns. I was also shown the Field Artillery Computer Equipment (FACE). This was the kit I would be trained to work with on arrival at my new unit. I had never seen a computer before except on the Television programme Tomorrow's World.

Infantry skills also needed to be learnt. We all travelled down to Hythe, in Kent, for a week of running around like maniacs, charging up and down hills doing section attacks, and creeping about ambushing each other at night. The hill running sorted out the fittest from the rest of us and they were earmarked as potential 29 Commando regiment guys from then on. During a night exercise I began to feel sick, possibly from some dodgy compo that we had eaten earlier, and puked up. We were practising ambushes in the pouring rain and it was all I could do to keep upright. Every time we stopped I was sick again, a horrible night for me.

To celebrate St. Barbera, for some reason the patron saint of the Royal Artillery, there was a compulsory church parade to attend. Most of us hardly knew what religion we were, let alone believed in a god. For the service we were to be dressed for the first time in our tailored No. 2 uniforms, peaked caps and bulled boots. I had to wear a pair of very fetching pyjama bottoms under the heavy woollen trousers, for the usual reason. A request went out for one volunteer from Alamein Troop to read the lesson in the garrison church, in front of a full house. Most of the guys would rather have fought Henry Cooper than read from the bible in front of an audience. I realised that quite a few would make a complete arse of the whole thing and would suffer dreadful embarrassment. It was time for the grammar school boy to help his mates out, so I put my name forward to the huge relief of the rest of them. One volunteer was always better than a pressed man. On the Sunday, the service and the reading was a doddle and I drew strength from having the balls to do it. I decided the old maxim of 'never volunteer for anything' was very limiting. From then on I volunteered for anything that sounded even slightly interesting and hoped for the best.

Sgt. Horwell asked us one Wednesday morning if anybody fancied trying out the dry ski slope owned by the garrison. I followed my new rule that I would volunteer for everything, so my hand shot up, with one or two others. On Wednesdays we had become used to the military tradition of enjoying a sports afternoon, for most this meant rugby, running or footy. I wasn't interested in any of those, at this time, but the skiing sounded fun.

After lunch we all paraded in the troop corridor in our sports gear, ready to go. It just happened that my aunty had knitted me a lovely white Arran jumper for Christmas. I stood lined up with all the lads in the footy shirts and tracky bottoms, looking a million dollars in my beautiful new knitwear. Horwell arrived and straight away marched up to me, looked me up and down disbelievingly and sarcastically asked,

"Who the fuck do you think you are, fucking Franz Klammer?"

He had a point.

I soon found out that the dry slope was very painful to fall over on, but it was a fun thing to try and I fancied learning to ski if I ever had the chance.

With only a couple of weeks to go before our passing out parade we practised hard at our drill, bulled our boots until they were like mirrors and began to feel like real soldiers. The new recruits were now jeered at by us when they marched like Biffos to the cookhouse. We had blossomed in fourteen weeks, toughened up mentally and physically and those of us that could cope with the discipline had quite a lot of fun too. The one or two who struggled to make the grade disappeared, as did the troublemakers and nutjobs. The army had no time for maniacs who just caused trouble wherever they went and they certainly didn't want guys that were softies, either.

They tested our behaviour under the influence of alcohol one evening. The troop had an official night out in the soldiers pub just outside the barracks main gate, which we all had to attend. We were encouraged to get a bit drunk with our instructors, who watched for signs of bolshiness, bullying or any other weird stuff when we were pissed. We all seemed to pass that test with flying colours but drill the next day was spectacularly painful with much puking at the back of the square. Carrying on with a hangover was another thing we had to get used to.

A few days before our pass out parade and dispersal to our units we were called into the corridor by Sgt. Horwell who was with a very posh captain and some of the other instructors. We lined up, wondering what was coming, then the officer addressed us.

"Good afternoon chaps. These are the Regiments that you will be posted to. Good luck, what!"

We knew little about the regiments in the artillery. Most were based over in Germany, a few back in England. We hadn't really had time to think about anything beyond finishing our basic training. We did know that one or two of the lads fancied 29 Commando based down in Plymouth. We had been informed that 50 Missile regiment never went to Northern Ireland, so most of us wanted to avoid them, if possible.

I was the first name on the list: "Fenton".

I came to attention. "Sir."

"You are going to 19 Field Regiment, The Highland Gunners, in Larkhill."

"Sir."

At this, the little group of staff and instructors burst out laughing. Sgt. Horwell, who by now had lost his gruff exterior and away from the drillyard had almost become like a knowledgeable friendly uncle to us, looked at me and grimaced. Fucking hell, I thought, why the response? What was wrong with 19 Regiment?

The rest of the names and regiments were read out. Several of my pals were also destined for 19 Regiment, a Jock regiment, although none of us came from Scotland. I didn't want to be going back so close to home. Bournemouth was only a fifty minutes drive away. There was nothing I could do about it except go with the flow. One very smart and keen London lad was off to The King's Troop, he bore the brunt of the mickey taking but I suspect he was rather proud.

The following morning we met the big, tough, back damaging, Rhodesian weapons trainer. He asked us what units we had been assigned to. When I told him mine, he stated ominously, "There are some very hard men in 19 Regiment."

Oh Jesus!

The day of our passing out parade dawned bright, cold and sunny. I was happy to have finished the training without any serious problems. My friends in Bournemouth had tried to sound knowledgeable when they said the training broke people down, then re-assembled them in the mould that the military wanted. That may have been the American way but not the British Army's style. I certainly didn't feel that I had been broken down in any way but certainly felt more confident, strong, grown up and capable. As a seventeen year old I could have left at any time, just walked away and gone home but I never felt that I wanted to.

Most of our parents came to see the parade where we paraded to the sound of the Royal Artillery Band. The March of the Grenadiers thundered out as we marched through the Arch for one last time before dispersing. One poor lad, however, missed that bit as he had fainted half way through the inspection by the visiting officer. Dad took a brilliant photo showing him flat out on the tarmac amongst rows of smart gunners trying not to snigger.

By lunchtime we had said our goodbyes, wished each other well and moved on with our lives, most of us never to see each other again.

Before heading for home, I was asked by the Army if I wanted to be part of their satisfied soldier scheme. In the 1970s the government was still trying to recruit young men into the military, rather than doing their level best to put them off. The scheme entailed me visiting my old school and giving a talk to any pupils that were interested in following in my footsteps. At the time, there was still a residue feeling of basic training being brutal, similar to national service. Most of the brutality had gone but it was certainly a tough life. The vital difference from conscription days was that the military did not want to retain soldiers in basic training who decided that the army life was not for them. Moaners wrecked it for everyone. I think that even the lads aged over eighteen would have been allowed to pack up and leave Woolwich if they had wanted to.

I agreed straight away to take part, volunteer for everything was my new way of thinking. So my task was to chat with anyone that was interested and tell them how I had fared during basic training. And for that, I was granted an extra week's leave. Going back into Bournemouth School ten months after I had left was an odd experience. In my smart No.2 uniform and twat hat I walked past a room where some of my friends were sweating away at an essay and I felt ten feet tall. They waved and smiled as I strolled by their window. Only about six boys and one CCF teacher turned up to listen to my experiences. Entry into the ranks was seen as being beneath most of the pupils.

The Highland Gunners.

During the Cold War the Royal Artillery was composed of dozens of regiments and tens of thousands of troops. All of them needed to be trained in live firing of field guns, missiles, or surveying techniques, meteorology, signalling and many other very specialist skills. Most of this took place at the Royal School of Artillery, at Larkhill on Salisbury Plain. To assist in this endeavour, a regiment with it's artillery guns was available to be used by the students during their training courses.

The artillery regiments rotated around different locations every five or six years. This was to stop them becoming stale and bored, gave everyone the chance of serving both in the UK and abroad and helped the levels of expertise stay high. For example, any unit that had served it's time at Larkhill was full of gunnery experts after their endless days on the ranges but the soldiers had lost many of the skills and experience of living in the field for weeks on end.

When I joined 19 Regiment. at Larkhill they were three years into a five year posting, before returning to Germany. Although notionally a Highland regiment that recruited around Dundee, many of the soldiers were from different parts of England. There weren't enough Scots wanting to join up with the right mentality to fill all of the posts. Therefore, the administration bods at Woolwich sent a suitable lad to whatever unit needed him. My local regiment was 27 Regt. the Hampshire Gunners, but they didn't need a command post assistant at the time I was being posted.

On my first day Dad dropped me off at the main gate with my trusty suitcase and kitbag. I was seventeen and a few months, five feet two inches tall and about nine stone eight pounds in weight. I needed to shave every couple of days. I smoked, drank a bit and didn't do much keep fit, it wasn't my thing in those days. I don't have a particular hobby, the CCF had been the nearest thing to one for a few years. I was quite good at many sports but not outstanding at any. I did have plenty of endurance, I could walk for days on end quite happily. I wasn't strong, nor a fighter, in fact, I hated conflict close up. I was a born optimist, had a good sense of humour and talked like a 'college boy arse'. I felt slightly privileged, coming from the seaside and with a fairly settled home life. I was fortunate to have received a good education, though I had little to show for it on paper. As I walked up to the main entrance I felt excited at what the future may bring.

After being welcomed by the guard commander, I was escorted across the camp to meet my new unit, 25 Field Battery. The battery was, as usual, out on the ranges, so a storeman took me up to my room. We picked up an old mattress and bedding on the way. The accommodation was a 1960s block on three floors, my room was on the top floor with the rest of Command Troop. The gun bunnies lived downstairs.

My bed space consisted of a metal framed bed, a battered metal locker and a small boot locker by my bed. Two other guys lived in the room but were not present when I arrived. Our lockers made a partition between us and the four guys next door. I wasn't very impressed. The only pleasant thing was the view of Stonehenge in the distance, about three miles away.

At tea-time the battery thundered back into the barracks. Eventually my roommates appeared, tired and grubby after their day's work. Carl was English, well spoken, from Royston and was obsessed with Motown music. Froggy, from Somerset, was a livewire, couldn't stop talking and smoking and was obviously a very bright lad. The blokes from the room next door also came in for a butchers at the new boy. Stevie from Bradford, a good looking guy who played bass guitar and an extraordinary character called Kev, who was larger than life in so many ways. Kev was one of those lads, handsome, strong as an ox, a fine sportsman and motorcyclist, bright and able to learn languages with ease. He was also a comedian who could tell jokes all day, mimic most people soon after meeting them and had a host of daft facial expressions. A very funny man indeed and brimming over with energy and confidence. His weakness, and we all have one, was the ladies. All four of these guys remained good friends of mine for many years.

That evening, Froggy told me the story of his first day in the battery. His first posting from Woolwich had been to the Parachute Artillery Regiment (7RHA). During his first few weeks there he had the misfortune to break his ankle whilst out on a run. He ended up having a few months at home rehabilitating then was sent to 25 Battery, which was, by then, deemed to be more suitable for him than 7RHA.

After he was shown his bedspace a giant acne riddled monster of a soldier, known as Mad Mick, appeared in his room.

"Are you the bloke from the Para's," Mick asked?

When poor little old Froggy nodded the big lad punched him so hard that Froggy flew across the room and hit the far wall. A couple more punches followed from big, oily fists, with love and hate tattooed across them. Froggy stood no chance whatsoever and ended up a heap on the floor. He was no more a fighter than I was, possibly less so.

"We don't like the Para's here," the ugly brute spat out as he left the room.

Strangely enough, a few months later, Froggy was at a disco in a local town, chatting up a girl when some civvy took offence at his dancing prowess. The guy was in the act of taking a swing at Froggy when the big brute appeared on the scene and almost whacked the man's head off of his shoulders with one mighty punch. Mad Mick smiled a yellow toothed smile of comradeship at Froggy and lurched back to the bar and his bottle of whiskey.

I settled in with the other young lads from Command Troop pretty easily. My small stature and open friendly attitude generally kept me out of trouble. For the first few months I wasn't much use to the battery as I didn't have a trade so I ended up helping tidying up the signals store and other boring tasks. Most of the lads were out on the ranges with the big guns four or five days a week, supporting the School of Artillery next door. The work for them was hard, tedious and very often, wet and cold. Early morning starts and late finishes were the norm. By the time Friday came everybody was knackered and ready for a beer or two. Most of the soldiers disappeared at the weekends. The married ones went home to their quarters, the singles went out partying if they had the wit, the money and somewhere to go to. A sad few unfortunates stayed in the barracks drinking heavily until the rest returned on Sunday evenings. I would get the bus or hitch-hike to Bournemouth and be home by opening time at The Pinecliffe. I washed and ironed my kit at home on a Saturday, before heading off to The Pinecliffe again, then on Sunday evening Dad would take me back to Larkhill.

The drive back to camp on a Sunday with the old man was just about the only time he and I spent alone together. As I only had a provisional license at the time, he was teaching me to drive and he did it pretty well. His car was a huge great 'Land Crab' Austin 1800 which was a pleasure to drive. We talked about sport all the way there and he listened to it on the radio on the way back home. He didn't see the journey as a chore as he loved driving on the quiet roads and was quite happy being out and about.

Those of us that had been away for the weekend dribbled back into the accommodation block with our uniforms on coat hangers over our arms, our heads full of tales of dubious sexual encounters and beer soaked parties. Much of it was exaggerated beyond belief and was received with derision and great hoots of laughter. Kev often had the tallest tale of incredible sexual exploits, usually ending in him having to make a sharp exit from a husband/boyfriend/coppers or taxi driver. There was always a story of a car breakdown, or a fight that had taken place, or of someone who had missed their train stop and woken up in Arbroath. Gradually the chatter quietened down by about midnight when only the sound of snoring, farting and the odd latecomer creeping in from afar, could be heard.

The first course I attended was Basic Signaller RA. Kev and a few other pals were there for the same training. We learnt how to use various military radios, set up aerials, use the correct voice procedure and the phonetic alphabet. All good fun. The highlight of the six week course was a three day exercise in the field where we practised the skills we had learnt. I was paired up with Kev. He was becoming a pretty good mate by this time. The students passed messages to and fro, changed frequencies and practised fire control voice procedure from the observation post to the command post. That was a complex skill in itself if a number of batteries were all taking part in the same fire mission. Or, if the situation warranted it, several regiments were all firing at the same target.

Just before we wrapped up for the end of course debrief, I was acting as Zero and had to send a message to all callsigns. Kev as callsign 1 should have been the first to reply to my message. He was tucked up in his sleeping bag in the back of our Land Rover. I sent my message from the front seat then realised that the switch on my microphone had stuck open.

What Kev and everyone else, including the directing staff heard was:

"Hello all stations, this is Zero, send sitrep over, fucking hell my fucking bastard pressel switch is stuck, bollocks."

Poor old Kev. He was staggering around outside, doubled up and almost wetting himself with glee at what he had heard. He was crying with laughter. The poor guy couldn't speak for about ten minutes, let alone send an intelligent message. Bollockings all round after that one.

Dartmouth and Tobermory

One morning I was summoned to the Troop Commander's office. A rare occurrence.

"Fenton, you come from Bournemouth, I believe, can you sail?"

I replied that I had sailed a bit with the Sea Scouts and just about knew my way around a yacht. I was then offered the chance of a week's sailing race from Gosport to St. Peter Port and back, onboard the Royal Artillery yacht, St. Barbera 111. That sounded more fun than Salisbury Plain in the mud and rain, with its endless shouting and loud bangs.

The RA Sailing Association owned several beautiful yachts, for the purpose of teaching adventure training to soldiers. The crew I met up with were all officers and experienced sailors so the only one doing any adventure training was me. I realised that I was the nod in the direction of the other ranks that had to be included in all sailing activities. It didn't bother me, they were friendly guys and the only rank on the boat was the skipper, the rest of us were judged on our experience at handling a boat.

We were going to be racing to St. Peter Port firstly, then back to Gosport after a stopover for one night, on the island. A course was set, bags were unpacked and watches established. As we cast off from Gosport I realised that Portsmouth harbour was exceptionally busy. It dawned on me that it was the weekend of the Queen's Silver Jubilee. We were seeing the ships making ready in The Solent to take part in the Spithead Review. As we left the harbour and turned to starboard towards the Needles, I could see small boats, frigates, destroyers, submarines and the Ark Royal, flagship of the Fleet. Lined up in the choppy waters on that memorable Friday afternoon sat more than 180 battleship grey fighting ships, representing Navies from across the Commonwealth. And we sailed right through the middle of them. What a sight it was and never to be repeated in such numbers. On closer inspection, as we made headway in a strong breeze, many of the boats looked old and tired and ready for the scrapheap.

Our yacht was a Camper and Nicholson 47. A navy blue and cream beauty, capable of ocean going cruising. We numbered ten altogether, three watches of three and the skipper. My berth was one of the small ones at the pointy end, just big enough to squeeze into amongst the sails and damp ropes. As we sped across the Channel we changed our sails several times to match the wind strength. I took my turn at the helm, under instruction from my watch leader. I was very keen to learn and felt on a par with the group of officers. They behaved and talked like the majority of my school mates, so I felt quite at ease with them.

As darkness fell, the stars appeared in a moonlit sky as we passed by the Castanets lighthouse off Cherbourg. The sound of the water rushing by the hull, the glow of the sails in the half light and the view of the flashing lighthouse were quite glorious and very memorable. I felt very much alive as the strong currents racing past France pulled us towards Jersey and our destination. We could go below when not on watch but most of us stayed up long into the night, talking of previous sailing adventures, drinking hot cocoa and living in the moment. The Skipper told me that the area we were crossing was notoriously dangerous for small craft so we had to keep a good distance offshore and away from the treacherous coast.

Early the next morning we entered the harbour where we safely moored up. We spent the day exploring the town then drinking gin and tonics onboard, whilst listening to Virginia Wade win the ladies title at Wimbledon. Whilst checking the steering gear that afternoon, the skipper found that we had a problem that caused us to pull out of the race. Nobody seemed too bothered about that so the trip turned into a jolly. It was decided we would head for the nearest English port, which happened to be Dartmouth, then sail along the English coast back to Gosport. I was just happy to be sailing, it didn't matter to me where we were going. Not that I had any say in it.

The following day we had an uneventful crossing and tea-time found us heading up the river Dart to a mooring close by the Britannia Naval College. A very noisy evening was spent at the Royal Dart Yacht Club where we showered, then ate and drank our fill. I decided that I rather liked this soldiering life. As we motored back out to sea the next morning, past the hundreds of moored yachts and the colourfully painted houses on Dartmouth's rocky hillsides, the thought came to me that one day I could enjoy living here. * *I moved to Dartmouth forty years later for a few years and sometimes crewed a racing boat that sailed from the same yacht club!*

The damaged steering gear held up well enough for us to return easterly along the coastline to base and after a clear up we said our goodbyes and headed back to our camps or homes, feeling happily tired out, weather-beaten and a little unsteady from the constant movement of the sea.

I must have passed muster because a few weeks later I was asked if I knew where Tobermory was? I knew it had to be in Scotland and replied I was keen to find out where. Three days later I was sat on the overnight train to Oban with a Welsh lad called Guy from 28 Battery. He had a wonderful valleys accent and a good easy going attitude. We were to make up a four man crew, with two officers from the regiment, to race in the Tobermory Regatta. This was my first trip over the border and I was tickled pink by the scenery. Oban and the nearby islands were particularly lovely and Tobermory itself, with it's famous colourful rows of terraced houses, was delightful. The sailing was marvellous but in our heavy old uncompetitive boat that was owned by one of the officer's fathers, we were never going to win anything. The winds around the rocky islands caused fierce squalls and even the best sailors could get caught out by their speed of arrival. If you had too much sail up in a light breeze, a sudden gust would almost broach your boat if you didn't let the sails out quickly enough.

One afternoon we were trying to squeeze every knot out of the game old tub. We had our biggest sails up and three of us leaning well out on the upper side to help keep her upright. A huge gust came whipping round the island, hit us hard and the wooden mast split with a thunderous crack, falling into the water amidst a tangle of sail, ropes and wires. Luckily, we all managed to hang on as the boat swung back way past upright and we all ended up waist deep in cold sea loch water for a few seconds before she finally stabilised. Much "buggering" and "oh shitting, what will Dad say?" followed, as we motored miserably back to the harbour where there was a boat builders workshop.

The owner of the workshop was obviously an old friend of the family and a couple of phone calls seemed to sort the whole thing out. A new aluminium mast was ordered for delivery the next week. I couldn't help thinking that the wealthy really do live in a different world from the rest of us. As Guy and myself returned to Larkhill the following morning, windburnt and tired, I wondered what adventure I could be paid to go on next time?

Home on the Range

Soldiering had to take priority, though, and I found myself sent on another course. I was now going to learn my military trade of command post assistant. Gunnery, since before Napoleon's day, has been the science of ballistics. Many variables have to be taken into account, the earth's rotation, weight of the shells, altitude of the target, wear of the barrels, even. Weather also played a major part, wind, air pressure and temperature all affecting accuracy. If the location of the guns was known to within a hundred metres or so and the grid reference of the target also pinpointed, then the guns could be expected to hit the target almost with the first round. Usually, one gun fired several shots until they just about hit the spot, whilst being adjusted onto the target by the observation post. Then the rest of the battery joined in, with all six guns firing at the same time.

It is possible for a battery of 105mm guns, spread out in roughly a circle a hundred metres across, to fire illuminating phosphorus shells high into the air in a straight line above, say, a road where enemy tanks are massing. Whilst those shells are falling slowly to earth on little parachutes, the guns can then redirect their fire to the tanks below, those shells falling before the flares go out. Pretty complicated stuff, especially when the crew are working out the firing data at four in the morning after being awake for maybe two days. Coffee and fags all round.

To make the calculations easier, quicker and more accurate, the job was computerised a few years before I joined up. The computer was housed in a huge green box about half the size of a fridge which was secured inside of the command post. The operator used a console with big soldier proof buttons and the screen had different coloured areas for different types of fire missions.

I found out fairly quickly that I just wasn't mentally suited to using computers. I struggled to remember the sequence of button pressing required to enter the data into the computer. It required a certain type of brain. My colour blindness found it difficult to make sense of the coloured zones on the screen. Frankly, I hated using the thing.

Before the advent of the computer, the whole job was done using maps and rulers, ranging tables, clever graphs and a bit of maths. I loved using those tools to do the job and became very quick at producing firing data. It used logic and mental arithmetic rather than sequential memory. Unfortunately, this old fashioned method was only ever used when the computer broke down or was switched off for a while during an exercise.

I passed the course well enough but in the field was quickly found wanting. The command post officer wanted operators who were slick, confident and experts at the computery stuff. I certainly wasn't and found myself relegated, with the other malcontents and mavericks, to the job of safety ack. We acted as a sort of referee to check if the rounds fired would land in the impact area on Salisbury Plain, rather than in one of the surrounding villages. Because of our careful checks, the only times there was a safety problem was when the soldier in charge of the gun would load more charge bags than was intended into the breech behind the shell. On these rare occasions the shell would overshoot, often by quite a few miles. Luckily, most of the land around the ranges was empty farmland anyway.

Safety crews spent their time cold and bored, the only fun part of the day was when your partner was connecting the field telephone to the range control office. If you timed it right you could crank the handle of your own telephone and give him a nasty little electric shock whilst he was desperately fiddling with the wires on his telephone, trying to attach them before you rang him. The Kray brothers had bought one of the same phones in a junk shop and used it to inflict pain on their rivals in rather different circumstances.

The other break from the monotony was lunchtime. A Bedford lorry would turn up on the gun position, the tailboard would be lowered and the storemen would dish out range stew to the hungry crews. Nobody bothered with mess tins or knives and forks. We simply queued up with our pals and when it was our turn, offer up a slice of bread, which the storeman would pour some lumpy stew onto. We then slapped another piece of bread on top and munched it down, finishing off with a long lick up our forearm to get the runny liquid cleaned off. All washed down with a mug of strong tea that tasted much like the stew.

I was pulled into the Battery Commander's office about the time of my eighteenth birthday and asked how long I would be signing up for. I had never given leaving the army a thought, even though I wasn't particularly enamoured with the artillery. I certainly didn't want to go back home and find a job in Bournemouth. That would have seemed like weakness to me, so I stayed and signed on for nine years. One could choose three, six or nine years. The longer you committed for, the higher your pay and the more chance of interesting opportunities coming your way.

This opened the door for me being given driver training, if nothing else. I could drive reasonably well by this time anyway but controlling a worn out old Land Rover took some practise. Just driving down a straight road was hard work, the steering had so much play in it that you moved your arms like a child with a pretend fire engine.

After a few pleasant 'cabbies' around the Wiltshire countryside I was deemed ready to sit my test. On the day, the regimental driving instructor sat me in the cab and asked me to drive to his mate's farm a couple of miles away with a bale of hay in the back that he had to deliver. We accomplished this task without any mishaps so he told me I had passed with flying colours. It only took about twenty minutes.

The Fire Brigades' Strike

Soldiers' pay in November 1977 was quite appalling. A private soldier, living in married accommodation took home thirty-two pounds a week. This measly amount was only two thirds of the national average industrial wage. There was nothing we could do about it except leave and find work elsewhere, but help came from an unexpected quarter just after my birthday. The Fire Brigades Union called a national strike over pay and conditions.

Rumours flew round barracks everywhere. Would we be called upon to help or not? A few days later that question was answered positively. 25 Battery found itself heading down to HMS Phoenix, the Royal Navy's fire training school, for some very hot and smoky training. The instructors gave us as much information as they could in one day, knowing that we were going to be in some very dangerous situations before very long. One snippet of knowledge was to wear plenty of layers of natural fibres to soak up the heat. Very good advice.

A couple of days later, six of us found ourselves tearing up the M6 to Southport RAF base where we manned a Green Goddess. They were old 1950s fire engines dragged out of retirement for the duration of the strike. We lived like lords on the RAF base. Crab Air really does have the best of everything. We even used napkins at the dinner table. Disappointingly, we returned back to Larkhill after two weeks without a single shout. The best memory of the fortnight was seeing Wild Willie Barratt on the Old Grey Whistle Test, introducing the nation to punk rock.

Meanwhile, across the UK, things had hotted up to such an extent that the whole battery was M6 bound shortly after our return. One troop was sent to Ashton-under-Lyne. My troop deployed to sunny Stockport where we found ourselves camping in a TA centre. Sixty of us on camp beds in the drill hall with a couple of bogs, an office and the good old ACC serving up wholesome food, day and night.

We worked for twenty four hours on, twenty four off. During the working day we practised running out hose, and pitching the ladders, whilst the drivers gamefully tried to operate the massive pumps safely. The problem was, there was nobody to teach us how to do things the right way. It was almost all guesswork and common sense. We wore wellies, old black waterproof leggings, combat jackets with army tin helmets on top. We looked like a bunch of spares.

The crew of the stand-by pump stayed awake and ready at all times. The boss sat by the telephone to answer any emergency calls. A police car was with the team to lead them to the address of the fire when it came in by phone. We loved every minute of our time firefighting and had a ball. There were plenty of fires, a few big ones too, because even a small kitchen fire quickly became a house fire. Without breathing apparatus it was impossible to penetrate thick smoke, even though we would have done if at all possible. The citizens of Greater Manchester loved us. Christmas was just around the corner and we became heroes in their eyes. Our TA centre had a noticeboard where members of the public would post their address and write something like this: Two lads for Xmas day dinner, 2pm. Most of us took up their kind offers and had a fine old time. Nobody ever had to buy a pint in the local pubs either. Even Debenhams gave us all a ten pounds voucher to spend in their store.

The work was hard and dangerous. Every fire was a huge learning curve but after a couple of weeks we found that we could handle most of the equipment pretty well. The difficult bit, as always in the army, was fitting the work in with the partying and still getting enough sleep. Christmas Day was my first one away from home but I found myself as a guest in someone's house, eating a huge lunch and trying unsuccessfully, as usual, to chat up their daughter.

After a month away a different unit took over from us. We left with fond memories, a couple of engagements to local girls, a few sore heads and damaged livers.

On arriving at Larkhill we went home for a couple of weeks of hard earned leave. I found myself going with Phil to a party that night. I drank one pint then promptly fell asleep on the floor in front of a live band, playing in the host's front room. I slept so soundly and for so long that some party goers thought I was dead.

Off the back of the eight week strike, that was, in fact, fully justified, the firemen received a decent pay rise but we came out of it with a thirty per cent rise ourselves. Sometimes pressure from the tabloids is a good thing for the working man. The pay still wasn't much to shout about but I could now just about afford to run a car.

Old Bangers

Even new cars in the 1970s broke down regularly, leaked water, wouldn't start and had many other faults. Some marques rusted away before your eyes in a matter of months. Built-in obsolescence was well-known about, too. Old cars, the kind young soldiers could afford, had all of these problems in spades. On a Friday afternoon, when the rush to the car park and the drive home took place, there would always be someone begging the rest of the lads for a push start, or even a tow round the square to get them going. Everyone was an amateur mechanic, well used to carrying out most jobs on a car. We bought our spares at scrapyards, fitted them ourselves and listened intently for the slightest change in our engine note that might spell impending disaster.

My first car was a massive Vauxhall with a column gear change and a front bench seat. I bought it off my friend's father for two hundred pounds and it was a pile of scrap. Dad spent a weekend working on it to improve things and at least after that it started and drove ok.

Phil and I had one weekend driving around Bournemouth posing in it and enjoying ourselves immensely. I came home the following Wednesday afternoon just because I wanted to drive my new car. By the time I had to leave home for Larkhill it had started snowing heavily. I had to be on parade for the ranges at seven o'clock in the morning, so I set out very carefully on my way back to the barracks.

The old Vauxhall was fitted with cross ply tyres, totally unsuitable for the conditions and the rear wheel drive worsened the lack of grip. I drove slowly and carefully, knowing the conditions were becoming treacherous not wanting to end up in a ditch. Halfway along the Ringwood By-pass the inevitable happened. I started sliding and found myself out of control, crossing the carriageway. There were three sets of headlights coming down the hill towards me. I couldn't do anything about it except brace myself for impact, which came a second later and was very loud indeed. Three cars piled into mine. As we had all been driving very slowly nobody was hurt but my big old bus was smashed to pieces all along the passenger's side. A Morgan that hit me was written off, sadly. We all stood at the roadside talking together about the rotten weather and waited for the police and breakdown lads to turn up. Due to the conditions I wasn't charged with any driving offences and the cops gave me a lift home. The regiment gave me the rest of the week off to recuperate.

Back to hitching home for a few more weeks before, one Friday evening, Dad opened the lounge curtains and pointed to a Morris Minor parked outside. He held a set of keys in his hand and had a big smile on his face. The old man had bought me a Moggy Minor.

It was nearly twenty years old and had a top speed of about forty five mph but was an endearing little car. In cold weather I parked it on top of a hill in case it failed to start in the morning, although I also had the back-up of the dreaded starting handle. A front wheel fell off one afternoon, prompting my brother to jump out whilst it was still moving sideways along the road. Dad and I bought a second hand engine for it, fitted it in a weekend and she became a flying machine. One evening Phil and I wound her up to 100mph, both of us holding the steering wheel and cheering madly as the wildly vibrating needle touched the ton. With Moggy being of a certain age, there was nowhere to mount a cassette player. I ended up fitting one under my seat which caused a dangerous bit of fiddling and looking down anytime I wanted to change the tape.

My Mate Phil.

Phil and I became inseparable buddies when I wasn't away with the army. We spent most weekends together. He stayed on at school to study for his A Levels with a view to trying for Sandhurst and a career in the military. A slightly built but tall charmer, who had a ready smile and a quick wit, he and Mum got on famously. Before long, he spent more time at my house than at his. Life was much more fun when he was around, often standing in our kitchen swinging his toast to cool it down, whilst telling tall stories about the night before. Like me he smoked and enjoyed his beer. Some people loved him but quite a few took exception to his attitude of cheeriness and good humoured mickey taking. It often landed him in trouble with guys who saw Phil as a threat. He received a few punches on the hooter from jealous lads and several well aimed slaps from outraged girls, too.

I was his wingman who watched his back and ran off with him laughing together when things were about to turn ugly. I couldn't have wished for a better mate.

Phil's grandmother owned a very pretty little villa just outside Torremolinos, in Spain, with a pool and beautiful views of the mountains and the sea. He was invited to spend three weeks there during the summer and told he could take a friend for company. 25 Battery kindly allowed me to shuffle my annual leave around, so the pair of us found ourselves at Gatwick airport ready to fly for the first time. We had bought one year passports from our local post office the week before.

To our delight, when we began exploring the environs we discovered a little local's bar, just down the road from Granny's. They sold San Miguel which we downed by the gallon then staggered back to the pool for a late night dip whilst listening to the crickets clicking away. We progressed to a daring night-time escapade. We would visit the bar for the evening then head into Torremolinos as things were quietening down in the pubs and restaurants. We would find a hotel swimming pool that was closed down for the night and hop over the wall, strip off and slip into the water. One night someone spotted us, security was called and we ended up legging it with our shoes on but most of our clothes were held in a hand. With the guard dashing round to cut us off, we jumped back over the wall and sped away up the road hooting with laughter. It was good harmless fun.

After a couple of weeks of sunbathing, swimming and drinking we became restless and decided to explore further afield. We decided to catch a bus along the coast to Gibraltar, have a look round then head for Cadiz and Seville, before returning to Granny's. Being young guys we could only just afford our San Miguel and our cigarettes and the bus fares. We didn't have any spare money for bed and breakfast so thought we would just see what happened with overnight stops.

The sun was scorchingly hot as we alighted from the bus in Algeciras and found our way to the crossing point to Gibraltar, where we thought we could show our passports and head onto the Rock. Not a chance, amigos! The border guards showed us short shrift, especially when Phil began arguing with them.

"But we are British," he said.

"No effing chance," they replied and they had the machine guns, so we left pronto. We had no idea that the border had been closed for many years due to some ridiculous political dispute.

We made our way to Cadiz where we found for the first time that warm countries can become very cold overnight. All we had with us was our toothbrushes and two small towels in a shopping bag. We didn't even have jackets to keep us warm. After several hours wandering around we sat on the beach where the sand still held some warmth and we dozed until sunrise. At least the sun coming up warmed things quickly. During the night some insects had found Phil's face to their liking and left him with a nasty itchy rash on his cheek.

We moved on to Seville and marvelled at the Cathedral, even though the sun, the heat and our rubbishy planning, was beginning to take it's toll on our mood. That evening we found ourselves chatting to an older English speaking Spaniard who took a liking to us and bought us several beers which we couldn't afford to buy ourselves. He was smoking dope, which we had never seen before and after getting into a taxi with him to go to a party we began to have doubts about his intentions towards us. After exchanging worried glances we managed to indicate a get-out plan to each other. At the next set of traffic lights we bailed out quickly, one from each side of the car and, not for the first time, legged it off into the night. We spent a truly unforgettable night lying in the entrance to a cinema on cold marble tiles, with our heads resting on the two little towels, freezing cold and numbed by the hard floor. We couldn't possibly sleep, so we passed the miserable night discussing what type of slavery or male prostitution we had just escaped from. In fact, the poor chap was probably just being friendly to two young Brits who weren't experienced enough at travelling to realise what a decent guy he was.

We arrived back at Granny's the next day, stinking, tired out, stiff, grumpy with each other but having learnt two important life lessons: Any idiot can be uncomfortable. And the 6Ps are true: Piss poor planning prevents proper performance.

We flew back to Gatwick two days later, Phil having just received his A level results which pleased him no end. He could now have a crack at getting into Sandhurst whilst I was heading back up to Scotland for a life-changing few weeks in the far North-West Highlands.

Lessons in Self-Sufficiency

En route to the Highlands, the five of us enjoyed a rather eye opening night out in Edinburgh. Bournemouth seemed very tame in comparison with Rose Street on a Friday night.

John Ridgway's School of Adventure was established by one of the pair of Parachute regiment soldiers who rowed the Atlantic in 1967. His partner on the historic first crossing being the indomitable Chay Blyth. And they didn't do it by the modern short route, they crossed from Cape Cod to Ireland without GPS or any other modern aids. Two very brave guys. The adventure school was based on one side of a sea loch with Ridgway's house and boat sheds nestled into the hillside just across the freezing cold water.

Our job was to provide radio coverage during a junior management course for IBM, the computer giant. We arrived a couple of days before the students did and settled into our cabin. Then we were introduced to the school's instructors and the trainers from IBM, all of whom seemed like a fine bunch, full of stories, jokes and energy. The instructors were a tough bunch of lads, very unmilitary, beardy, hippy, mountaineering types. They had recently completed the Whitbread Round the World Race on board the school's 57ft yacht and had rather mixed views on John Ridgways ideas of leadership. I fell generally into his camp, the more I heard and read about him.

The course students, high-flyers, aged in their twenties, thought they had been booked on a relaxing couple of weeks sailing, kayaking and hill-walking. They enjoyed the rail trip to Inverness, where they jumped on the waiting coach to speed them to Ardmore and the school. They received rather a rude awakening when the coach pulled into a layby, miles from anywhere and they were told brusquely to get their walking gear on but leave everything else on the coach.

The rather shocked and now fully awake students changed behind the coach, whilst we stood around chatting and laughing. We knew what was coming next. Having been split into six groups of six, my group met their trainer (Ian), instructor (Tony) and army signaller (me) then had to decide between them who their first leader would be. Tony then asked the rather confused group if they needed any map reading tuition. Being a rather arrogant bunch they declined the offer.

The whole point of the week's exercise was to create conditions where the management skills of the participants were put under a very fierce spotlight. Fatigue, hunger, cold, confusion and general bodily soreness all helped to lower the morale and mental state of the students very quickly. Once they had reached a very low ebb, their true nature couldn't be hidden from the staff's watchful gaze.

Their chosen leader plotted a course from our location to a grid reference about eight miles away and off we went over the moors and hills. The landscape is some of the best in the world and I thoroughly enjoyed every minute of the week spent yomping around from place to place. We summitted the mighty Foinaven one beautiful morning, I was going really well, causing Ian to label me a mountain goat. My Ten Tors training and walking holidays fully paid off. Every now and then I radioed into base to let the school know our location and how things were progressing. The rest of the time I was fascinated by the performance of the young up-and-coming managers. Every time they became disorientated or lost, Tony bollocked them for not asking for some map reading training on day one. They had to complete tasks, such as getting the barrel over the stream without it touching the ground. The usual sort of thing, but if you haven't slept for over twenty hours it is a huge mental problem.

On day six we traipsed along a track to a small, rickety, old shed, with a village hall table set up along the back wall. The incongruous sight of Mr. John Ridgway dressed in a pinstripe business suit sat at the table, met our eyes as we filed in. There was an egg box on the table in front of him. With little preamble he told them in his best Sandhurst voice, "I now need you to march to a location at x."

This was about sixty miles away and completely beyond the dishevelled bunch of weary young people. The one with a bit of spirit left piped up and asked for food. Ridgway then played his masterstroke, he opened the egg box and offered them five raw eggs. To their credit, they shared out the eggs by slurping a bit and passing them round. (I heard later that on more than one occasion, eggs had been thrown in John Ridgway's direction at this stage). They then left the shed and made an effort to sort themselves out for the long march ahead. At this stage Ian stepped in and told them this part of the course was over and they could jump in the minibus for a comfortable ride to the adventure school which they hadn't yet seen.

In my opinion, a few had coped reasonably well but others just fell apart when things became difficult. They team rowed frequently, the guy with a big mouth was a shadow of his former arrogant self but the quiet girl was the natural leader when the chips were down. I learnt a few things about motivation, leadership and keeping going when things look bleak. Most of all: don't be the moaner, in a tight situation it helps nobody.

The young managers spent a few days having a lengthy, honest and very personal debrief in their teams. I heard that some of them found this part very difficult indeed. One or two arrogant young chaps found their personal faults being fully exposed and discussed by their peers for perhaps the first time in their lives.

Meanwhile, us signallers spent our time walking, kayaking and sailing and making the most of the facilities. Shortly before home time, there was an end of course meal and shindig at the Rhiconich Hotel, about five miles away. We dressed as smartly as we could and enjoyed Highland hospitality, with haggis, bagpipes, singing and much boozing. I left before the end because I was worn out with all the fresh air and exercise, plus a few pints of heavy knocked me for six.

I was awoken in the night by a racket going on in the doorway to our wooden hut. Bob, one of the signallers, appeared in the hut a bit groggy and looking mightily bashed up and bruised. Not uncommon for soldiers after a party, though. It transpired that Bob and our Bombardier named Dave had been driving the old Land Rover back from the pub when it somehow crashed off the road and rolled over. Dave crawled into the back of the wagon and pulled the unconscious Bob from the now burning wreck. As the location was only a mile or so away, Bob limped back to our hut but Dave stayed put until first light. He thought a bit of fresh air might be a good thing before he met our officer for some explaining. An ex-commando and a tough, good bloke, he must have been freezing, sat on that hillside overnight. His commando's Dennison smock was part of the burnt out and melted shell of a vehicle and its contents that we gawped at the next morning.

Amazingly, nothing much was said back at the regiment. A replacement vehicle was brought up to us two days later for our journey back south.

The whole Ridgway experience had a profound effect on me as an eighteen year old. I had coped well with the physical side, got on well with the trainers and mixed easily with the instructors. I fell in love with the remote beauty of the area and pledged to come back again. John's philosophy helped mould my views on life and how it should be lived. Self-reliance, an optimistic outlook and looking after your kit as if it is irreplaceable, are the main themes and they made good sense to me, though it took a few more years for me to grow up enough to make those rules a lasting way of life.

I felt mightily proud when John wrote a short note in his autobiography that I purchased on the day we left. 'Remember those mince pies,' he had written. (On a night exercise he had left his paper bag of pies on the seat of a vehicle which I had then sat on and crushed, causing much hilarity amongst the rest of the group).* *I next met John when my old army pal Clive and I, were holidaying in the area in 2012. He and his wife, Marie Christine, were on fine form. They cooked us breakfast as we reminisced about the burnt out Land Rover, now sunken in the peat bog in which it had rolled into.*

We had been granted one week's leave so I arranged to meet my brother, Dean, at Glenridding campsite in the Lakes. Shortly after crossing the border Dave pulled our new transport into a lay-by by the M6-A66 Penrith roundabout where I leapt out shouting my goodbyes. As they chugged off in a cloud of smoke back down the motorway, I threw my rucksack over a shoulder and started marching down the dual-carriageway towards Blencathra and Glenridding.

Hikers and Bikers.

I was full of youthful energy but fairly soon the famous Lake District wind and rain found me miles from shelter in the gathering gloom. I had nowhere to stop so strode on hoping to find a bus shelter or somewhere with a roof, maybe an old barn. The wind picked up further, whilst the trees dropped twigs and leaves which swirled around my feet. I had to walk in the centre of the lane, catching an odd glimpse of tarmac when the moon scudded out from behind the racing clouds. Sometimes I stumbled onto the muddy verge then re-adjusted my direction back towards the middle. By now I was dripping wet. The Army didn't issue us with waterproofs and I hadn't my own wet weather gear. My brand new red JRSA fleece that I was proudly wearing was waterlogged but at least it kept me warm. In the early hours I came upon the entrance to a caravan park. I was pretty much all in by this time, so I nipped through the entrance and headed for the toilet block. Oh, thank god for that, it was toasty warm. I had a smoke, made a brew with my little stove and sat on the floor to rest. I must have dozed for a couple of hours because when I peeped outside it was dawn and the wind had abated a bit. After another quick cuppa, which was washed down with some compo cheese and biscuits I packed up, made sure there was no mess left behind and continued my journey.

As I finally hobbled along the path to our rendezvous at about 8am my brother jumped out from behind a drystone wall and pretended to attack me with a bloody great branch. An impressive hillwalker, at five feet four inches his body reminded me of a Pygmy, with little arms and a pot belly but his thighs and calves were that of a Turkish Olympic weightlifter. He looked like two different bodies put together in one. Unfortunately, our hiking holiday passed all too quickly and I found myself on parade the following Monday morning for another week on the ranges armed with my map and big protractor.

I arrived back at Larkhill just in time to celebrate Kev's nineteenth birthday. We decided to head to Bournemouth and The Pinecliffe for a few beers. Kev had recently bought himself a lovely Honda 250 so we leapt on and fired her up. I was used to being pillion with Dad and straight away knew that Kev could handle the bike with ease. Dean and his pal Howard joined us in the pub where pint after pint of lager was piled up for Kev to work his way through. He manfully tried to keep downing them before he ominously toddled off to the bogs just before closing time. After a while I thought I should go and check up on him. I saw his legs lying on the floor inside a cubicle and managed to squeeze through the door to get to him. His chin ran with dribble and he was obviously horribly drunk. I gathered the other two boozers and between us we dragged Kev out of the bogs, through the passageway and into the fresh air. My brother and I supported his top half as we staggered homewards, his feet dragging along on the pavement. When we reached home we crept in through the side gate and dumped him on a damp bed in the cabin then chucked a couple of blankets over him. I went to bed indoors, feeling pretty grim myself by this time. I could not believe my eyes when Kev woke me at 5.30 am all ready to go and looking fine, except that the toes of his shoes had nearly been worn away by the dragging home. We jumped on the Honda about ten minutes later, still as drunk as Lords. A couple of pints of milk, nicked off a doorstep, helped sober us up and we made it back to camp in one piece with about a minute to spare.

Ace Mobile Force, Norway.

One of the units in the regiment, 13 Battery, was part of NATO's Ace Mobile Force. Their task was to help secure Europe's northern flank. Part of their training for this role was to spend three months every winter in Norway, firing their 105mm guns and practising soldiering in the cold conditions. And each year they asked for volunteers from the rest of the regiment to go along as re-broadcasting signals crews. As usual, I raised my hand, anything to get off the ranges and Norway sounded a good place to visit.

I became part of a crew of three, myself, Tippy and our boss Alan. Two other similar threesomes joined us from other battery's, including, I was delighted to see, my old pal Scouse from basic training.

We suffered with our allocation of equipment because we weren't known to the storemen handing it out. They just chucked the left-over old rubbish at us. Our tent was three layers thick to keep the cold out but we found out when we pitched it in the snow that all of the zips had broken. We lost loads of much needed warmth through the gaps. We loved the thicker arctic issue sleeping bags. It was a shame nobody told Tippy and I that we should take our normal issue sleeping bag as well, to put inside them. So we ended up freezing at night. Where we were heading for you couldn't afford to make mistakes like that.

I was the crew driver and thoroughly enjoyed learning about the Volvo BV206 Snowcat. It came with three seats in the front, gull wing doors and a top speed of about twenty mph. It was designed primarily for use on snow and had wide rubber tracks. I had never driven anything remotely like it. All our kit was kept in a trailer section behind. The heater in our trailer never worked, so we couldn't use that part, it was just too cold to sit in there without hot air blowing around.

Towards the end of November 1978 we paraded on the square then mounted our vehicles and set off in convoy for Marchwood docks, near Southampton. At 20mph it took an age to drive there but finally we arrived and were directed onto the deck of the RFA ship Sir Galahad.

We chained the Snowcat to the deck then found our bunks way below sea level. Cramped doesn't really describe it. The bunks had a headroom of about twenty four inches and lay four high alongside a narrow gangway. There seemed to be dozens of us in one cabin. The Chinese crew served up tiny amounts of food on tin trays and hardly spoke any English. I fondly remembered various times I had been in the Solent as I stood on the deck watching Southampton and the Isle of Wight gradually disappear. The cruise down the Channel was calm but once we passed through the Straits of Dover and turned to port the seas began to become a bit more lively. Before an hour was up, the first lads had started to go quiet and look for somewhere to be alone. By the time darkness fell almost all of us were honking and puking over the side. I'm not too bad in a rough sea if I am busy but sitting around getting bored causes you to think about the wave action. We spent a horrendous four days and nights crossing the North Sea to Trondheim. All of us were mightily relieved and a bit lighter in weight when we pulled into the shelter of the fjord running up to the harbour. The scenery was majestic and before long we docked then unchained our Snowcat. Soon we were on our way to the Norwegian Army camp where we would base ourselves for the duration.

The weather was below freezing continuously and whilst working on our vehicles we wore plenty of layers of clothing. This included some very sexy padded trousers that you could remove without taking your boots off. We also wore lovely warm sheepskin hats with long warm sideburns that Velcroed under our chins. Much of the army parade ground bullshit didn't matter here, keeping warm, safe and the equipment functioning was all that mattered. We completed a drivers course which taught us how to manoeuvre our vehicles across ice, deep snow and other obstacles.

I was also re-introduced to skis. This time it was the famous army planks. Aptly named, the planks had a bit of an upturn at the front and bindings to fit them to an army boot with a special squared off toe piece. We tried them on and straight away just fell down all over the place with gales of laughter. Legs sliding everywhere, guys falling awkwardly, then going down with cramp and being unable to move. Lads falling on their arses then standing up for about a second then tumbling over again. It was absolutely hilarious and I couldn't believe we would ever learn how to ski on these old bits of painted wood. Of course, the old hands, some of whom had been to Norway ten or fifteen times, just glided past us serenely, killing themselves laughing.

After a couple of days us novices progressed to being able to shuffle round like old fogies, only falling down occasionally. The next challenge to be overcome was how to travel long distances cross country, being towed behind a snowcat. To practise this difficult skill, two long ropes lay on the ground, tied to the back of the vehicle. Sixteen of us, two lines of eight, picked up our rope and held tight with one arm. The other arm held our ski sticks. We all looked very very pensive, in our white camo and russki hats. As soon as the driver engaged gear and pulled forwards with a slight jerk we all instantly fell over, hooting with laughter. After sorting ourselves out, wiping the snow off our faces and calming down a bit we readied ourselves again. Tighter went the rope as the vehicle moved away, then a quick jerk and down most of us went howling with glee once again. One or two heroes managed to keep their balance. This charade went on for a couple of hours but eventually we learnt that if we shuffled forward as the rope went tight we could stay upright for a few hundred yards. Of course, if the bloke in front of you on the rope crossed one ski over the other and fell, you just piled straight into his skis and crashed head first into the snow with him.

During our few weeks of cold weather training around the camp we sometimes ventured out in the evenings. One time we visited a local restaurant. There were no pubs, but the eatery was so expensive we couldn't afford a single thing on the menu. We met some local guys in the gents who pulled out a bottle full of a clear coloured liquid which they offered us to try. Moonshine, they called it, the strongest drink I have ever tasted. Evidently, most of the Norgies hadn't enough money to buy alcohol so they brewed their own and kept going to the bog for a swig when they went out for a meal. Needs must.

We took the train to Trondheim one Saturday for a bit of culture. A beautiful and interesting city it certainly was but again, we would have needed to pool our financial resources to buy a sausage roll. We wandered round for a few hours then caught the train home feeling rather poor.

A few days later we set off as a rebroadcast crew into the snow covered mountains of southern Norway. Our job was to be a link between the OP and the guns as their transmissions couldn't cross the high mountains. We had orders to sit atop one of those mountains, freezing our nuts off and rebroadcasting their messages from one to the other.

Our chosen spot was on a snow covered plateau at about five thousand feet altitude. The landscape was similar to the rounded hills of North Yorkshire Moors but the sky was a beautiful clear blue and even the freezing snow had a bluish tinge to it. We parked the snowcat, quickly pitched our clapped out old tent, then threw a white camouflage net over the top.

Alan manned the radio whilst I made a much needed brew on our naphthalene fuelled stove. We moved our personal kit into the increasingly crowded tent and settled in. Over the first few days the temperature dropped markedly, reaching minus forty two degrees centigrade at its lowest. Tippy and I had trouble keeping warm in our sleeping bags even with every item of clothing on. We kept our boots in our bags with us and they still froze. We manned the radios two hours on and four off, the man on duty drinking cocoa by the bucketful. Radio Luxemburg was the night time signaller's friend too.

If we needed a pee at night we had to dress and go outside the tent. Several times when I was outside weeing very quickly, I marvelled at the Northern Lights shimmering away in the clear sky. An incredible once in a lifetime spectacle to witness from our remote location. I knew it was very special and I was privileged to be there. When not on duty there wasn't much we needed to do. When the temperatures plummeted we put a ban on being outside for more than ten minutes. It just wasn't safe. How on earth anyone could actually do any fighting in that cold was beyond me. Keeping alive took all your efforts. A couple of times on slightly warmer days, I donned my skis and headed for the top of the nearest hill. The views stunned me. The snow was so clean and white that it seemed to have a blue hue to it. The sky itself was the clearest I have ever seen and the tops of the hills had a touch of pinkness to them. There were no houses, airplane trails, birds or animal tracks anywhere. The only sign of life was our little tent with our snowcat parked next to it at the far end of my ski tracks, back down the hill. I couldn't stay out for long even when the sun was at it's highest because my extremities began to suffer from the cold.

One morning I took our cooker outside the tent to re-fuel it with naphtha. The fuel works fine at low temperatures but has the decidedly dodgy characteristic of burning without a flame. Like an idiot, whilst refuelling, I spilt some on my legs so when I lit the stove to make sure it was working properly my trouser legs caught fire but I didn't realise straight away, until things heated up very quickly. I ended up sitting on my arse, caught up in the cam net, desperately flapping at my legs with snow and my heavily gloved hands. No harm done but I was taught a serious lesson. Be bloody careful whatever you are doing when you are hours from safety if something goes tits up.

One morning we received a very entertaining message on the radio. A member of our crew had to pretend to have broken a leg. The other two had to treat the break, make an improvised stretcher, then have the poor sod airlifted away to hospital by helicopter. Because Al was the boss and me the driver, Tippy was picked as the very unwilling victim. We made him dress in all of his clothes, whilst we made a stretcher from a pair of skis. We bagged him in his sleeping bag and sent an SOS message about our casualty. Tippy kept wanting another pee before we tied him to the skis but once we had him all bagged up he could hardly move.

Soon we heard the unmistakable Wocka Wocka of an incoming chopper. I dressed and nipped outside to look for it in the blazing sun. The temperature was about minus twenty that morning but calm and clear. I waved the small helicopter down as best I could. I hadn't been trained to do this sort of thing. Once it touched down the pilot slowed the rotors and jumped out.

He strode over to me and asked "Hello, have you got any smokes?"

I replied, "Yes, I've got some roll-ups in the tent."

He looked at me as if I was some sort of imbecile. "No son, coloured smokes, to give us an idea of the wind direction when we try to land."

I replied in the negative. More poor planning. A very pensive Tippy was then lashed to a skid on the outside of the helicopter. The poor guy hated the cold anyway, even before being exposed to a freezing wind and unable to move, or even look where he was going. The pilot checked the bindings, told Tippy he would be fine, then gave us the thumbs up and off they went, with Tippy shitting himself, no doubt.

A couple of days later end-ex was called and not before time. We had suffered a bit of what they called frost-nip. A precursor to frost-bite that does no lasting damage if the fingers and toes are warmed up again. Al and I packed up slowly, very aware that we would never come back and it was good to try to memorise the views. We had slept very little during our stay but had managed to do our job properly, with no major mishaps and had learnt many things about cold weather survival.

Our rendezvous was Hjerkinn railway station. If somebody mentions the name Hjerkinn to many British soldiers of a certain age, the soldiers will be reminded of the cold and snow and have mixed memories. I wouldn't have missed the time up there for the world. Just before dark we met up with the other re-broadcast teams and swapped stories. We unanimously decided to sleep in the railway's waiting room that night. We would carry on our descent off the mountains and back to our barracks the following morning. The luxury of putting my sleeping bag down on a thin Karrimat with plenty of room around me, brewing up in the warm and dry and not having to wear all my clothes to keep warm was a wonderful thing. We all slept like logs that night, luxuriating in not being in a cramped tent with two hairy-arsed mates. The next morning I suspect we all threw away one of our socks.

A few days later, we found ourselves back on the dockside in Trondheim. We re-embarked then fixed the chains securing our faithful snowcat to the deck in case of a rough passage. Us rebro crews then joined the hundreds of bored squaddies on the dockside watching proceedings. Everyone was demob happy, wanting to get back to Blighty then away on some well-deserved leave.

It was below freezing as usual and the overcast February day grew ever colder. We smoked and mucked about like young men do but avoided getting onboard until the last minute. A squadron of Scorpion mini-tanks had begun carefully making their way down the loading ramp and disappearing into the hull of the dull grey ship. The tide had been going out for hours and as it did so, the ramp from the dockside became steeper and steeper.

We all watched in silence as we realised that the drivers were struggling to steer a straight course down the ramp. Eventually, one unlucky chap finally lost control as his eight ton armoured vehicle slid slowly towards the edge of the ramp. In a second, he leapt out whilst his commander shot out of his turret like a Polaris missile and also jumped away to safety. Not a moment too soon as a few seconds later the scorpion toppled over the edge and hit the water with a mighty splash. Every single squaddie watching gasped, then let out a rousing cheer and burst out laughing. Incredible stuff. Much shouting and bollocking by officers and NCO's followed. The next morning, when we finally cast off for home, a very seaweedy

Scorpion was firmly chained to the deck, having been lifted back out of the drink overnight by a huge great Norgy crane.

Before I left for my delayed Christmas break, I was informed that our posting to Larkhill was coming to an end and we would be moving to Dortmund in Germany during the summer/autumn. I was quite happy with that. We had heard plenty about life in BAOR and it sounded fun. The overseas allowance would help, too. Phil had recently attended a Regular Commissions Board officer's selection interview but had unfortunately been turned down. So he would be leaving Bournemouth for Portsmouth Poly to start a quantity surveyors degree. My old pal Simon from Primary school also failed. I am positive that both of them would have made the grade, given the chance. Oddly enough, another friend who was a bit of an oddball, passed, went to Sandhurst, then was found out and binned after a few months.

Last days in Bournemouth

We were determined to make the most of our last few months in Bournemouth. Two carefree teenagers with an old banger, just enough money, a few girlfriends and a great pub to socialize in. The Pinecliffe hosted a live band seven nights a week. Some played great sixties tunes, Elvis, Frank Sinatra, The Stones. One much-loved performer was a Dave Allen looky-likey who played an organ and sang old love songs like 'Goodnight, Irene'. Hippo was everyone's favourite, they always gigged on a Friday to a full-house. We drank and smoked far too much, sang along, laughed, and always went home thoroughly inebriated. During one mad session I picked up a soda syphon from the bar and sprayed everyone around me with it, whilst laughing hysterically. God knows how I escaped a ban or even a good thumping.

Much time was spent fixing the car or just cruising around in it, though it was very hard to look cool in a twenty year old grey Moggie with one green wing. Saturday night might find us gatecrashing a party with a pitifully small amount of beer as a token gesture, or heading into Bournemouth to go to a club.

Phil and I decided it was time to make a sharp exit from the fag end of one of those parties. We had, no doubt, drank copious amounts of weak beer and wanted to keep the night going a bit longer. Dawn had just broken, somewhere in Bournemouth. The town was still and quiet.

"How do you fancy an early morning sail?" he asked, as he jumped onto his trusty Yamaha Fuzzy.

A few seconds later we put-putted away, two up with no helmets, on our way to his Dad's prized 14ft dinghy, stored at Mudeford. We made it across town without being seen and before the sun peeped above Hengistbury Head Coastguard's station, we leapt into the little boat and headed for The Run. The Run was a particularly tricky tidal race between the estuary and the sea. Depending on the tides, it could be flowing very fast, either going in, or out of the estuary. Luckily, for us it was an ebb tide and we roared with delight as we shot down through the straits and reached a calm, blue sea. A couple of hours sailing saw us beginning to tire from the night's dancing, drinking and having a good time. We decided to sail to the empty beach, drop the sails and have a little lie down for ten minutes. Of course, we had no water or any other provisions with us. We lay along the two hard wooden benches and promptly fell asleep, the noise of the water gently slopping against the hull helping us to drift off.

"Hey Dad, there's two blokes in it!"

The kiddie looked down at me and smiled hesitantly. I tried to smile back but my lips had dried out and stuck together. My eyes squinted in the strong, hot sun. Where the hell was I? Who was this bloody kid? Why did my body hurt so much? I heard a familiar groan from the opposite gunwale and things gradually became clearer.

"Uuuuurrgh, my head," Phil cried through a parched throat. He sat up, his face was flat on one side from lying on the wooden bench and covered in dribble that had dried on.

I sat up and looked about me, my head thumping with dehydration and sunburn.

"Oh Jesus, we are in deep shit Cliff," he croaked, "the sea is miles away."

Judging from the height of the sun, it was apparent that we must have slept for several hours. The sea had retreated a couple of hundred yards and our dinghy was high and dry on the sand. Our heads thumped horribly as Phil began to heave on the rope at the front, like a tug-of-war anchorman, whilst I and a gang of laughing kids pushed from behind.

Somehow, after much shoving, tacking, swearing and complaining about our throbbing headaches we made it back to the mooring and tidied the dinghy away as if it had never been touched. How I managed to get back home, I have no idea but we never repeated that little nautical adventure.

Mum and Dad had decided to go on a fortnight's holiday that autumn, so would be away for the middle weekend when I came home from Larkhill. Phil and I thought we would invite a few friends round after the pub shut, for a bit of a do. Somehow, the entire clientele of the Pinecliffe heard we were throwing a party and decided to come round with their pals. Loads of my schoolmates appeared too. By the time Match of the Day came on the little telly in our kitchen there were well over a hundred singing, drinking, laughing, partygoers, in my parents' lovely guest house. I was beside myself and stood in the road appeasing the neighbours who found it all to be amusing. Luckily, most of the revellers drifted away quietly and only about twenty friends stayed the night. Every single one of our beds was occupied. When we arose we all cleaned the place up and all day Sunday we kept the windows wide open and disposed of dozens of bottles and cans. I kept an eye down the road half expecting to see Dad driving home from holiday early, something he is known for. We got away with it but years later Mum hinted that she knew something had gone on. It would have been very interesting if Dad had come back at about midnight, to meet twenty cheering Manchester United supporters in his kitchen and a house full of drinkers, dancing and chatting each other up.

Part Three 1978-1981

The move to Dortmund.

I was picked for the regimental advance party, which meant heading over to Dortmund a few weeks before the rest of the guys followed. Our job was to prepare the barracks and check all the kit being handed over. I sold my beloved Moggie to a friend who had ducked out of coming to Germany. Within a week the other front wheel had fallen off, much to his chagrin and to my amusement.

I had become very close to a lovely girl and spent most of my free time that summer with her. Many soldiers going overseas feel a strong need to keep a link back home and I was no different. Unfortunately, our relationship only lasted a short while due to my youth and lack of life experience. I didn't think it fair to keep her waiting for me when I was so far away and stupidly gave her up.

We flew from Luton to Dusseldorf and thereafter by coach to our new home. The British Army took over Wehrmacht barracks en masse in 1945 and their heritage showed. The Germans built them to last, the large accommodation blocks consisted of three floors with dozens of four man rooms and communal ablutions. BAOR camps usually had several of these buildings for housing the troops, surrounding a large parade ground. There were also long lines of garages for parking armoured vehicles, a cookhouse, stores and all sorts of other smaller buildings scattered around. They struck me as somewhat drab, to say the least, usually being faced with dark grey stones, with cobbled roads between the accommodation blocks. Our camp was right next to the B1 autobahn in the area where traffic on the road slowed down coming into the outskirts of Dortmund. We heard constant traffic noise and fumes, day and night.

After my first day working in the camp, I settled into my four man room on the top floor and after a last cuppa and a fag, switched off the light and fell asleep. The next thing I experienced was a resounding boom and the sensation of the building moving for a second. Wow! What the hell was that? There was pandemonium in the camp with soldiers running around all over the place. As I hardly knew my way around I just watched out of the window with a couple of colleagues. It transpired that a member of the IRA had climbed the perimeter wall and planted a homemade bomb against the back of our building. It had detonated at about 6am without causing any substantial damage. That was a nice welcome to Deutschland and a reminder that we would probably be off to Ireland before very long.

We spent the next few weeks carting large square wooden boxes up the stairs and into the bedrooms of the guys who would be arriving soon. These MFO boxes held all the kit of soldiers, wherever they were being posted around the globe. Some other lads busied themselves signing for all the vehicles and their kit which was being handed over by the unit that was leaving.

Early in September the rest of the regiment arrived. We all spent a few evenings out on the lash getting used to the very lovely Dortmunder beer. The town was famous for it's five breweries and the smell of hops pervaded the air, especially when the brewery chimneys were cleaned.

Each battery housed a bar on the ground floor which was managed by one of the gunners. I think the idea was that if we drank cheap beer on the premises we wouldn't be out in the town causing mayhem. Rumour had it that 19 Regiment. had left Germany in disgrace after the last deployment but while I was there I heard of very little trouble. The biggest crime seemed to be lads taking a taxi to the camp gates from the pub, then fleeing past the guardroom at high speed without paying the irate driver. Fighting was rare but drunkenness was part of everyday life.

I shared a room with three good lads. Tippy of the helicopter flight in Norway fame, Martyn, the Army high jump champion and Clive, a lad from Sheffield. Clive and I first met a few months previously when a shooting club was proposed by our Sgt. Major. Clive and I both turned up to join the club and we hit it off straight away. He was a quality runner and all-round athlete. At school with Seb Coe, he wasn't far behind in ability. A tall middle-class lad, he was a very rare tee-totaller, looked like a proper soldier and could blag the best jobs by sweet-talking our officers. He was one of those guys that everybody liked and, on the very rare occasion he found himself on guard duty, he was automatically awarded stickman and the night off. He looked smarter than the rest of us shortarses, stout lads, twice a day shavers and assorted bags of shite.

Our daily life quickly settled into a routine. At seven o clock a junior NCO would come around the block and wake everyone up. Wash, shave, breakfast, then on parade at eight. Nearly every morning we stood in open order outside our block whilst a lieutenant inspected us. Any little speck or bit of fluff could result in extra duties. Three extra guard duties awarded for a tiny bit of dirt on a boot, or something equally trivial, was a real pain in the arse. The same guys always picked up the extras, the favoured ones got away with it. The American Army calls it chicken shit and it was one of those things that tipped the balance between enjoying our soldiering, or calling it a day and getting out.

After the parade it was all hands to the gun park where we kept our vehicles. Our battery was equipped with Abbot self-propelled guns. Like a tank but smaller and fires artillery shells up to twelve miles without having to see the target. Our command posts and observation post crews used a 432 tracked armoured vehicle. It was basically a large metal box on tracks.

Days in the gun park revolved around vehicle maintenance, cleaning and messing about. Our vehicles needed regular work on them as they had plenty of miles on the clock and showed their age. Many had begun service in the early 1960s.

We knocked off at 4pm, when the married guys would head off to their quarters whilst us single blokes would all go and lie on our pits for an hour before dinner. Feeling horribly groggy when we woke up, we would saunter over to the cookhouse with bedspread marks on our cheeks, a sign of a good kip. The food was nourishing and there was more than enough. We never went hungry. Then it was off to the battery bar or to the town for the more adventurous and the shaggers.

Beer was an ever present part of army life and not always in a good way. A few of our lads had serious alcohol problems in Larkhill and when they arrived back in Dortmund things deteriorated for them. The difficulty for us young lads in Dortmund, was that we couldn't go home at weekends to escape the drunken excesses. One maniac, in particular, would haunt the accommodation in the early hours, completely out of his mind on booze. He was a big, sturdy bloke who might appear in our room at 2am and start talking Glaswegian gibberish, whilst dribbling and sweating and poking his poor victim with a grubby finger.

At nineteen years of age he scared me. If I had been twenty nine I would have dealt with him in about five seconds and he wouldn't have troubled anyone again.

As the weeks became months, and the drinking became boring, a few of us turned to fitness for the first time. I took up running with my roommates several times a week and Kev even joined us, dressed in a bin liner to help him sweat more. Clive was the standout runner but as time went by the rest of us improved and started to enjoy training seriously. We tried boxing a few times. Six of us would go to the gym where the first two donned gloves and boxed for one minute. One stayed in the ring and fought everyone, one after another. By about the fourth minute, with tiring arms, it was hard to defend yourself very well. The last one stayed in to fight the others. We pulled our punches a bit, nobody wanted to badly hurt their pals but once or twice someone received a hit that doubled them up or made their nose bleed. Usually their concerned mate apologised.

On one of our regular Wednesday sports afternoons, our BSM marched us to the gym for a milling session. We lined up in size from left to right and had to fight the lad next to us, in the ring, with our mates cheering us on. Dad had taught me the basics of boxing. Fighting my pals a few times helped too. When the whistle blew I waded into my opponent without mercy. Neither of us were fighters but I had some limited skill and thought it best to get stuck in hard before he managed to hurt me. The fight was stopped by the referee after less than a minute and my pals cheered loudly. Later on, the regimental boxing instructor came up to me and said, "I saw you earlier, how about joining the team and training seriously?"

I declined. At that age I didn't have the balls for things like that. A few years later I would have jumped at the opportunity.

The sport I did take up was hockey. It was much more my thing in those days. I played for the regiment and we had some great games against other units. We played on the square which caused our sticks to wear down very quickly. Our only tactic was to get the ball forward to Jennings who hardly ever missed a goal scoring opportunity.

One Sunday morning I found myself having to drive the cross-country team to a race an hour away from camp. Max was the team captain and asked me to chuck my plimmys and shorts in the Land Rover, just in case. As usual, one of the lads called off and I was press-ganged into the team for a six mile race. Six miles! I had never run that far in my life. The whistle blew and off I jogged whilst the rest shot ahead. I avoided coming last but hardly troubled the engraver and had awful blisters for a week. However, a change was beginning to occur within me, from being a boozing, smoking, teenager, without much of a care about my health and fitness, to becoming a guy who trained regularly. I now drank maybe only once a week. At the same time and partly because of the new fitness regime, I was gaining in confidence. The immature teenager was slowly developing into an adult with a voice that demanded to be heard and increasingly becoming an independent spirit.

Training for War

Our role in West Germany, along with the American Army, was to stop a Russian invasion of Europe. NATO and the USSR glowered at each other across the border in an uneasy peace. They both knew that a war would escalate to nuclear weapons being fired and that wasn't what either wanted. But, if we hadn't been based across western Europe they could have just walked in, so our presence was very necessary. British Army troops were spread across a number of towns where the indigenous population, with a few rare exceptions, accepted us. Their daughters married the young soldiers, whilst our spending often kept the local economy afloat.

Several times a year regiments went on exercise to train realistically for war. Most years, entire divisions would train as one fighting force, and every now and then even bigger large-scale deployments and exercises took place. Sometimes, even mobilising Territorial Army units from the UK to back up the regulars.

There was also a very unpopular regular event called Active Edge. In case of Russian invasion we had to be able to deploy to our war positions quickly. So we occasionally practised. The first we ever knew of it was our orderly NCO waking us up in the middle of the night yelling "active edge." Fucking hell! Up we all got, grumbling and moaning. Vehicles started, weapons drawn and signed for, then off down the B1 at high speed to our defensive positions. The fun bit was trying to get the drunks sorted out and into their vehicles. Some pisshead always happened to be coming through the camp gates just as we sped off. They would smile and wave with their legs buckling under them and their bratwurst mit pommes frites falling on the ground. They caught up with us later. I once had to chuck Kev in the back of our Land Rover and into his sleeping bag when he had turned up pissed just after an Active Edge was announced. He was giggling and mucking about and trying to tell me about some poor, unfortunate, girl he had shagged. During his lurid tale, I had to collect guns, stores, our kit and a very sleepy Max from his quarters. Then Kev slept off his session with a big grin on his face whilst I drove non-stop for about eight hours.

Before one of the large-scale exercises, I had tried to get some green paint from the quartermaster's stores for the front bumper of my Land Rover. Old Charlie just swore at me every time I tried and said he didn't have any, so I gave up. Come the big line-up on the square and my recce truck was the leading one for the whole regiment. I was going to be on point for a very long convoy heading for Luneburg Heath at exactly twenty two mph. We all stood to attention in front of our vehicles awaiting the command "Mount." Max was to my left and Kev the other side. The RSM took one look at the shiny metal work behind me and instantly turned a funny maroon colour. He was in my face in two second and demanded to know what the fuckin' 'ell I was playing at?

I just about managed to squeak, without any wee coming out, that the stores wouldn't let me have any paint. I knew I had fucked up badly and was heading for a difficult time. The upshot of the incident was that gallons of paint appeared within one minute and the whole battery was confined to camp for two days when we returned from the three week exercise. Oh bollocks, I really was in trouble. So for the duration of our time in the field, big, ugly Sgt. McDuncan was after me and was going to commit murder if he managed to get hold of me. He worked on the gun position, where I had to be at least a few times a day. The gun crews found it highly amusing, whenever they saw me racing across their position with my theodolites and tripods and SLR and webbing, trying to hide from big Sgt. Mac. They pointed from the top of their Abbots and shouted out gleefully, "there he goes, get him Mac."

Being in the field on exercise toughened up all us young lads considerably. We slept where and when we could, often just a pile of bodies in sleeping bags on the ground by our vehicles. Maybe with an oily old tarp on top to keep off the rain. On one divisional exercise I went seventy two hours without sleep. The first twelve hours was the drive from barracks to the exercise area. We stopped for a quick piss then carried on leading the Abbots at their low cruising speed. We dug in, drove, recce'd positions, drove, cooked and repeated. By the end I could hardly see, let alone drive or work my theodolites. We thought nothing of two hours sleep a night for a week. That was par for the course. Not so hard when you are twenty years old.

One thing we had to endure was stand-to. This was the first light and last light ritual of forming a perimeter around your position in case the enemy planned an attack. Crawling out of a warm sleeping bag after two hours gonk, to lie in the cold dewy grass for half an hour, was character building, to say the least.

Fried egg banjos kept us going and we had some good laughs at times, too. Kev and I once set up and levelled our theodolites in an empty field and waited for the guns to turn up. They were still nowhere to be seen hours later, when a herd of cows decided to take a look at the two camouflaged shortarses standing in their pasture. We couldn't shoo them away and the more we waved and yelled the more inquisitive they became. We were licked, our kit was licked, the tripods fell over and the gun markers all got trampled into the ground. Satisfied that there was nothing to eat here, they moved on leaving behind two very licked, sticky young squaddies. The guns still didn't arrive and darkness began to fall. We could hear fifty five ton Chieftain tanks somewhere in the distance, their huge engines roaring. Darkness became total and the bloody great tanks came closer and closer. Their exhausts make an unmistakable noise as they continually change revs. The giant armoured beasts clatter and crash as they smash up the countryside. I pulled out our little right-angled torch, fitted with a red disk to stop too much light showing, ready to wave it in their direction.

"That'll feckin' 'elp 'Arry," Kev said.

We stood around, smoking and chatting and listening, trying to tell how close they were but finally they quietened their roar and went to fight elsewhere. We knew that a few guys had been squashed under their tracks, usually run over when sleeping in the dark.

A few days later, whilst having a couple of days off from the exercise, the regiment was parked up in some woods on Luneburg Heath. I was sent for and told to report to the guard commander. The plan was that the RSM and nine other senior NCOs, were going to the nearest bar for some R&R (rest and recuperation) and I was going to drive them there and back. These were the career soldiers that ran the regiment, all highly respected and a bunch of tough guys that a twenty year old like me would annoy at his peril. Sid, the RSM, and I had already had a run in that ended rather worse for me than it did for him.

I was given the duty Land Rover keys just as they all arrived in their clean combats and waterproofs. We piled in and set off for the pub, about a forty minute drive down a winding lane, with overhanging trees blowing around in the howling gale. I decided to drive as if I was taking my driving test. Nice and steady, partly because the bloke sitting next to me was huge, ugly, and very powerful. If I braked sharply he would end up with the transfer box knob whacking him in the nuts, which probably wouldn't go down too well with him. When we arrived at the Gasthaus they piled into the pub, with Sid telling me to be back at 2359hrs to pick them up.

I duly did so, making sure I was good and early. Out they came, a little the worse for wear and much more talkative. By now the rain was coming down like stair rods and the wind was blowing even stronger. The two lucky ones in the front settled down in their seats whilst the lads in the back crammed in together. I turned on the wipers and the lights, then off we chugged back down the country lane. The lights on those old landies were almost useless on a bright dry night, let alone in a storm. In this downpour I was struggling to see very far ahead at all. Then, the wiper motor packed up. Oh Jesus. Now what? We had to keep going, we had no comms and I was the only one sober. I slowed right down and realised I could just about make out enough of the road to plot a course down the middle. The rest of them had to put out their cigarettes. I needed total darkness to be able to see through the windscreen that was running with water. Each bend had me sweating but in some way I was enjoying the challenge of getting them back to camp safely. Finally, after over an hour I could make out the camp in the distance. What a relief. When we stopped and they began to de-bus, the big lad who had been sitting against me turned and said, "That was the best bit of driving I have witnessed in many a long year son, thanks." One of the most meaningful compliments I have ever received.

On some of the bigger exercises Kev and I crewed a Ferret scout car, which was an early 1960s design, weighed four tons and sported a Daimler engine. We all loved using them. The driver sat very low down, with a steering wheel that was oddly angled with the top part closest to his body. He had a small armoured hatch in front which he lowered to see over when he was driving. To the left and right hung two other tiny windows that could be pulled closed. The tricky little catches on these mangled many a driver's fingers. Tippy once zigzagged out of our convoy and onto the autobahn hard shoulder with his pinkies shut tight in the armoured window. He had to steer to a stop one-handed and was crying out in agony. They also had a habit of toppling over on rough ground, causing the commander, who stood behind the driver and had his top half out of the vehicle, to be crushed. As well as all this potential pain, the clutch pedal had a tendency to hit back with huge force on your foot when you changed gear, almost breaking your ankle. They certainly did not design scout cars with comfort in mind.

The vehicle batteries hid away well down in the bottom of the Ferret and maintenance on them was a nightmare. I was once upside down with my feet out of the commander's hatch, adjustable in hand, tightening a battery terminal. I could only move the metal adjustable about an eighth of an inch without touching the metal body and causing a huge spark, a puff of smoke and a loud bang! Not good for your nerves.

One long boring afternoon in the gun park, a group of us hui around passing the time, watching a Ferret crew trying in vain to take off the spare wheel using a large spider brace. They couldn't loosen any of the nuts so Mr. Big Right Arm Kev, saw his chance to show off in front of everyone. I held his beret whilst he gripped the wheel brace tightly and gave it his best shot. We all watched intently, egging him on. Suddenly the spider slipped off the nut causing Kev to hit his elbow with tremendous force on the armoured plate next to the wheel. Oh Jesus Christ! He was cross-eyed in agony and hopping about holding his arm and speechless with pain. We all roared with laughter and nearly fell over laughing and jeering at his injury.

Cars and Bars

We found out that we ended each month with some spare cash, a good job too, because we worked long and hard for our money. So some of us decided to start buying cars again and getting out a bit further afield than the bars downtown. Our local overseas allowance meant that the days of old British rust buckets could end. Big Toyota's started to appear in the car park, then a beautiful TR6, Tippy purchased a Volvo 1800 Saint mobile and after having saved two hundred pounds each month for a year I bought an MG Midget, only two years old and British racing green in colour. It looked fabulous, though actually it wasn't a particularly good design of car. One summer evening a group of us friends happened to be standing outside the battery block chatting and larking around. We all turned our heads to gawp at the thunderous roar from an ancient and knackered black Porsche 911 coming our way down the cobbles. Kev, thinking he had topped us all, pulled up in front of the amazed bunch feeling very pleased with himself but as he stopped a front headlight kept going, fell off into the gutter and rolled away.

The autobahn heading to Zeebrugge was like a racetrack on a Friday afternoon if we had been granted some leave. We crossed Holland only stopping for a few seconds at the border posts and reached the docks in a few hours. The ill-fated Townsend Thoresen ferry was well known to most of us BAOR soldiers. Cars usually had a full complement of squaddies sharing the fuel and the ferry ticket. Very early one December morning I drove off the ferry and through a sleepy Dover, for the mad dash to home. I was bombing along a dual carriageway just as dawn was breaking. I crested a hill singing along to Pink Floyd, trying hard to stay awake. Suddenly, the front tyres hit ice causing my back end to spin round. I was going through 360 degrees at 70mph, like on a fairground waltzer, in my lovely little car. Somehow, I stayed in the centre of the road, avoiding all the hazards and as the car slowed down the front started to grip and I regained control, shaking like a leaf, and carried on in a straight line.

I was back home for a Fenton family Christmas. My uncle Colin and his wife Ita often came to stay, so, with Clarice and Phil often around too, we had a big happy crowd to feed. Mum always managed to excel with the grub and Dad always lightened up when his brother was around.

Colin was the youngest of the six brothers and sisters. He was the highly entertaining sibling that the others all loved. He ran the family news service in Oxford, on one occasion nearly beating the police to the Great Train Robbers hideout. When he married Ita, a lovely young artistic lady from Limerick, he took her to the Isle of Man for their honeymoon. What he didn't tell her was that he had shipped his Matchless motorbike over there and would be racing in the Manxman races during their week's holiday. He was a regular starter in the races and qualified for the TT but work commitments wouldn't allow him to make the step up in competition.

On Christmas Eve the Fenton males plus a couple of friends decided to nip out to the pub for a beer or two. The ladies were delighted to get some peace for a few hours, no doubt. We headed for the Commodore, on the clifftop not far from home. As we entered us youngsters fought our way to the back, so Colin was forced to buy the first round. I noticed a three piece band was singing Moon River. My favourite.

We all asked for beer as ever, expecting Dad to order a half of lager to sip through the evening.

"I'll have a whisky Col," he said, to our utter amazement.

We drank at our usual speed, the band played merrily on and Dad drank a whisky every time we bought a round. One or two of his friends noticed he was drinking for the first time in many years and bought him a glass, too. By late evening the six of us were in fine form, as were the rest of the customers. The band began singing Christmas songs, old favourites that we all knew. Then, god knows how, the Fenton choir found itself on stage behind the mikes. None of us could sing a note but there we were, including Dad, belting out White Christmas with the crowd joining in and watching Dad closely for any sign of collapse.

On our way home we stopped at a few houses to give them a quick rendition of Good King Wenceslas for good measure. Dad made it home but was beginning to go a bit quiet. We shushed each other as we crept indoors, making a hell of a row and giggling like kids. Good old Mum, she had put the turkey in the sink to thaw out, before going to bed. Oh no! Dad had turned green and was heading desperately for the sink. In the nick of time, demonstrating all of his fine tuned motorcyclists reactions, Colin swept the huge bird from the sink milliseconds before Dad arrived. Poor thing, he didn't reappear again until Boxing Day.

Caving in the M

A few days later I was heading to the Mendips in Somers~.
taste of caving. My brother was a stalwart of his university caving ~
A few members of the club had decided to spend some time at their
old cottage near Wookey Hole. The more experienced cavers wore old,
battered wetsuits, with holes patched over and rips fixed with bits of
gaffer tape. I sported a pair of old army coveralls which proved
themselves completely unsuitable when climbing underground
waterfalls, or for splashing through knee deep streams several hundred
metres underground. We all carried miners lamps, fixed to our plastic
safety helmets.

The caving club's hut was an old quarry workers cottage that had
been turned into very basic accommodation for twenty or so cavers.
The ground floor consisted of two large rooms, both incredibly squalid
and filthy. A kitchen with several old, battered electric ovens, and a sink
full of grease, opened to a lounge, complete with grubby old sofas,
armchairs and a lovely big fireplace full of logs. Upstairs held rows of
rickety bunk beds, some with mattresses, some without. The whole
place would have been condemned by any official on grounds of filth,
fire regs, overcrowding, etc, etc. but it was a wonderful place for
students to escape to and full of energy, humour, story telling, music,
adventure and life.

Mostly but not exclusively, male, the inhabitants lived in a very
different world to the one I inhabited. To a man, they had long hair and
scraggy beards. Dressed in baggy holed jumpers, filthy old combats and
climbing boots, they must have looked at me with amusement.
However, they were a hardy breed who would think nothing of being
underground for twelve hours, getting cold and wet and crawling for
miles through narrow passages. When they eventually appeared back
into the daylight they would often scoff a plate of homemade spag bol.
This would then be washed down with huge quantities of beer whilst

arty games well into the night. That lifestyle required some
. to keep up for a week.

y first day of caving started fairly tamely with a large cavern that
walked into. The passage gradually became tighter and tighter as we
,rogressed. We ended up crawling, before coming to an underground
pool which we could stand up by and look into. A rope had been tied
to a rock at the back of the cave and it disappeared into the murk. Dean
explained that if I chose to hold the rope and pull my way along it
underwater I would resurface in the next part of the cave system a few
yards further along. I declined but his student pal Bunce showed me
how it was done. Bunce was a Bromley boy who would go on to be a
cave tour guide and leading light of the Irish caving scene. He waded
into the very cold water, grinned and disappeared beneath the surface.
With a kick of his boots he was gone. All went quiet. Blimey, I thought.
A couple of minutes later he re-appeared with a mighty splash and a big
gasp for breath. I said I would love to have a go but needed a wetsuit
before I could. Phew, I escaped that one.

That evening the partying ensued. They played guitars, sang, split
logs with a bloody great axe in the fireplace and told hilarious caving
stories, often about rescues they had taken part in. The games mimicked
caving life. Climbing through a wooden chair without touching the
ground was a favourite. Circumnavigating the room in the quickest
possible time without touching the floor was another. One of the
heroes of the famous Thailand schoolkids cave rescue was there, at the
time a young student with a guitar and long hair.

As things started to quieten down in the early hours, Bunce
suggested we go caving. In for a penny, I thought, so Bunce, my
brother, and I, dressed in our soggy old gear and headed off to the
nearest cave. It happened to be a few hundred yards from the hut and
was called St. Dunstan's Well Cave. It was known as a collectors piece
in the caving world. We entered the dark, damp passage and sobered
up quickly as we crawled and crouched our way along. After about
thirty yards we came to the interesting feature that makes this cave
special. A feature known in the potholing world as a duck. All I could
see was a little pond on the cave floor at the end of the passage. The

pond was no bigger than a yard across. Bunce explained that to progress further into the cave you had to lay on your back in the water with your feet on the ceiling. You then took a deep breath and pushed your head underwater and straightened out your body. With any luck you surfaced about three feet further on past the small obstruction. It was a bit like the u-bend in a toilet so was named Domestos Bend in the guide for that reason. If all went to plan, you came up the other side gasping for air and laughing like a drain. Bunce readied himself in position, smiled and ducked down then his feet followed and he was gone. Jesus, my turn next. I was very sober by now and dripping wet. I lay down quickly, said bye to my brother and pushed hard with my feet whilst dipping my head down into the water. Half a second later I could hear Bunce laughing as I emerged soaking and coughing. My brother followed a minute later and we carried on. The cave continued for another ten yards then it ended with a short passage that was almost too small to squeeze into. The last short passage sloped downwards at forty five degrees. We turned round and headed out, now beginning to tire and getting very cold. Of course, we had no choice but to go through the duck again but we didn't hang around this time and were back in the warmth of the hut within twenty minutes.

A few years later my brother and some college friends did the trip again. Though, this time the lead man, having navigated the duck, crawled into the small sloping end passage and tried to go through it, not realising it was a dead end. And he became firmly wedged in upside down at forty five degrees with just his feet showing. Panic stations! A full-blown rescue operation began, teams were called out including a caving doctor. Everyone who was involved at the sharp end had to negotiate the duck with their equipment, ropes and other stuff. The doctor gave the trapped lad an injection to calm him down and to relax his muscles. After five hours of the rescue team pulling on ropes around his feet, he eventually emerged. His eyes and head were so swollen he was unrecognisable. That was the final straw for my brother and his rescued pal. Over the previous years they had a few brushes with death underground but after that episode they never caved again.

Training for Northern Ireland.

When I arrived back at Dortmund after my leave, there was a buzz about the camp. The regiment had been warned that a tour of Northern Ireland was coming up. It was pencilled in to commence in the summer. My friends and I liked the idea of going over there to see if we could cope with a different type of soldiering. Most of the lads that didn't fancy it had left, or transferred, when we moved to Germany. Training for our new role was to begin fairly soon with a week long series of lectures from a specialist team. I decided not to tell Mum that we would be in Ireland as she would be a nervous wreck for the duration of my time there. I eventually organised a kind friend, Smudge Smith, who stayed behind with the rear party, to forward any mail from Mum over to me.

We sat down for our first lecture feeling a wee bit nervous about what to expect. Irish fiddle music was playing on the loudspeakers to get us into the mood. Our commanding officer made a short speech then handed over to the training team. They were all Ireland veterans, mostly infantry and superbly professional. The week flew by and we learnt a great deal. All useful information that would help keep us alive. We viewed some pretty terrible slides of the aftermath of the atrocities that went on over the water. Wholescale, indiscriminate, bloody slaughter, in some cases. Food for thought for us young lads. The regiment had last served in Ireland in 1974 and many of the young gunners that walked the streets of Belfast on that tour had since become experienced bombardiers and sergeants.

Our destination, after much rumour, turned out to be Co. Fermanagh, a beautiful but very wet collection of small towns and villages, running alongside the border with the south. I was more than happy with a rural tour as I enjoyed walking in the countryside and being out in nature, even if there happened to be folk around trying to kill you. Ours was the first artillery unit to be sent to the border during the Troubles. Although, our location was nothing like as hazardous as South Armagh, along the border on the other side of the island.

25 Battery was being split into two equal troops, one was heading to Lisnaskea, and the one I was in was assigned to Rosslea, just over a mile from the border with Southern Ireland. I was put into a brick of four guys with Mick, my old boss from firefighting days, Martyn, my good pal, and Dave our machine gunner.

Now we knew where we would be based things really livened up. The next part of our training was a visit to the famous Tin City. This was a mock-up village, complete with pub, shops and houses. Mainly made from corrugated tin, we could practise patrolling the narrow streets and learn how to control a rioting mob. The mob were soldiers from other units, who volunteered to spend time there and thoroughly enjoyed causing mayhem.

I found the whole process fascinating and loved every minute of it, except one. It had been drummed into us from the beginning, that if we can see a bomb, the bomb can see us. On our second day of training we had found a dummy car bomb, sealed off the area then put a cordon round it. The video cameras caught me peeping round a street corner to look at the suspicious car. At the debrief the following morning the instructor asked,

"Who the feckin' 'ell is that dickhead trying to get his head blown off?"

My grinning pals piped up, "It's 'Arry, he's over 'ere." Cheers, lads.

One evening I was on guard in a watchtower, when I saw something move in a bedroom window perhaps a hundred metres away. I kept watching with rising trepidation and realised I really was looking at a bloke with a gun about to take aim in my direction. We had been issued a type of plastic low velocity bullet for our rifles for this very situation. I cocked my weapon, took careful aim from the shoulder, then let fly with a round, hitting the target. The gunman was made of plywood. That pleased me greatly, more than making up for the dickhead moment.

We visited the ranges a few times to improve our weapon handling skills and on the final one we held a battery competition which I won with a two inch group, at three hundred metres. My prize was a huge great night sight, to be fitted to my rifle. The rifle itself was heavy enough on it's own, without another few kilos added on.

Rural patrolling was another infantry skill that we picked up, being taught by a very bright corporal from the Sherwood Foresters. I loved making rendezvous, ambushing and carrying heavy rucksacks through the countryside. During that part of the training we found ourselves thoroughly exhausted at times from lack of sleep. One night I found myself walking along a track on patrol, whilst just about nodding off. During one long ambush, where twelve of us lay in wait for hours, I looked around, whispered "oi" and found that I was the only one still awake.

The next day we met as a battery for a lunch stop and sat down in the middle of a field awaiting the cooks to turn up with some grub. I went through the make safe procedure with my SLR, my mate Dave checked it was empty, then I fired a blank round at the ground in front of me. BANG! Then followed a moment's silence before all my mates nearly died laughing. A negligent discharge meant I was in deep shit. A week later, I was marched into the Battery Commander's office in my best uniform for a bollocking, then marched back out and up to the CO's office for punishment. The RSM, who had given me plenty of grief with the shiny front bumper incident, met me outside his door and snarled. He doubled me round the square for ten minutes, then back to the CO's office. In I went, sweating and puffing hard, unable to speak, received another bollocking and a two hundred pounds fine, two weeks pay, left turn, march out, eff right eff right. Ouch.

Then I was hit by some surprising news. The isolated units in the remote villages would need a medic, as we were long distances on dangerous roads from the regiment's doctor. It was decided I was the man for Rosslea, so I was going to be sent to Aldershot in a couple of days time, for an eight weeks course. A couple of other lads from other batteries received the same news. I was surprised at the urgency but happy to go and left for Blighty immediately.

My best mate Phil, was by this time studying at Portsmouth Polytechnic and living in a hall of residence. This happened to be about an hours drive from Ash Vale where the basic medics course was to begin on the following Monday. We arranged that I would live in his room at the Poly and he would move in with his girlfriend for the duration. So every morning I would get up, have a free brekkie in the hall of residence then bomb up the A27 to Ash Vale in my Midget, getting there in time for a 9am start. God knows what the canteen ladies thought, as they served me eggs and bacon in my army uniform. I obviously shouldn't have been ligging breakfast every morning but they never said a dickie bird. It was wonderful to be free of the military from teatime until the first class the following morning, spending my free time with Phil and his many student friends.

The course itself was interesting enough but almost useless for operations in Northern Ireland. It was designed for looking after soldiers in the sickbay back at base. The regiment, meanwhile, flew over to Co. Fermanagh during our last week in Ash Vale. The three of us from 19 Regiment politely asked the course leader if we could be excused the final few days, so that we could rejoin our unit. He, equally politely, told us to fuck off.

My last night with Phil before I left for the airport was a bit of a classic. The pair of us settled into an Italian restaurant and ordered two giant plates of spag bol. Three bottles of wine washed it down, no doubt with dozens of cigarettes. We moved on to a disco and drank some more. I have no idea where we ended up next. The following morning, I found myself being woken by Phil's girlfriend at her flat. I was lying on her kitchen floor with my head out of the open back door, on the concrete step, feeling a bit delicate to say the least. Phil was comatose nearby, looking terrible and groaning, his hair full of bits of carrot. Poor old June was used to this sort of fiasco in the mornings. We looked at the clock and an awful realisation struck, my train was leaving Portsmouth harbour for Gatwick in about a quarter of an hour's time.

Fourteen and three quarter frantic minutes later, I sprinted along the platform with Phil hard on my heels, still half dressed and laughing my head off. I leapt onto the slowly moving train as Phil threw my suitcase in after me. The bloody thing wasn't shut and all my kit flew across the passageway. Never mind, I had made it. Good old Phil jogged down the platform, smiling and waving, still half-cut and covered in food stains.

County Fermanagh 1980

After a night back in Dortmund, the three of us newly qualified medics and a few other odds and sods found ourselves on the tarmac at Wuppertal airport, dressed in combats, carrying our weapons and suitcases. We all climbed aboard an incredibly noisy Hercules transport plane and found a webbing seat to settle down into. The bog was a bucket at the back behind a little curtain. The flight was a chance for a long overdue kip. I woke up just before we touched down at Aldergrove airport, outside Belfast. Here we go then we thought, as we trooped off the big green bird. The first stop was customs. What, you're joking? I had packed my case with a four months supply of roll-up tobacco, not realising I might be stopped by customs and searched. My stash was impounded, along with everyone else's. A nice little earner for somebody.

We then made our way to a quiet area of the airport where we climbed into a large old removals lorry. Somebody was given a few rounds of ammunition, the backdoor was shut and away we rattled out of the airport. Blimey, three nights before I had been, unsuccessfully as usual, chatting up a very pretty student in a smart club and now I was lying on the floor of an old covert vehicle heading for the border.

Rosslea police station stood on a slight rise on a road, a few hundred yards from the village. A mile down the road in the other direction was the Southern Irish border. The station had seen plenty of action over the years, including a gun fight on the staircase and mortar attacks. The police lived in the surrounding area, driving to work for their shifts just like coppers everywhere. The difference being, that these guys were targeted day and night and could never feel safe. Real heroes.

Us soldiers occupied three portacabins in the carpark and had taken over part of the cop shop too. We had our own ACC cook, a tv room and a washing and cleaning cabin. The base was surrounded by corrugated iron to a height of about twenty feet and three sangers, modern pillboxes, stood on towers in the corners of the land. The whole footprint of the base was tiny, if a helicopter had to come in with supplies, it landed on the school field a few hundred yards down the road.

The only safe way to get from regimental headquarters forty miles away was by helicopter, the roads being too dangerous for us to travel along due to the risk of culvert bombs. That was why the troop needed a medic, to carry out simple first aid tasks. If something was beyond his limited knowledge and skills the medic could telephone the regimental doctor for advice. Surprisingly, I had not been taught a thing about dealing with gunshot wounds or blast injuries. I would have to rely on common sense and plenty of field dressings if anything major happened. If it did, picking up the phone would have been the last thing on my mind.

I was delighted to meet my friends who had been there for a week already. They all seemed pretty happy with things and had saved me a bedspace in their cabin. I was shown around, including a visit to one of the sangers. The sanger was accessed by a trapdoor, once inside the ten foot square blast proof box you had a good view through the front opening. A GPMG machine gun was fixed to the opening with a long belt of shining 7.62mm rounds hanging from it. That was a very reassuring piece of kit to have on your side, if an attack was launched on the base.

Our role was to protect the community from IRA attacks and to gather low level intelligence. To do these things, we disappeared into the countryside, then reappeared briefly to carry out car stops and searches. We never hung around long enough for the IRA to organise an attack on us before moving on. We searched old buildings for guns and explosives whilst providing a presence around the farming community, in an attempt to give them some protection. If the bad guys planned a hit on someone, they could never be sure we weren't hiding close by, ready to mess up their day.

Usually we patrolled with eight or twelve soldiers and we stayed out for up to six days. On our return we washed our kit, tried to get some kip, ate loads of nosh and spent many long and lonely hours up in the sangers. When we patrolled, we walked miles across the hills in daylight, then, after dark, slipped deep into a conifer plantation. Nobody could have approached our hideaway without alerting the guy on stag, who would hear twigs snapping underfoot. Most nights we managed a few hours rest before moving on. We lived on compo rations, with breakfast usually consisting of a can of bacon roll heated on a hexi burner. The grease was washed down with strong army coffee and an oatmeal block. Ace.

One evening we crept into a hayshed and set up an ambush facing the farmer's front door. Our intelligence cell had information that the farmhouse was to be targeted. The owner was to be murdered on his front step when he opened the door in the dark, like so many others. We sat quietly watching throughout the night with our guns ready but nobody came. Early the next morning we met the farmer's friendly wife. Our troop lived a very isolated, rough life, away from female company and home comforts. So when she invited us, in two groups, into her huge, warm farmhouse kitchen for a massive fry up, we loved it. What a memorable morning that was. A kitchen never felt so homely.

As the tour wore on, tiredness crept in more and more. One night I was talking with Mick in the control room when a voice can over the intercom from the front sanger,

"Where the feck is Spanner, he should have relieved me ten minutes ago?"

I told Mick I would go and find Spanner, who was a good friend of mine. The ugly old sod was fast asleep in his warm pit. I shook his shoulder to wake him. Nothing. Dead to the world.

"Spanner mate, wake up, you're on stag ten minutes ago."

Still nothing. He was completely done in. I pulled him by the shoulders out of his bed and onto the floor. Finally, he roused and opened his eyes. "What the feck?"

"Come on Mate, you're late on stag," I said.

He finally came to, then staggered off to his post, to receive a bollocking from the guy he relieved, no doubt.

It was also Spanner whom I had to relieve a few nights later. I dressed and crept quietly outside for the 4am until 6am stag. I climbed up to the trapdoor in the sanger floor, then pushed it. It wouldn't budge. I tried again but no, it was firmly closed. I called out Spanner's name, now becoming a bit concerned. Was he ok? After a few moments I heard the noise of someone moving around above me. I pushed the trapdoor and realised what had happened. The daft bugger had sat on the floor for a couple of minutes then nodded off.

One wet and windy night I was again in the control room with Mick and another guy, a wild but hugely entertaining bloke called Blackey. A young cockney geezer called Gary was up in the front sanger, freezing his nuts off with the wind howling through the front opening. We devised a little scheme to make sure he stayed awake through his stag.

Blackey quietly climbed up the back of the sanger onto the roof above Gary's head. We gave him a few minutes to get up into position then said to Gary through the intercom:

"One of the other sangers thinks he heard something from in front of your position, can you poke your head out and have a butcher's?"

As Gary dutifully leant out the front opening, Blackey's upside down gargoyle head appeared out of the darkness just in front of his face. In the control room all we heard was Blackey's blood curdling roar and half a second later, Gary's terrified scream. The poor kid must have been absolutely petrified for a moment, though he laughed afterwards back in the warmth of the control room, after changing his trousers.

Thankfully, I wasn't called upon to do much medical work. One big lad had an abcess in a very painful area which I drained a few times with a syringe, whilst receiving instructions over the phone. A few of the guys had ticks to be removed and cleaned up. That was about it. Very few of us ever booked sick anyway and nobody became ill with colds or flu during our tour. Fresh air, good food and plenty of exercise works wonders.

Things changed the day one of our police officers was targeted by the IRA and shot dead at his home. Decisions must have been made at a high level, because our tactics changed. We received orders to dig in and build a sandbagged sanger in a field by a road overlooking the border. Before this, our plan was always to be mobile, but after the tragic death we went static. A few days into our time at this location, a pair of us had walked back to the sanger for a cuppa after finishing our turn keeping watch on the road. We brewed up and Martyn handed me an orange,

"Happy birthday Harry," he said.

It was my twenty first. The rest of the boys chipped in with a can of compo steak and kidney pud, a real treat. Top of the Pops was on the tranny and we listened to the DJ announcing Adam and the Ants as this week's no.1. Just as the opening drum roll sounded on the radio, a crack, crack, crack, of shots whistled over our shelter. We fucking helled, piling out of the entrance, grabbing our guns on the way. By this time, the guys on the road had fired back, including Big Phil's Bren gun booming away. A few more shots came back over our heads as we ran up to the road to join in.

The gunmen raced back over the border very quickly on a motorbike. All hell broke loose on the radio following our "contact, wait out," report. We checked that nobody was missing or had been shot. We reassured each other then gradually things calmed down. Nobody amongst us was very concerned by the shooting. We knew it was coming once we received the order to stay put in the open. The new tactic was designed to take the pressure off the police for a while. A helicopter equipped with Nitesun soon appeared to illuminate the scene of the crime but nothing much was found, except a dead goat that we must have shot. Their weapon was thought to be an American M60 machine gun. They obviously weren't much good with it, all the rounds flew several feet over our heads.

The only other shooting incident happened when a patrol from our troop was crossing some fields in the middle of nowhere, a few weeks later. A gunman popped up and fired some shots at the tail end charlie. He fired back and they exchanged shots, nobody being hit by any of the rounds. The terrorist then disappeared quickly, before the rest of the patrol could engage with him. That was it for shootings on our tour but we felt more in danger from booby traps and culvert bombs under roads. We always avoided gateways and stiles, so to cross a field we made our way to the thickest part of the hedge and forced our way through or climbed fences away from the gates. There was plenty of laughing at lads falling over fences or getting their huge rucksacks stuck on brambles and hawthorns.

I was only scared on one occasion during the tour. We had been out patrolling for a few days and somewhere along the way had befriended a black and white border collie. He came with us when we slipped into a plantation for a few hours kip. We ate, then slept. I was woken for stag in the early hours and stayed very awake as the border was only a few hundred yards away. The nearness of the border kept us on high alert. I had my night sight with me and used it to scan the woods every few minutes. Our new friend, Spot the dog, began to get agitated. Ears up, hackles starting to rise, deep low growl. Something or someone was out there, coming our way and I was the only bloke on guard. I listened, frantically scanning the trees with my sight but couldn't see anything except wood. I was very nervous, as was the dog who kept growling. Should I wake the exhausted patrol or not? My heart thumped in my chest as I wondered what to do. Wake everyone to be on the safe side, or not? Cock my weapon and fire a round? Surely I would hear anybody getting anywhere near? After a few very long, lonely minutes, the dog calmed and became bored with whatever was out there. Thank god for that. It was probably a badger or a deer.

My time in Rosslea came to an end in early December and, on the whole, I was pleased to have experienced the nearest thing to proper soldiering that I was likely to face. The lads of the troop performed brilliantly, working hard with no fallouts or major rows. It helped that our boss was a sensible bloke that we all respected, who never put a foot wrong. Our regiment, thankfully, had a good tour with no major casualties. On the Spring morning back in Germany, when the CO handed us our General Service (NI) medals we all stood a little bit taller.

Biathlon

When I arrived back in Dortmund I was asked by a young officer who I had worked with previously, if I could ski? Too right I could, where are we going? He asked my friend Stevie and I if we would like to be members of the regimental ski-ing team. If so, we would be training for a month down in Andermatt, before going on to the 3 Division Championships in January.

The next morning the pair of us found ourselves driving in my cramped little Midget over to Petty France in London to collect our ten year passports, compliments of the MOD. When we arrived at the office they took some photos and delivered the passports within the hour. Government service, it said inside them. Who, us? Spies? We then hot-footed it across France and into Switzerland where we met snow for the first time. We arrived in Andermatt late at night and had a very quick meeting with our instructor. He was an Olympic standard cross-country skier who had one of those roles everyone in the military dreams of. Teaching ski-ing in the winter, adventure training in the summer and being well paid at the same time. He told us that we should have started two days previously, so had a fair bit of catching up to do. We had spent the previous several months walking with heavy rucksacs, carrying weapons, having hardly run anywhere since about June. Our expertise at langlauf ski racing was also non-existent too but we very much wanted to learn and give it our best shot.

The setting was absolutely fabulous. A beautiful hotel, us all in single or twin rooms with plenty of good quality snow. This was more like it. The only problem was the lack of food for guys using up four or five thousand calories a day. Thin soup with a roll is not enough for lunch if you have been cross-country ski-ing all morning. The hotel was onto a good payday. Our training was relentless, we weren't there to muck about and we had to give it our all. It was full on nackering, running up the hills, then skiing as fast as possible on the flat. My technique was a bit crap to say the least but I began to enjoy the feeling of pushing myself harder physically than ever before. I cut down my smoking to one in the morning and one before bed. By the time the third week came we felt capable on the skis, could run up the slopes with them on, then push on hard over the summit of the slope. On the final Saturday we competed in a twenty kilometre race. I finished somewhere in the middle but during the debrief, the video footage showed me creeping along like a short arsed, wooden, clockwork toy.

"Who the feck is that?" the chief instructor asked, amazed at my poor technique.

I kept my head well down whilst Stevie, sat next to me, nearly pissed himself.

We finished the months training with a boozy end of course party, then packed to leave the next morning. Over breakfast we heard of John Lennon's sad murder in New York. Stevie and I motored away in heavy snow towards Calais and the UK where we spent a well-earned couple of weeks leave.

With that out of the way and a good bit of the hard fitness training undone with too much food and beer, we joined the rest of the team. Together we set off for Zwiesel down near the Czech border. This was where the Divisional Championships took place. We took our trusty SLR's as our event was the biathlon. This very challenging sport included ski-ing and also firing at targets situated at the halfway point in the race. Breathing control was everything during the shooting stage.

The racing was very competitive, with the best finishers going on to represent the division in the British Army Championships. As first timers we stood no chance but enjoyed the experience. One of the highlights for me was recognising a smiling face at the finishing line after a twenty kilometre race. Sgt. Horwell, my basic training instructor and I shook hands, then chatted and reminisced like old pals. I was still no Franz Klammer!

The beginning of the End.

By the middle of February I was back in the gun park, cleaning vehicles with a diesel covered rag. I was bored out of my mind and wanting to be doing anything other than facing the drudgery of daily life in the artillery. A radical change had occurred in me during the previous year or so. I was not a big drinker by the standards of the day so I found that I gradually became more and more disillusioned with the drinking culture.

I had finally realised that running is a pleasure in itself once you get to a reasonable level of fitness. After a certain amount of training you really do stop getting painful stitches after a few hundred yards. As before, a few of my mates felt much the same, so we kept up our levels of fitness by running together several times a week.

Things like the guard duty rota started to really hack me off. Some of us seemed to be on guard every couple of weeks, whilst some teachers' pets hardly ever had their name on the list. Complaining would just have made things worse. On one such evening, nine of us marched onto the square, highly polished and ironed. We were waiting for the duty officer to inspect us, then award the stickman the night off, for being the smartest. As the young officer approached, my old buddy Carl let out a huge fart. It could have been heard two hundred metres away. Eight of us immediately started shaking, sweating and desperately trying not to laugh. We resembled the Roman soldiers during the Bigus Dickus scene in Life of Brian. Holding in the mirth made it worse, of course. The only one not in obvious distress was Carl. The officer looked us all up and down one at a time, his face a fury. He was thinking our suppressed laughter was caused by something we found funny about his marching. He arrived at Carl, noticing he looked calm, serious and soldierly, and promptly awarded him the night off. As stickman Carl marched past me, back to his room for the evening, he winked and smiled. Nice one mate.

Snow Queen

The ability of the British Soldier to have a go, fail miserably, laugh at himself, then get drunk, has helped him through some tough situations over the years. This was all too evident when some of us travelled to Bavaria to take part in operation Snow Queen. Most units in BAOR owned or borrowed a house somewhere up in the mountains. Soldiers could go to have a break, learn to ski, get pissed and do some adventure training. So myself and a gang of mates found ourselves staying in a beautiful wooden house near Fussen for a fortnight's downhill ski-ing. Some of us could ski a bit but none of us were proficient downhillers. I could langlauf competently but had never tried downhill ski-ing. Our first morning on the slopes was something to behold. The German skiers looked on in amazement at this rag-tag bunch of clowns, dressed like travellers in half military clothes, half cheap nylon waterproofs. We couldn't even get up the slope on a T-bar without falling off, then being dragged up sideways. Our lads could be seen snow ploughing very slowly sideways across slopes, whilst the locals bombed past them, missing the randomly sliding squaddie by inches. We laughed, we fell over, we hurt ourselves but we pressed on and gradually learnt to stand up, turn and aim downhill a bit. The Germans loved the show, finding the badly dressed maniacs to be highly amusing entertainment.

Incredibly, about a third of our number didn't even try getting onto the slopes. They gathered in the viewing area attached to the bar at the bottom of the hill. In comfort they watched the rest of us valiantly falling over time and time again, while they got hammered on schnapps and lager. Everytime we stood with them for a breather they slumped lower in their seats and talked less coherently. By the end of the fortnight there was a permanent area of seats set out for them by the bar owner.

We gradually improved but those gains brought with it increasing bravado and more spectacular crashes. We watched Big Stevie flying past us down a slope like a true professional, gathering tremendous speed in the tuck position. Then we realised he had no idea how to slow down but was too terrified to move a muscle. He just got faster and faster until he hit a bump then smash! Down he went in a gigantic whirl of arms, legs, skis and poles. Followed by much cheering and hilarity from us and the locals.

Being squaddies, we thought we had much more prowess than was the case. So, at the end of the first week we decided to conquer the black run at the top of the mountain. Even though, at this stage, we often still fell over when we just stood and chatted to each other. Up in the cable car we went, heading to the mountain top dressed in our NATO woolley pulleys and bobble hats. At the summit we started to have second thoughts. We looked over the edge and saw how steep it really was. The cafe with our drunk pals sitting outside was a tiny speck way, way below. The Germans, of course, just piled down over the edge without pause. We felt like we should be roped together to go down that thing! One lad fell over just standing there, nevertheless, he saw no reason why he couldn't ski down a black run. That's a soldier's optimism for you. Off we all went and within ten yards began to fall and slide for dozens of yards. Occasionally, one of us would get going properly then chicken out, tumbling over on purpose before gaining too much velocity. Seeing someone snow ploughing really slowly across the slope, then turning at the end and being unable to get back into the opposite snow plough, so they rocketed off down the hill at high speed, screaming and laughing, was just so funny. We all made it down in the end with no bodily damage except bruises and agreed that it was time for some beer.

We drank like only soldiers do, danced at some long forgotten club with the girls there. Sometimes we danced with each other if the girls said no, which they usually did. We ate huge quantities of bratwurst mit pommes frites and generally had a great time. Usually fairly well behaved, I found myself necking Pernod for the only time in my life and later on shinning up a hotel flagpole to steal a giant Bavarian blue and white flag which came back to Dortmund with me at the end of the second week.

Belsen, Hohne, and the Great Race.

Shortly after our return to camp I was pulled into the battery office.
"Fenton, you are to start working in the garrison medical centre from next Monday," I was brusquely informed.

I was devastated. I had been promised, before I went on the medics course before the Ireland tour, that I would never have to work in the medical centre. However, there was nothing I could do but report there and see what happened. I ended up working in the pharmacy giving out pills to the sickies which wasn't too unpleasant but it wasn't soldiering. I was called in on one occasion to help hold down a lad who came in with a huge abscess on his thigh. We all held a limb whilst the doctor burst it. Eeek! When he had cleared away the pus I could see right inside the guy's leg where the muscle had been eaten away. Fascinating stuff, I learnt quite a bit of useful first aid in the few months that I worked there.

The battery then began another series of build-up training exercises in the field, so Kev and I found ourselves back in our Ferret crashing around the forests of Luneburg Heath. There were moments of great humour amongst the rain and lack of sleep. One wet night we set up our theodolites and out of the darkness a young gunner ran up to us. He was sent from his Abbot to be given a bearing to be applied to his gun's sight. The bearing was always a four figure number. We told him, he repeated the number, then ran off. A moment later he returned. "What was it again?" he asked.

Off he went, only to reappear yet again.

"Sorry, I forgot it," he trembled.

Kev grabbed a chinagraph pencil and asked the lad to take off his beret, then wrote the number on his forehead, before he scampered away again. A minute or two later we could hear the lad's gun commander laughing his head off in the darkness.

Driving in the dark across the countryside is a tricky skill to learn. Our vehicles had a tiny little convoy light which glowed white underneath the back of the vehicle, for the one behind to follow in the dark. The lead vehicle would follow a guide with a red torch. Much whispered cursing and shushing would go on, trees would be driven into and vehicles sometimes became bogged down, causing even more swearing and bollocking. After two weeks of dashing from one gun position to another, we took a break for a weekend at Hohne camp. (Everyone except Max and I, that is. He decided to have me drive him around the ranges to recce possible gun positions for the next week. Everyone else kipped for two days.)

Hohne had the hilarity of communal showers, something not for the faint hearted. The water stayed hot for about five minutes so you couldn't mess around and with thirty of you going in together the "don't bend down in front of him" and "look at the size of that," jokes abounded. The way to survive was to never show weakness and to keep laughing. Once out of the showers we practised the old army trick of wiping the water off ourselves by hand, before using the issued green towels which just spread the water around without drying you. Towels were only good for whipping each other whilst we dressed.

The shower jokes weren't in evidence on the Sunday when we all paid a visit to Bergen-Belsen, the WW2 concentration camp. We stood silent and could hardly believe that anyone could be so cruel to other human beings. A horrible, horrible place.

One of the great characters in the battery was a guy of Polish descent, Sgt. Charlie Dodds. Always smiling and laughing, he was one of those blokes who could get away with murder with his cheeky chappie attitude. His crew loved him and his type was priceless when morale needed raising or someone needed bringing down off their high horse. Such a scenario occurred on the Sunday afternoon, at the start of the regimental cross-country race, which we all had to take part in. Six hundred of us lined up, laughing and taking the piss out of each other in the mud, waiting for the big send off. On a wooden podium stood the CO and his wife, specially driven all the way from Dortmund for the task. She was going to fire a starting pistol in the air and off we would dash. After a short speech by the CO she raised the gun ready to fire it. Just then, Charlie shouted at the top of his voice "GO!" So off we went, racing away, roaring our heads off at the sight of this smartly dressed lady wondering what the fuck was going on and what the hell was she doing there anyway.

I amazed myself by finishing in twenty sixth place. The fitness training was beginning to pay off. It was becoming a very important part of my world. I could feel that being fitter was helping me grow in stature in all aspects of my life.

The Sandpoint Six

However, next on the horizon was the trip we had all longed for. BATUS stands for British Army Training Area Suffield, near Medicine Hat, Alberta, Canada. The Army trained regularly on the prairies of Alberta. It was the only place an entire battlegroup could practise warfare and fire it's big guns in a 360 degree circle. The training area was many times bigger than Salisbury Plain, or Luneburg Heath in Germany, where we normally held our exercises. Our battle group consisted of us, the Royal Highland Fusiliers (RHF) and the Tankies from the south-west of England, The Armoured Farmers, as they were known. Loads of other smaller units of engineers, transport, etc, made up the whole fighting unit of several thousand men.

25 Battery flew on an RAF jet configured with the passenger seats facing the rear. It is safer to fly that way but it felt a bit weird. We landed at Keflavik airport in Iceland to refuel, then set off again, having gained a new country for our tally. Our great circle took us over Hudson Bay. Above which, we watched the setting sun just lightly touch the snow covered distant horizon, then ascend again. For me, that was a truly magical spectacle. Equally enthralling, but in a very different way, was seeing the highrise blocks of Calgary coming into view. Against the backdrop of the flat landscape for miles around, with the purple Rocky mountains jagged outlines on the horizon, it was like being in the opening shot of an American movie.

We settled into our camp and acclimatised to the heat for a few days. There appeared to be a slightly more laid back attitude from our bosses, which was very much welcome. Being in Canada, with it's huge skies and massive open countryside, plus the sunshine and the very different culture, ensured there was a smile on all our faces.

We went out onto the vast prairie on manoeuvres where instead of the usual mud and rain, we experienced heat and dust. It was glorious. One or two guys taking their shovels for a recce, heard the unmistakable clacking of an angry rattlesnake guarding it's territory. Not what you want to hear with your pants down but a great help to those constipated by compo rations!

We met up with the tankies on the vehicle washdown at the end of exercises and I was very jealous of them. Their Chieftain tanks looked magnificent and the lads in black had a very laid back lifestyle. If I had been as independently minded at seventeen years old as I was at twenty one, I would have told the recruiters, "it's the tank regiment for me or I go home."

At the end of our rigorous two months training on the Prairie we had the fantastic chance to see a bit of Canada before the regiment flew home. We were given a week's leave and the officers encouraged and assisted us to go and do something adventurous. One guy flew down to Chicago and others disappeared to see Niagara Falls. A few stayed in camp and drank themselves stupid, of course.

I wondered about going to Toronto to try to solve an old family mystery: My great grandparents, Willie Fenton and Jessie McPherson, had been brought up in Aberdeenshire. They made a living running a chandlers shop by the harbour. Just before the first world war, they moved to Manchester where their two sons worked as journalists. One of them, John, my grandfather, eventually made his way to Oxford, where my story began. But, the other son, Billy, took his young family across the Atlantic to Toronto. Very little was known about Billy and his family by Dad. All he knew was that Billy had several children and became a famous sports journalist. My idea was to go into the Toronto Times offices where I would ask if they had heard of Billy Fenton. Surely some old reporter would remember him? After a bit of research I quickly changed my mind, it was too expensive to get to Toronto.

However, over the next few decades I kept thinking about my family in Canada. None of my uncles had any idea who Billy was, even. Eventually, thanks to the internet I made a breakthrough. Billy had been inducted into the Canadian Soccer Hall of Fame in 2006. During his career he had written an article about footy every day for forty four years and was known in Canada as "Mr Football." Through a bit of perseverance I managed to find the addresses of two of his granddaughters. The upshot of all this was that Judie, Ruth and I, had a wonderfully emotional meet up in Paris in 2019. Almost certainly, the first get together of the two sides of the family for over one hundred years.

Instead of tracking down Billy, I came up with a plan for a trip and gathered a few pals to join me.

So, on the Saturday of our week's leave, Al, Kev, Joe, Stevie, Vic and I, found ourselves collecting a Chevrolet Caprice Classic estate car from a rental in Calgary and excitedly piling in. The car was as big as one of our armoured vehicles, with a five litre engine and plenty of room for six with all our gear. We headed off for the border feeling like extras from Easy Rider. Somebody in the car then produced a little bag of dope. I had never tried cannabis before but decided, in for a penny, so I gave it a go. Kev was next to me on the huge back seat. As a group, we decided that the driver mustn't smoke any and had to keep his window open whilst we sped along. I was passed the joint and took a couple of drags. Kev was already giggling and I joined in. Before long five of us were crying with laughter and splitting our sides. It was so funny that we actually hurt ourselves. Just catching Kev's eye set me off into another bout of hilarity and tears of laughter. We gradually calmed down and although it was great fun, it wasn't something to be repeated very often. We stopped at a rest stop on a most beautiful road through the mountains and worked out how far we had driven in the past few hours. A very short distance was the answer. Vic, the driver, thought he was doing about seventy miles an hour but was as stoned as the rest of us by passive smoking and had been toddling along at about twenty. Crossing the border into America later on was a bit of a worry as the guard had a good look at us and our rather smelly car.

After the best part of a day's driving, we pulled into a small town somewhere in Idaho and headed for the bar. The folk there welcomed us with open arms. Most of them had never met live English guys before. We had arrived in timber country where people worked hard, drank hard and all wore checked shirts and had fingers missing from working in the big mill saws, even the girls.

We drank, they drank, then we slept it off in and around our car. The following morning we demolished a breakfast of hashbrowns with maple syrup and coffee then moved off, heading south through the glorious Yellowstone National Park. We saw black bears, gophers, giant redwoods and beautiful mountains and rivers. The time of our young lives.

Continuing our trip, we pulled into the main street of Sandpoint, Idaho. A small but very lovely lakeside town, surrounded by forests and ranches. Truly stunning. However, as a bunch of lads in our early twenties, all we wanted to do was sample the delights of 'Shenanighans, The Cowgirl Corral', the bar that we spied across the road.

I ordered six glasses of Coors beer and took a seat at the almost empty bar. We had arrived very early in the evening and the two girls sat nearby perked up when they heard my accent. Englishmen! The other lads picked up their freezing cold beers and wandered off. I fell into a conversation with the girl sitting on the stool closest to me. I think she must have been appreciative of a conversation that wasn't about timber. Connie and I sat there for hours chatting each other up and having a great time whilst Stevie moved in on her friend.

Meanwhile, the bars filled up with locals who, as ever on our trip, seemed an extremely sociable crowd. In the large bar at the rear stood a huge contraption that we didn't recognise at first. It looked like a giant school PT pommel horse and was surrounded by cushioned mats. When someone told us that it was a mechanical bucking bronco we straight away knew the evening was going to be a memorable one.

Once the evening warmed up a bit the DJ asked for the first volunteer to try his luck. Alan, my pal from the Norway trip, was the first to climb on the monster's back. The audience of oldies sat around the room knew just what was coming. The DJ shouted go and pressed a button which started the bucking action. Within half a second Alan was tossed off to a roar of delight from the onlookers. Up we all went, one at a time, to try our luck and all of us met a similar fate. Tossed off in a few seconds, sometimes less. As we all drank more and learnt how to hang on, things improved a little. Vic even managed a couple of rotations and a one handed wave before he was thrown. The crowd of Americans loved every minute of it and cheered on our efforts.

At the same time I was continuing my cosy chat at the bar with my new American friend and Stevie was making good progress with his girl. The evening drew to a close and we said our goodbyes to the DJ and the rest of the drinkers. Stevie and I headed to the girls apartment, all four of us much the worse for wear. When we settled down in their apartment I couldn't believe that a large bong appeared and was prepared for use. Pink Floyd was on the music system, all four of us ended up in the same big bed..........

The next morning, five of us made the rendezvous back at the car. Kev was nowhere to be seen. He had disappeared at closing time, maybe with an unfortunate female. After a couple of hours of breakfast and hanging about we decided to speak to the local cops. We wondered if he happened to have been banged up for the night. To our delight, they put out an APB for our missing mate. About an hour later, he wandered up to our car with a huge grin on his fizzog and sold us a very unlikely yarn about his night of passion with Miss Idaho or maybe an actress. Typical Kev, in actual fact, he had probably slept on his own in a bus stop.

Back as a group once again we motored north to Spokane. Not liking the look of the town we U-turned and made for Banff. This was more our scene, we spent the evening sitting in a hot spring talking, laughing and reminiscing about our trip.

On the long journey back to Calgary the next morning through the Yellowstone National Park I decided that, after my one joint and a puff on a bong, drugs didn't suit me. I think the rest of the guys felt the same. There was only one lad back in Dortmund who smoked cannabis regularly and he was a cook. Nobody else, to my knowledge, went near it. Beer was our drug of choice when we wanted to party.

We handed our faithful old Chevvy back to the rental in one piece and after working out the mileage fee, we all chipped in our last few dollars to pay it. We walked out of the garage with twenty one cents between us. Phew! What a priceless week that was.

Adventure Training in the Rockies

Back at BATUS the battle group prepared to leave Canada for it's bases back in Germany. A call went out for volunteers to spend a few weeks adventure training in The Rocky Mountains, near Banff. Unbelievably, only a few showed interest. I could understand the married lads wanting to go home to their wives and families but surely all the single blokes would rather go adventuring than hanging around in the gun park back in Dortmund? I was the only one of the Sandpoint Six who volunteered for the trip up into the mountains.

The coach trip was sensational. Our destination was a small military campsite somewhere in the Jasper National Park. Huge mountains surrounded our tents on three sides, whilst to our front was a river feeding off the glaciers to the north. The scenery knocked my Lake District into a cocked hat, lovely though it is.

A couple of rows of trusty old eight man canvas tents awaited us. We all claimed a bed space in the tent allocated to us. I was fortunate enough to be pitched in with seven lads from the Royal Highland Fusiliers. Glaswegians to a man, they were a delight to spend a few weeks with. One of them was a miniature Billy Connelly. He played a guitar, sang, told jokes and kept his pals amused with his stories of Glasgow life. They accepted me from the off, I was just another young soldier out to make the most of things and happy to muck in with them.

The first night we sat around a huge bonfire and became acquainted with each other and the lads from The Armoured Farmers. I was so pleased to meet a gang of guys who spoke with the southern rural accent that I knew so well from home. Many of them came from Dorset and Devon. Singing, eating and taking the mickey was the game before we finally headed off to our pits.

Up bright and early, we met the small number of staff who kept the place running. The plan was that we would spend a week or so on the different activities, canoeing, glacier walking and hill walking. Between each activity there would be a couple of days back in camp. Sounded good to me. Firstly, everyone that wanted to take part in the canoe trip had to prove that they could swim two hundred yards in cold water. Cold? We could see the glacier that bore it in the distance. The instructor pointed to a canoe way out in the river with a little figure sitting in it waving at us.

"Swim out to the canoe, duck under, then swim back," he said.

"Oh, bollocks," we said as one, our nuts shrinking at the very thought.

Then, one nutter shouted out "Aaaaaaarrrghhh," quickly stripped off his clothes, then ran headlong towards the narrow beach. Not wanting to look like effeminate tossers, the rest of us ripped our kit off. Yelling "banzai," or "yeehaa," we chased after him. We couldn't muck about acclimatising, we would have chickened out, so we just ran in then dived. All forty of us. It was by far the coldest water I had ever swam in. Chest-clampingly cold. But we all somehow made it to the canoe, ducked under, spluttered, fucking-helled, and swam back. Wow, that was bracing, to say the least.

Our adventure training group's stay in Jasper was the first of the summer season. The alpine hut that the army used was way up above the snow line and had been emptied by the last group to use it the previous autumn. This meant that a huge load of kit needed to be transported up there by somebody. That somebody was all of us. My team was starting with the glacier walking week, our first aim for the day was the alpine hut anyway. Because we had rations, clothes and skis for a week's touring, we carried very little of the hut's itinerary for the summer. The others found themselves equipped with a variety of bizarre items on their antlike trek to seven or eight thousand feet. The unluckiest big lad was carting a bloody great wooden table on his back. When we arrived at the hut they dumped the stuff inside, turned round, waved and disappeared back down the mountain to the campsite.

Our instructor was a good guy. A hardy outdoor type from the Army Physical Training Corps and what a marvellous job he had. He explained that we would be skiing up the glacier for a few days, staying at a different hut each night. We sorted ourselves out, divvied up the group stores into our rucksacks, donned the skis and prepared to set off. Our skis were the much reviled army planks with ankle boots. Because we expected to climb several thousand feet of virgin snow, we fixed Beaver skins to our boots. These synthetic skins helped the hapless skier from sliding backwards when he tried to make progress uphill. After my bi-athlon training the previous winter I felt confident that I could cope with the skiing. For me, this was real living, the sort of experience that I put up with the gun park and the endless exercises for. The views of the snow covered peaks, the whiteness of the glacier, the valley covered in trees below us and the tiny river curling away into the distance, just knocked me sideways. I could hardly believe we were being paid to do this? And most of the guys said no thanks, can we go back to Dortmund please? Unbelievable.

The nine of us skied with no real dramas, for several hours a day. We fell plenty of times but improved as the week went on. When we arrived at the next one in the series of the fibreglass shelters at the end of each day, we brewed up, cooked, cleaned up, then went to sleep within two minutes of lying down. On our last day we prepared to descend from the hut leaving our warm down coats and skis for the next group. As I looked about me and took in the glacial scenery one last time I knew I had experienced something incredibly special.

Back at the base camp we recovered for a day, lying around in our big smelly tent. My Jocks had a thing about Reo Speedwagon, who's music played on their cassette player all day. After dark, they sang the band's songs round the bonfire, accompanied by their guitarist. The Tankies only had one tune, Yellow Bird, which they murdered endlessly when it was their turn to give us a song. Us gunners didn't even have our one to sing, to our shame.

After a short training session on a small lake, our next trip was by kayak and canoe down the river. We loaded tents and provisions into the boats and off we paddled downstream. Progress was easy with the flow but the occasional tiny rapids caused us some trepidation. Once again, we found ourselves in the most beautiful wild scenery imaginable with icy clear water, snow-peaked mountains all around, blue skies and trees. Landscapes full of tall pine trees, wherever you looked below the snow line.

After several hours of paddling we spotted our campsite and pulled into the bank. Families of Canadians sat around, interested in the strange accents of the new waterborne arrivals. They had travelled by pick-up trucks with huge aluminium Winnebagos attached and provisions for weeks of camping. In a short while we had made camp, brewed tea and began socialising with the holidaymakers. They couldn't have been more generous, plying us with food, beer and warm hospitality. I had noticed that all Canadian men, wherever we travelled, came in two sizes, large and huge. Their giant frames usually clothed in thick checked shirts and jeans. The Jocks and I seemed positively Lilliputian compared, except one lad in the group who was a body-builder with more muscle than noggin. Him and a much smaller guy actually had a beer-fuelled fight that night in front of everybody, which caused much jeering and derision, from both their pals and the Canadians.

We spent the week cruising down the river, stopping at campsites every night, always meeting a generous reception when we pitched up. The guitar and the singing helped us fit in, everyone loves a sing-song round a campfire. We must have been a long distance downstream when the trailer caught up with us after a week's kayaking. We loaded up and motored back to camp with aching shoulders, sore arses and some more great memories.

Next up for our group of happy campers was the hill walking phase.

I have noticed over the years that if a hundred or so blokes are together in a group, certain characters are always present: The natural leader, the comedian, the grot, the know-all, the athlete, the shagger, happy drunk and violent drunk, fat bastard, the good looking one, teacher's pet, and the one we all really hate, the pervy guy. Our leader for the week's hillwalking was an officer from my regiment who was that one, the creepy pervy guy. Being very much a run of the mill unit, we rarely attracted the posh officer class. Most of our bosses came from grammar schools, or lesser known private schools. They generally mucked in, played hard, worked hard and we all accepted the differences in upbringing between us. Except this chap. He played at being one of us in the battery bar, then turned nasty in the field. He enjoyed the power he had over us gunners. We all hated him with a passion. I was fascinated to see what the straight-talking, no nonsense, Glaswegian lads would make of him.

Our truck dropped us off a few miles from the camp on yet another brilliantly clear, warm morning. We heaved on our hefty rucksacks, looking at the peaks way up above us with trepidation. A path led up the trail through the tall pine trees that covered every mountain up to the snowline. The officer led the way, map and compass held in his fat, pasty fingers. Within ten minutes we had all passed him then put about two hundred yards between us. The Jocks had his number already. "Who the feck is that c*nt, wee man? Is he for real?" they asked me.

"The fat bastard won't be sleeping in my tent, the fecker, he'd completely fill it." And so on.

I was in stitches, they felt just like the lads back at 19 Regiment. Our route passed through bear country which troubled us somewhat. We had seen plenty of them raiding the roadside bins and they had a reputation for not taking prisoners, especially if they had their young nearby. The ringleader amongst the Scots came up with a crude but very workable plan if we ran into an angry bear. "Hey lads, listen up, if we see a big fuckin' angry bear coming our way, the nearest one of us to that fat numpty cripples him straight away, then we all leggit." I truly believe that is what they would have done without a second thought.

We never did, which in some ways, was a pity. We walked miles up and down hills, camping wild in our little bivvys every night. We passed through a few old Native Indian campsites, seeing some incredible scenery on our way along the trails. The officer trudged along, always a bit behind the rest of us. When we stopped for a brew, or for the night, he was shunned and it served him right. You reap what you sow.

We walked back into our camp after several days away and felt ready for a good long rest. I realised that I hadn't phoned home for weeks and Mum would be wondering where I was, as I had long ago made a rule to get in touch at least once a month. I hitched into the local village and found a phone box. I was suffering from the young soldiers perennial problem, lack of money. I was flat broke. I thought about it for a minute then picked up the receiver and dialled the operator and asked to make a reverse charge call. Mum had forgotten I was in Canada and straight away accepted it, thinking I may be stuck somewhere. A quick "Hello, I'm ok, bye," cost her eleven pounds and she never let me forget it.

Back at camp for our last night, we partied wildly. The Tankies and I swam naked in the icy water, the Jocks sang their Reo Speedwagon songs round the bonfire and after a good few beers we all slept like only tired squaddies can.

The next day we packed up, said our goodbyes to the staff, then headed for the airport and Germany. I was very sad to be leaving a wonderful country and some lovely, friendly, generous people. I felt depressed to be heading back to normal army life too. I mused that decisions needed to be made about my future before much more time had passed.

Time to say Goodbye.

I squeezed in another caving trip with my brother's club, this time to Yorkshire, during a bit of annual leave. Whilst arranging things he asked me if I could go past a female student's house in Buckinghamshire and give her a lift up north. By the end of the fortnight Jeanette and I had become fairly close.

The following Monday morning I was summoned to Max's office. I received a devastating order from him. As I was his driver/op/crew on the reconnaissance truck and he was the officer in charge of gun troop, for some daft reason it was decided that I was to move to gun troop immediately. I couldn't believe it. Since I joined 25 Battery I had, like all the technical gunners, been in Command Troop. None of my friends worked on the guns, although the gun bunny's and us lads on the top floor worked, played and drank together. I was in disbelief that the battery could be so lacking in empathy for a soldier who generally worked hard and didn't cause much trouble. Because of this ridiculous decision, he was almost certain to follow a few of his mates out of the camp gates into civvy street. If you can't beat them, leave them. Clive, Carl and Tippy had all bought themselves out recently. With each sad goodbye to a good friend, life becomes a bit duller. I moved my mattress and kit out of the room I shared with three old pals and found myself a bed space downstairs. The next morning I paraded with gun troop who wondered what the fuck college boy was standing with them for. My pals all hooted in derision at me as I walked past and called me a feckin' gun bunny. Squaddie humour at it's best, I suppose

I tried to get on with things but the die was cast. I reasoned that I had done most of the exciting and enjoyable things the army had to offer me. Canada had been the last one to tick off. The future looked like endless months of hanging around the gun park, interspersed with weeks in the rain on exercise. Yes, we had great comradeship and a lot of fun but moving to Gun Troop ruined all that.

The end wasn't far off.

During a long weekend off in September I flew from Dusseldorf to Heathrow, then hopped onto a bus to Jeanette's house to surprise her. She surprised me more because she had just gone back to Aberystwyth for a few weeks, to go caving and job hunting. It was now Friday teatime and I was standing on her mum's front door step. What to do? Ridiculously, I decided to hitch-hike up to Aber to see her. The M1 passed close by and before long I was hammering up to Birmingham in a big truck. The driver dropped me off and a couple of short lifts later I found myself at a roundabout on the A44, heading for mid Wales. Sometime during the night I walked across Leominster before getting another lift and bought coffee and crisps in an all night garage. The further I travelled, the more capable and self-reliant I felt. Daybreak saw me walking triumphantly down the hill into Aberystwyth and to my brother's rented house. He will know where she is, I thought, I could go and make her breakfast. Imagine my thoughts when my brother's flatmate answered the door and said "Sorry Harry, they are all away caving until tomorrow night." Jesus Christ!

I hung around and rested in my brother's horrible, festering digs. Late on the Sunday they all crashed through the door laughing and joking about their trip away. Jeanette and I slept on his filthy lounge floor. Early the next morning I jumped on a bus to London, then from Heathrow, I made my way back to camp by plane and train.

The four days had been a real test of endurance, little sleep, miles of walking and freezing laybys, for a quick chat with a girl I was very interested in. I was pleased to have made it back in time and was thankful I had cleaned my uniform before going away. On parade the following morning the hammer blow came.

Our epaulettes carried a small RA badge with a little brass backplate underneath, holding it in place. The inspecting officer found a thumbprint on one of mine and awarded me four extra duties. The miserable bastard. Because it was autumn this was bound to mean two weekends sweeping leaves in the rain. Couldn't these people see that our lot was hard enough without all this nonsense? Immediately after the parade I went to see the battery clerk. There and then, I applied for premature voluntary release from the Army. Things had gone way beyond a joke.

I told Mum that I was leaving and she warned me not to, the same way she warned me not to join in the first place. The job situation in the UK was pretty desperate but as an eternal optimist, I reasoned that I would be ok. The battery sergeant major, a miserable piece of work who did little to help anyone who wasn't one of his favourites, told me that I would end up living under Bournemouth Pier. He was one of those oldies that was scared of reaching forty years of age when he would have to face the big, wide world.

My one big problem was my MG. Due to not, at that time, being financially savvy, I had landed myself with a rather big debt with the NAAFI. One that I had to pay off before I could leave. One of the lads in the battery saved my bacon, by offering to buy the car from me over a period of time with monthly payments. It seemed a way out, he was a pal who I had known for three or four years and appeared to be trustworthy.

I had a final medical, compulsory for anyone leaving, then handed in most of my kit. In those days we had to keep one combat uniform. If it all went tits up with the Russians, we could be called up quickly to come back and get killed. One set of combats would be more than enough. I also paid nine hundred pounds for the privilege of buying myself out of my contract early.

My last day was a Friday so the battery bar was opened early in my honour for a leaving party. Everyone came, the battery commander made a speech in which he thanked me for my work, we all drank far too much and my friends gave me a leaving present of a watch and a sleeping bag. For life under the pier, no doubt.

The next morning I took the train to Zeebrugge, a quick ferry crossing, then another train to Woolwich for my final bit of paperwork. On the 15th December I handed in my ID card and walked out through the gate for the last time. Tellingly, I set off into a heavy snowstorm.

Part Four 1982-1988

Beginning a New Life

I was twenty two years old, full of beans and excited about my new future, whatever it may hold. I had no idea what I would end up doing workwise, or where I wanted to live. I just needed to be free from overbearing military discipline and away from barrack room life.

As I walked down the hill towards the railway station I smoked my last cigarette. My plan for a year or so had been to give up the fags when I left. My life was changing so it would just be another small difference. It was a good job that I wanted to stop because I was completely broke, the car having drained my finances for a long time. The lesson to never overstretch myself with debt ever again was being well and truly learnt. Every penny became a prisoner from then on. I certainly couldn't afford the luxury of cigarettes, I could hardly afford a rail ticket to get across London.

My first choice for a new career was the fire service, having loved the excitement of being involved in the big strike up in Manchester a few years previously. I fired off an application to London Fire Brigade and thought I was in with a good chance. That fell flat when they very quickly wrote back a very short note stating that nobody living outside the GLC area would be considered for employment. Dammit.

From my home back in Bournemouth I set out every evening for a run. My progress astounded me. Within a month or so of giving up the fags I was easily running ten or twelve miles some nights. I was stopping because I was hungry and bored, not because I was fatigued. My thought was that the fire brigades would have quite demanding physical requirements, so I needed to be as fit as possible to put on a good show.

To earn some money in the short term I started work at a local garage as a forecourt attendant.Serving petrol to the oldies. It was really embarrassing but at least I was working, able to give Mum a bit of cash for my keep. After a few weeks I had saved enough from the old dears tips on the forecourt to buy some transport. A car was out of the question, however, the local motorbike shop displayed a shiny second hand Honda 250 in the window. The same as Kev's old one. I'd never ridden a motorbike before but I had pillioned with Dad many times and decided it couldn't be that hard to master. I paid for the motorbike and rode it out of the shop onto Boscombe High Street, getting the hang of the gears as I steered my way through the traffic. Two days later I set off on an epic journey to Portsmouth to meet up with Phil, Judith and Jeanette for a couple of days. Somehow I survived the lorries and the corners, neither of which I found to be much fun.

Back home again, Oxfordshire Fire Service had replied positively to my application, so a few weeks later I found myself sitting their entrance exam. Bizarrely, I found myself in a fire station just down the road from my early days nursery school in Headington. I spent the afternoon with a couple of hundred other desperate lads vying with each other to be accepted. We climbed ladders, ran out lengths of hose and carried each other round the drillyard. Two weeks later Mum gave me the morning post, a letter from Oxfordshire. I opened it with trepidation. Failed! It hadn't been a complete waste of time, however, as going through the process had taught me the right way to prepare myself for any other brigade's selection panels.

Living at home was comfortable but not what an outgoing young guy was looking for, so I decided to head for the bright lights of London. I sold the Honda because I quickly realised that motorbiking wasn't in my genes. With the money I bought a lovely lime green Marina Coupe rust bucket. I arrived in the Smoke, found digs in Harrow on the Hill and bought the Evening Standard for the jobs pages.

My hopes of finding work rose when I spotted a couple of likely jobs in the centre of London. How exciting. Off I went, very naively, for the interviews. The first company wanted security guards to work at Covent Garden. They rejected me because I was too small and not tough looking. Fair enough. The second interview took place in a big private house in Wimbledon. I never quite understood what they wanted from me but I suspect they liked my gunnery skills and ran an agency for hired guns, working in Africa. I gave them a wide berth.

Walking back to my digs in Harrow later that day I noticed a sign in an office window advertising for staff. It was The Pinkerton Agency, recently set up in the UK, looking for new employees. I opened the door, introduced myself to the ex-naval officer running the show and was taken on virtually on the spot. A job is a job and my funds had nearly dried up.

My trustworthy pal in Dortmund had let me down badly. The monthly cheques he had promised to send had not appeared. Not a single one. He was now three months behind on payments. Meanwhile, I was still paying NAAFI for the car he had bought from me. I dropped into a solicitors office and paid him to write a letter to the army on my behalf.

My first job for the Pinkertons was easy but dull and very badly paid. A global hotel chain owned a mansion just outside London and it needed to be guarded during the hours of darkness. My job was to sit in the foyer, go on patrol round the grounds and through the offices every couple of hours and be a presence. For twelve hour shifts, six nights a week. They worked American hours, take it or leave it. I was bored beyond anything I had ever known before.

Even with those shifts I wasn't earning enough to pay my bills. So I picked up some lunchtime hours washing up in an old folks home down the road from my room. I also had the perk of some free grub there, which helped.

Pinkertons gave me a little Fiat van and a patrol job after completing a couple of months as a static guard. My new role was to drive around some car showrooms, an anodising factory and visit a hotel in Wembley. It was more than a bit unnerving creeping around at night in these places. The factory had a giant tank of acid on one floor which I often thought would be good for chucking my body in if I disturbed a gang of robbers. I kept an iron 'napper tapper' up my sleeve, just in case.

The huge hotel in Wembley had twenty odd floors and a clocking in system that checked my route along every floor. I would arrive there about 5am dead on my feet and starving. As I crept along the corridors past the bedrooms, I would pilfer food off the trays left outside the rooms from the previous night. Needs must, and I definitely needed it.

Very early one morning, just as the sun was coming over the horizon somewhere near Luton, the inevitable happened. I nodded off driving down the M1 and veered off the carriageway. I snapped awake and regained control, somehow missing the barriers. That was my wake up call. I resigned from the company later that day. There had to be something better.

As there was still no word or cheque from Dortmund I decided the time had come for decisive action. I hitched to Dover, took the ferry to good old Zeebrugge and continued hitching to Dortmund, intent on having a rather frank discussion with my friend. When I jumped out of my final lifts car across the road from the maingate I knew it was too quiet. The bloody regiment was only away on exercise for the next two weeks. Thankfully, the provost sergeant, the much loved Paddy Rowlands, let me in for a word with the paymaster. He was an old member of the hockey team I played for and knew me fairly well. We sat down for a chat and drank coffee while I explained the car situation to him. On hearing my tale he was not a happy bunny and agreed to sort it out as soon as the regiment came back to camp. He was as good as his word. He bollocked the guy, then made him write out enough cheques to cover the debt, dated them all monthly, then the pay office kept sending them to me until the debt was cleared. Top man. It was very fortunate for me that I had played regimental hockey.

Arriving back in Harrow after a long return hitch, I packed up my car boot full of possessions and moved in with Jeanette. She found herself a very good job in Watford where she lived, working in a laboratory. That helped the money problem but I still needed a job. Lady luck smiled again, our housemate worked for a company that was looking for an assistant gardener. Off I went for a quick chat with the head gardener. We hit it off straight away, so I started working there the next day. Heavy outdoor work with wonderful, filling canteen lunches was much more to my liking than security night watchman stuff and I thoroughly enjoyed my time mowing and pruning.

I dropped into Watford police station one morning with fleeting thoughts of joining the force. They took one look at me, then said don't bother applying if you aren't five feet eight inches tall. I even spoke to the Sgt. in the army careers office with the vague notion of going back into the military. He explained that, since the very recent Falklands conflict, they had more than enough recruits, so wouldn't even consider a PVR re-application.

Dorset or Hertfordshire?

I was still posting off applications to various fire brigades. My school and my military background must have ticked the right boxes because I was asked to attend for interview at both Dorset and Hertfordshire fire brigade's in the next few weeks. I drove across to Hertford and was impressed by the training staff immediately. After a morning running around the drill yard doing the usual tests I was called back for the afternoon session. Twenty of us sat the maths exam, then waited, sweating profusely and chatting nervously with each other. After a while the chap came back in and called out about half the names. They filed out and must have not made the grade because they were gone. Those of us remaining then carried on with the English test. Same thing again, names were called out. When I heard mine, my heart sank. I picked up my coat and headed for the door. Once the instructor had shoved us out of the door he said, "Cheer up lads, you lot passed!"

The poor sods still in the room cleared out and we went back in for the next step. Our eyesight was crudely tested with the alphabet chart. Then came the colour vision test. I was nervous about this one but was shown four strings of coloured wool and had to identify red, blue, green and yellow. Even I could pass that.

Our chest measurement had to be at least thirty six inches with a two inch expansion. I only just about passed but was deemed good enough. I noticed that the guys doing the testing were informally chatting with us about our jobs, family, and sports history. They had begun to check our backgrounds for any dodgy characters amongst us. I only just made the five feet six inch marker with a wee bit of heel raising. They didn't look down, the ex-army thing helping again.

I had ticked all the boxes so far. The next step was an interview with a senior officer. I walked into the room, shook hands and sat down. The large, mustachioed chap looked at me and said to my delight, "Ex-gunner eh, same as me, what regiment?"

I knew then that I was home and dry. We talked about my service and I asked a few questions about the job, which only seemed polite. I could have hugged him when he told me I only had one test left to do and it shouldn't be a problem for me.

A couple of days later I attended the same tests in Bournemouth, which went ok too. Then back to Herts for the last hurdle with them. I think it was a speciality of Hertfordshire. It went under the name of the fitness test but they were looking for something else from the candidate. A very fit looking young instructor met me in the changing room and introduced himself as Station Officer Powell. He took me into the drill yard alone and asked me to run round the tarmac a few times to warm up. I did that, thankful for all my evening runs and wondered what was coming next. He then told me to climb the internal ladder up to the top of the tower in the corner of the yard. Up I went like a rat up a drainpipe, eager to please. As I climbed he raised his voice and started giving me verbal abuse about my slowness. I couldn't go much faster so he just blew up. "Get down here you lazy bastard," he screamed.

Blimey! Of course, to an ex-squaddie the language was water off a duck's back. I'd been sworn at by large, angry men with PhDs in effing and blinding. Percy Powell was O'level standard by comparison.

Round and round the yard he sent me, getting me to work really hard, press-ups, squats, "come on you soft git, speed up," etc etc.

Then we quickly moved into the headquarters building and I ran up and down the six floors several times whilst Powell barked and yelled in my ear. "You squaddies are a useless bunch of *****," and so on. I just kept working and ignored him.

Then suddenly, he just stopped me and said, "Well done Harry, you passed."

Not only was it a very functional test of my fitness and agility it served the purpose of checking if I would react badly when under a bit of pressure. The old John Ridgway tactic. Maybe they only tested the ex-military guys in this way. Looking for the nutters. I applauded the idea and very much liked the way this brigade did things.

I caught the train back home and was met with a letter from Dorset, my preferred choice of fire brigade. I had passed everything so far with Dorset and had made it to the final twenty eight. Of those, just eight would be given an appointment. What to do?

Herts had offered me a new career and a starting date on their recruits course in a few weeks time. Dorset dangled the carrot but was it worth the risk of losing everything to get the dream job in Bournemouth? After much deliberation, I plumped for the bird in the hand and chose Hertfordshire. It was one of the hardest decisions I have ever had to make.

Recruit Training

Most brigades sent their new recruits off to regional training schools but Herts ran their own small courses internally at the brigade headquarters in Hertford. The duration of the course was fourteen weeks, after which the firemen became probationers for two years. Two experienced old timers ran the courses in a very military basic training style. The main differences from the military being, firstly, that we went home at night and, secondly, about half of our learning time was spent, not in the drillyard but in the classroom. Firemanship is a science and firefighting can be a very dangerous game if both the practical and technical skills are not learnt properly.

I met the other eleven lads in the locker room on the first morning. The usual characters showed themselves. A tough old sea-dog from the Fleet Air Arm was the first one to stand out. Another well built guy was an obsessive body-builder who appeared to live only on peanuts. There was also a lad who only looked about fifteen years old, who's Dad had been in the brigade. They were joined by a few tradesmen. These guys had completed apprenticeships but found that they couldn't stand their chosen trade and wanted a bit more excitement. I hadn't met chaps like them before, hard workers who could make things, fix stuff and think their way around mechanical problems. One poor lad, an ex-part time fireman, proved to be completely useless, panicking whenever he had to think for himself. As always, there was the tall, handsome, smug git who, as the course progressed, found himself ostracised from the rest of the team, who stuck together and helped one another as much as we could.

We had come in for our kit issue the week before and I was dismayed by the heavy woollen trousers we wore. I had to wear something underneath them because of the dreaded itch. I eventually paid a seamstress to add silk liners to them. The rest of the uniform was comfortable enough except for the giant steel toe capped wellies. We wore yellow trawlermen's plastic leggings, which needed plenty of scrubbing with vim in the evenings to remove the scuff marks. Apart from the scrubbing, it was far easier to be smart in dark blue than in my old green uniform. The three of us ex-forces lads gave advice on bulling wellies and ironing shirts if asked by the other lads. This time round, there was little danger of our kit being lobbed out of the window. The discipline was strict but it was hammered into us that self-discipline was the thing in the fire brigade. If you arrived at work late, or forgot how to use a piece of equipment, then somebody could die because of your idleness. It was also drummed into us from day one, that we always had to find a solution to any problem, however difficult or dangerous. It was a given that sometime in our career, we may have to put our life on the line to save another human being. If you weren't willing to do so, the door was over there. As our instructor said, "we can't call the fire brigade to help us out!"

After the first day I travelled the fifteen odd miles across Hertfordshire with three other lads from the Watford area. Traffic was always terribly heavy and we drove at about twenty miles an hour the whole way. We spent the journey doing questions and answers sessions in readiness for the exams coming up.

We learnt a minimal amount of drill, just enough of the open order march routine to allow for a morning inspection. There was too much interesting and important information to learn, without bothering about marching round and round all day. When firemen have to march they actually just walk. When they halt, they just shuffle to a bit of a shambolic stop, often crashing into each other.

The fire service drill manual was the bible for our training outdoors. We began with the simple task of opening a fire hydrant pit, connecting a hydrant pillar then running out a length of hose from it. Followed by adding more hoses and branches (nozzles). Everything was done by numbers, as per the book. Shouting and yelling without good reason was frowned upon in the fire service, the instructors informed us. You only raise your voice to give orders.

Flapping around like a headless chicken, achieving the square root of F all, was seen as a major crime.

Once we had mastered this stuff on the ground, we progressed to pitching the smallest ladders. Then we started climbing the ladders, first very slowly, then as we gained confidence, a bit quicker and eventually we practically just ran up them, our hands barely touching the rounds. Trust came in to play here as someone had to heel the bottom of the ladder as you climbed it.

We saw some old hook ladders lying around and asked our instructor about them. They consisted of a twenty foot long one section ladder with a three feet long jagged bill on one end. They were used to gain access where bigger ladders wouldn't reach. To use one, you sat on a window-sill whilst holding the ladder upright, and smashed the window of the floor above with the bill. You then allowed the bill to grip the window sill above by pulling down hard and presumably checking it had a good purchase. You then proceeded to get onto the ladder and climb up it, before repeating the process until you had reached the floor on fire, or your nerve gave out. It was said that many good young recruits had to leave the service because they just couldn't overcome the fear of getting onto the ladder and climbing up it, so the brigades ditched them. I suspected I would have been another one of those good young recruits with the brown trousers and knocking knees.

Next in our training programme came the ten metre ladder. It was a big unwieldy beast that needed four strong lads to carry and pitch. The handling poles had to be expertly used or it could topple over in a wind. It also had the scary characteristic of lifting its head off the building as you were all running up it. It was standard issue in all British fire brigades and had mostly replaced the magnificent old wheeled escape ladder, as made famous by old pictures of London burning during the Blitz.

We had great fun manoeuvring our wheeled escape off the back of the fire engine, round the yard and up to the tower. The No.1 had to shout out commands to get the crew to slow one wheel down to change the direction, whilst he and a couple of others pushed it along. Once it was in position the crew had to crank big handles like maniacs to elevate, then launch the ladder into the window opening. It was all energetic stuff, done at the double with plenty of loud commands and we loved it.

We became skilled in knot tying, running out hoses and using pumps. Fire engines carry a portable pump for use when pumping water from a river or a pool that the main pump can't get near to. The lightweight pump was powered by a car engine and was by no means lightweight. Four of us would lift it and carry it round the yard cursing and swearing then set it up by the huge tank of water located underground. Getting it started by pulling a string could be a very fraught time for the operator. The crew were calling desperately for water, the instructor was yelling in your ear and the pump, despite you nackering yourself twenty or thirty times pulling the string, just spluttered and refused to start. Choke out, choke in! Someone always got it going in the end.

The main pumps at the rear of the fire engines usually pumped five hundred gallons a minute, the older ones, twice that amount. More than enough power came down the hoseline to push over somebody holding the end of it if the water arrived rapidly with too much force. Worse, if the man on the end of the hose was clinging to a ladder he could be pulled off it and fall when the water arrived. So the pump operator had to know his stuff and the instructor had to be ready to jump in and make things safe if the trainee messed up. I was mindful of the huge pumps we had attempted to operate during our army firefighting days with the operators receiving a woeful lack of training in their use.

After a couple of hours outside running hose and pitching ladders we would move into the classroom with tired muscles, pumping with adrenaline from all the charging around. Classroom lessons included building construction, fire chemistry, hydraulics, legislation relevant to our job, etc, etc. I found the whole thing absolutely fascinating and was determined to give this new career my best shot. I had found school boring with many of the lessons way above my head so did badly but this was stuff I could understand, learn and remember. I also had no trouble handling the work outside and was very confident being in charge of a crew. I was a much more mature person than the young lad that joined the military. Partly because I had grown much fitter and stronger. Also, my experiences in the military boosted my ability to handle the things civilian life would throw at me.

Once we had become rapid ladder climbers, well used to working from the third and fourth floor of the tower, a new challenge was introduced that tested one or two of the recruits.

The carry-down needed more bravery to be the victim than the rescuer, in fact. We pitched the big red escape ladder up to the third floor then the instructors demonstrated how to do a good carry down. When they finished they both looked red faced, puffed out and the victim had obviously hurt his balls because he kept wincing.

I was told to be the first to give it a go, with Andy, the weightlifter, asked to nip up to the third floor to be rescued. A safety harness was clipped to Andy's belt when he got up there in case he fell during the rescue.

Up the ladder I dashed, jumped into the building, put him on my back in a fireman's lift position and climbed back onto the ladder. So far so good. I began a very slow descent, my knees taking the strain of the muscle bound weight on my shoulders. As I moved slowly down the ladder, the weight appeared to become less and less. This was a doddle.

Up above me all hell broke out. Andy hadn't fancied going down the ladder face down on a little bloke's shoulders, so once we cleared the tower he just hung onto the ladder with his hands and as I descended he stayed put and rolled off my back. For this he received an almighty bollocking, was mocked for days by the rest of us and was always used as the body in future. Everyone else coped with the carry down but we all joined the instructor with sore nuts for the rest of the day.

We spent an interesting few lessons being taught how to enter buildings through doors, windows and skylights without being injured. We learnt how to search rooms without getting hopelessly disoriented and unable to find our way back out to safety. Searching technique involved shuffling along whilst keeping one arm on the wall and another in front of your face. A very slow process especially when your partner keeps tripping over furniture in the dark. Our instructors told us that the cardinal sin of firefighting is to search a building without finding a casualty that is in it. Speed and aggression, though, were needed as well as thoroughness, since anybody trapped upstairs by a fire could perish if we faffed around being too cautious downstairs.

The last phase of our course involved learning how to use breathing apparatus and how to fight fires inside buildings whilst wearing BA. Time and time again, it was impressed on us, by our experienced instructors, that firemen cannot fight a fire from outside the building. If you did not get in there and attack the seat of the fire, we were told, then you may as well stay back at your fire station playing volleyball or drinking tea.

The heavy steel compressed air cylinders took a bit of getting used to as did the facemasks. It just needed plenty of practise. Our air supply lasted up to forty five minutes, less if you worked hard or were a big lad. The BA set had a whistle attached which was set to go off when about ten minutes air supply was left. We trained to be leaving the building just as it started to peep. We practised hauling heavy canvas hoses into the firehouse, finding the fire, then spraying some water onto it whilst other crews searched the building, all in complete darkness, with heat, smoke, fumes and noise with furniture scattered around to trip us up.

The casualties we searched for with our sweeping feet weighed about twelve stones. Much harder to find were the child sized dummies. They could be hidden in a draw or on top of a wardrobe. When we found a large dummy casualty we would try to lift them up between two of us, before carrying them to safety whilst not getting lost on our way out. Confusion and chaos often reigned. We knew the instructors hovered nearby dressed completely in black, watching our every move. Sometimes a facemask would appear out of the black and demand in a muffled voice "how much air have you got left?" If you forgot to keep an eye on your air pressure gauge you risked a bollocking in training but much worse in a real fire situation.

Along with the whistle, pressure gauge and torch we also carried a short length of cord. Usually when search teams entered a building the pair of firemen went inside clipped together. This stopped the team from becoming separated in the murk. Another piece of safety equipment that we had to learn to use was the guide line. This is a sixty metre long rope that is used to lay a safe route deep into a building, so teams can follow it straight to the seat of the action. Laying the rope in the dark whilst tied together can be a very difficult task, especially when it is hot, noisy and the route is blocked with rubbish, furniture, pallets or debris. Occasionally, our teams found themselves completely tangled up in their guide line and personal line and needed saving by the instructors. Our knot tying skills had to be first-class because the casualties sometimes had to be rescued by having a knot tied around them, then hauled through a hatch and lowered off the side of the building. Calmness, a sense of direction in the dark and a bit of determination to get the job done was what was needed to be a success at this game.

When we ended a hard training exercise we cooled off in the drillyard, knackered but exhilarated at having completed the task together. Usually we dripped sweat from our sodden underclothes as we stood about covered in grime and soot. Whoever had messed up had the piss taken out of them and lessons learnt sunk in. Soon it would be for real.

One afternoon just before the end of the course we did some leadership exercises. Once again, using the John Ridgway military idea of applying some stress to find out how we then behaved. I was put into a team of three with the youngest lad on the course in charge. Our task was the old favourite of getting the barrel over the river with a few planks and a ball of string, etc. The young lad was lost, he had no idea what to do. Because I had more experience with this sort of thing, I came up with a plan fairly quickly. But, because of my army training, I didn't feel I should butt in and take charge, he was the boss, I was just a bod.

We muddled through but afterwards I was taken on one side and given a serious talking to. I was told that not speaking up and taking charge cost me the best recruit award. The instructor pointed out to me that this was the fire brigade, not the army, and anyone on the crew might come up with the best solution to a problem and if they did they had to pipe up. That was one of the reasons that fire brigades liked to recruit tradesmen and guys with life experience. They are usually people that are used to solving practical problems. An important lesson learnt by me. Funnily enough, the young lad won best recruit!

The next morning with all our exams passed, we sat waiting to be told which would be our fire stations. For some psychological reason, Red Watch always sounded more exciting than blue, green or white. Hertfordshire had sixteen full-time fire stations, so the brigade could post recruits fairly close to their home address if vacancies permitted. The one we all wanted was Garston, my local station on the edge of Watford, just off the busy dual-carriageway intersection that was soon to become the M1-M25 junction. We all wished for that station because the six wheeled Range Rover emergency tender, equipped with a multitude of rescue gear, was based there and it was imagined to be super-cool by us impressionable young fireys.

The training officer read through the list of our names and our postings. Most guys nodded and smiled when they heard. One poor sod groaned whilst the rest of us mocked and laughed, he was off to the quietest backwater fire station out in the sticks.

My heart was in my mouth, I didn't want to put up with a long drive in my dodgy old Marina four times a week. Getting through the rush hour traffic was a nightmare across Herts and getting worse every year. When the new M25 opened it was going to be hell travelling around.

"Fenton," he said, looking for me around the room. "Garston, Red Watch."

A cacophony of whistles and cheers from the rest of them. "Well done, 'Arry."

I was delighted. The best fire station in the county and only a short walk from home. What could go wrong?

Old John, our instructor, pulled me to one side later in the day.

"You have a problem on your watch," he told me, looking grim. Bloody hell, not again.

He explained that I was joining a close-knit team of old guys whose knowledge and skill at firemanship was top notch but who might not welcome an ambitious young upstart, full of new ideas and energy. My presence would mean they would have to put the tea-pot down for a while and train like other fire stations did. My mind was cast back to when I was posted to 19 Regiment, and all the training staff burst out laughing. I was confident that if I could cope with that, the old timers at Garston shouldn't cause me too many problems.

We had come to the end of our very interesting and physical fourteen weeks and just wanted to get onto a fire engine for real. We emptied our lockers, shook hands with each other, said goodbye to the training team and off we went. That was the last I saw or heard of most of them.

Garston Fire Station

I visited my new workplace a few days before starting there, to drop off my kit and meet the watch. My first impression was of the size of them all. The station officer, Phil, was over six foot tall and at least sixteen stones of muscle, toughened by a working life as a builder in his time off. He was delighted that I was an ex-gunner as he had served in the artillery during his national service. That explained his deafness!

The sub. officer, Danny, was a friendly bloke with a ready smile and a 'stuff them' attitude. An ex member of 2 Battalion the Parachute Regiment, and the proverbial brick shithouse, on his days off he did any work he could find, from gardening to painting and decorating.

Roger, the leading hand, was a proud ex Coldstream Guardsman who towered over me. His fiddle was removals, his dodgy back bore witness to a life humping furniture around.

Tony and Dell stuck together and provided the meals for the troops. Tony, a tall, strong, car mechanic from Luton, with goalkeepers hands. Dell earnt his extra money as a skilled carpenter. This pair were the leaders of the fireman on the shop floor and the first BA team into anything dodgy. Dell was one of those cheeky London chappies that was never down in the dumps, who earnt more money fiddling than he received from the fire brigade. He was also remarkably lucky. There was no point entering a raffle if Dell had bought a ticket, he always won first prize. On one celebrated occasion, he ordered a television from Comet that was delivered a week later. A few days after that another one arrived, which he cheerfully thanked the driver for and sold a while later.

Brain, a french polisher, was the sprog who had only been there for about ten years when I arrived. He was delighted when I became the new boy and the butt of the mickey taking, which took the pressure off him for a while.

Dave, ex Royal Navy, was the odd man out. A very talented scrum half for a local rugby club in Watford, Dave was very much an individual who hated the job and didn't mix with the rest of the guys. He left for pastures new, shortly after my arrival.

The chap I replaced was the biggest of them all. A six foot seven giant who had represented England at basketball. Bloody hell, he was over a foot taller than me.

They all wanted to know a bit about me, so I sat at the bar drinking a couple of pints with them as I told them my story. I was amazed that they had permission to drink on duty. Evidently, it was the done thing after 9.30 pm, once all the work was finished, to sit at the bar and have a beer or two. I never did, because of my increasingly low tolerance to alcohol and I needed all my wits about me when at work. But one or two of them quite happily downed three pints every single night shift of their working lives, with seemingly no effect on their performance whatsoever. The bar was a throwback to the days of the seventy two and fifty six hour weeks, when almost all the men's time was spent at the fire station, so their social life had to be there too.

The main thing they wanted to know about me was what I was going to do on the side as my fiddle. All of them treated the fire brigade as a cross between a boys club and a hobby. To them, their other work was far more important and interesting. This was what I had been warned about by my instructor, John Hall, at the training school. Because of the high skill level of the team, they hardly needed to train, so I would find it difficult to get them out into the yard to practise my skills. They all worked with tools, ladders, and heavy equipment during their days off, so the last thing they had on their minds when they put their uniforms on was more heavy lifting and running around a drillyard. They simply had no need to. For most of them another source of income was imperative because a fireman's wage wasn't enough to maintain a decent standard of living. Plus the fact, working a two days on, two nights on, four days and nights off, shift system, gave firemen six days off in eight. You had to do something to fill your time.

The watch had sensibly based their fire brigade hours around this way of life. Lights off at eleven pm sharp and death to anyone that made a noise in the dormitory or turned on a light after that time. Beds had to be made beforehand so as not to wake sleeping beauties by mucking about with your locker. Dinner was always at nine thirty pm, breakfast at seven am. Breakfast was a substantial fry up with cereal and toast. It meant we could all go off to our day jobs without going home to eat. They had it very well organised and efficient, just like the fire brigade should be.

On the day when I started working at Garston, I walked the mile from home with a huge feeling of nervousness, the most I had felt since going out on my first patrol in Ireland. It was a similar feeling of expectation and excitement, with a bit of anxiety about my performance. Would we be called to a house fire at five past eight in the morning, with me having to search the premises in BA for little children? Or maybe the tannoy would inform us of a major RTA on the M1 with carnage spread across the carriageways.

As it happened, my first shout was more typical of what firemen deal with every day. A tree stump on fire. When the alarm bleeped I kept my cool and followed the rest of them at the same speed down the stairs. By the time we reached the appliance we knew it was just a tree on fire. I was still thrilled to get a shout of any sort before tea break on day one. Some guys go for weeks before they break their duck and by then are like coiled springs, jumping every time their tannoy clicks or hums. The drive was interesting even though we cruised down the high street at a sedate pace. We arrived by the playing fields and looked across at a burning stump surrounded by kids on BMX bikes. Phil told me to fill a bucket with water then follow the rest of them across the field. I dutifully did what I was told and doubled after them. The other three stood together taking the piss out of the new boy. Phil looked at me expectantly and just said, "go on then 'Arry." I chucked all of the water at the fire in one woosh, missing most of the burning areas. The three stooges laughed out loud. Phil called me a f'ing C-word and asked what the f they taught us at training school these days? Suitably bollocked, I was sent scurrying back for another bucketfull. Dell then proceeded to use the water carefully, scooshing it out by the handful onto the flames, putting it out quickly and easily.

"There you go, 'Arry my son," he said, "that's how it's done." He smiled at me, probably remembering being the boy himself.

We had been told that a good fireman can learn something from every fire he attends. On the drive back for our delayed cuppa I realised there the old saying was correct. There was a hell of a lot more to this job than meets the eye.

I was quite happy to have the mickey taken for a while. That was expected in this kind of work. It's all part of growing up, as long as the boundary isn't crossed and bullying begins, which for me it never did. I was very confident in my abilities by this time and also felt that the three older ex-squaddies on the watch quite liked having me around, we had a common bond from day one.

My wait for a serious fire wasn't a long one. The following dayshift the tannoy sounded and directed us to a house fire a mile or so away with a warning of persons reported. This meant that the control room had been informed by the 999 caller, that people may be in the building that was on fire. Firemen always gave it 100% to get on their appliance and out the doors as quickly as humanly possible on these occasions. Even the oldies that prided themselves on being calm and measured in everything they did, could be seen dashing hell for leather to the appliance bay.

The drivers loved these calls because they could really pull out all the stops to get to the incident as quickly as possible. They had to think about the guys in the back struggling desperately to get their BA sets whilst being thrown around but their first thought was for anyone trapped by the fire. At these times we drove the wrong way round roundabouts, squeezed through the narrowest gaps, flew round corners on two wheels and swore loudly out of the cab windows at anybody that dared to slow us down. Most road users tried desperately hard to help us by mounting pavements or just pulling over until we had passed by.

En route to the house fire, Phil glanced at the three of us in the back and barked out the order.

"Dell, Tony, BA, Harry, you are BA control."

For a minute I was angry and confused. Why wouldn't he let me be one of the BA team? Did he not think I was up to it? Then it occurred to me that the situation wasn't about me, a novice at this stuff, it was about the folk possibly still in a burning house. The two experienced men had been chosen to get into the house. My chance would come in time.

Smoke was billowing from a first floor window as we raced down the side road to the semi-detached house. The coppers had already arrived, they were talking to a woman in the front garden who was panicking about something in the house. We stopped and leapt out, going to work quickly and quietly. I pulled on the hose reel for the two BA men to take with them, whilst the driver operated the pump at the rear. The BA men masked up in a few seconds, checked their air, then handed me their plastic name tags which I slid into our BA wearers control board. Then they hurried up the front drive and disappeared into the burning building. Smoke continued to billow from the window as a crowd began to build up across the road. I crouched low as I fed the hose reel through the front entrance for the guys now heading up the staircase.

A fire engine from Watford came hurtling along the road to join us and a second BA team prepared to go in to search the house whilst our lads fought the fire. The second team reappeared from the smoke into fresh air after a minute or so, with the inert body of a large dog being carried between them. The poor thing had died of smoke inhalation upstairs. No humans or other animals had been affected by the fire. The poor lady who lived there was distraught about her pet.

The lads upstairs dealt with the fire in a few minutes, then opened all of the windows to release the smoke. Phil sent a message back to control that it was all over and we would be heading home soon. He gave me a tour of the house to have a look at the fire and water damage. The rooms stank of bitter burnt plastic and poisonous smoke, a smell I became very familiar with. Dell and Tony sat in the back of the fire engine, pumping with adrenaline, stinking of smoke and dripping with sweat. We had done a good job, quickly and with no fuss. The attempted oxygen therapy for the poor old Mutt failed, much to our dismay, so we departed, leaving the cops looking after the bereft owner.

Phil, the Station Officer, cajoled the watch to train, purely for my benefit. They grumbled good-naturedly but training helped pass their day a bit quicker. If something was going on there was always a chance one of the crew would muck up, giving us all the opportunity to take the mickey. I noticed that the words of command for pitching ladders, that we had shouted with such purpose during recruits training, became redundant once you joined a shift. Everyone holding the ladder knew where it was going so why make a row about it?

The watch gave a nod to fitness training with an evening volleyball session if they felt in the mood. What I lacked in height, I made up for with effort, until in one particularly boisterous game, I landed squarely with my foot on Roger's foot then agonisingly went over on my ankle. Within five minutes it had swollen badly and I was off home whilst I could still operate the clutch on my car. Seven weeks at home with my purple and yellow foot up, was the result.

The watch barely saw flames whilst I was on sick leave and I quickly settled back in, taking care never to jump up again when playing volleyball. It really didn't matter if we lost, I told myself. One quiet evening we sat around the bar, feeling good after a huge plate of spag bol, cuddling a Guinness or, in my case, lemonade. Just before we all crept off to bed, the phone rang. Phil and Danny glanced at each other quizzically. Something unusual was going on but I wasn't sure what it was. Phil returned after a couple of minutes of quiet conversation on the phone.

"We have a callout to the A41, near so and so, appliance and emergency tender, no horns or lights, the cops are in attendance."

The older firemen gave each other a knowing look, something was up. Fantastic!

We slipped quietly out of the appliance bay and drove a few miles to where the traffic cops and a very unhappy man in overalls, obviously the driver, were standing behind a huge wrecking truck. The giant vehicle carried a big crane and winch behind the cab. It was the sort of vehicle that lifts the front of lorries off the ground and tows them away. The double axle back wheels stood taller than me. A police traffic car was parked underneath a street light, about two hundred yards back down the dual-carriageway. A line of cones diverted any cars around the police vehicle and the tow truck, though the road was fortunately empty of other traffic. A lone traffic cone sat in front of the police car.

We positioned our appliances and jumped out, Phil and Danny approached the coppers whilst we opened the lockers, ready to grab whatever was needed. What the hell was going on, we asked each other?

We soon found out when the guvnors returned and gave us our instructions. It was apparent that a lady had run in front of the truck, probably suicidally, and become wedged between a pair of the giant rear wheels. There was nothing the driver could have done to stop or swerve out of the way. She was assumed to have been an inmate of the nearby mental hospital and had managed to escape.

Our gruesome task was to somehow get the body, or what was left of it, from out between the wheels. Dell suggested a hose reel, with a bit of pressure, to wash her out. It was the most practical idea we could come up with. We laid out a tarpaulin nearby to collect the parts. I could feel that I was being watched for my reaction to all this gore. I wasn't bothered by it, she was dead, out of pain and not recognisably human. I remembered seeing similar horror during our initial NI training week, when some terrible footage of the Troubles was shown to us.

We did the best and most respectful job we could and turned off the hose, then gathered around the tarp. looking down, realising together that something was missing.

A copper strolled up, "Her head is under that cone, in front of our motor," he answered before we asked.

Phil looked at me. "Arry, get a bucket and go and fetch it, would you?" he asked.

This was my big test then. Off I went with my bucket, raised the cone and, blimey, there was indeed a head lying on the road. I picked it up without looking at it, popped it in the bucket and slowly walked back. Phil pointed to the middle of the tarp. I tipped up the bucket and the head fell onto the hard surface from a couple of inches. Bonk! Everyone grimaced. On the way back to the station Phil turned to me and said "Well done, 'Arry." I had passed the gore test.

The Gnome

Very few firemen enjoyed studying. We worked with our hands and used common sense to work out problems on the fireground. However, to progress up the ranks you had to pass the relevant exams. Almost as soon as I arrived at Garston I was asked if I would be sitting the leading fireman's technical exam in the spring. As the paper covered much of what I had learnt during my basic training and I was ambitious, I said yes, of course. All of the information that was needed to pass the technical exams was found in the set of Home Office books on firemanship. They became my bible for the next few years, I collected all of them and eventually learnt the more important contents almost word for word.

Those that passed the technical exam in the Spring could attend the practical exam in the Autumn. It was the same for the Sub. Officers exams, Spring and Autumn, with the Station Officer's two day technical exam taking place each February, open to anyone who had passed the four previous ones. All the fire brigades used the same exam papers, which were administered by the Home Office and carried out the practical tests using examining officers from different brigades to keep it as fair as possible.

A few dozen of us sat the leading fireman's technical exam in a school hall. I found it easy enough. My passing it, meant that the watch would have to devote some time out in the drill yard so I could practise for the practical exam. The format was simple enough and not beyond anyone with a bit of confidence. The candidate, dressed in his freshly scrubbed firegear, had to march onto the drillyard and stop just in front of the chief examiner. After saluting him, he would be given a piece of paper with instructions for a crew who were standing waiting by their fire engine. Maybe something like: Pitch the 10.5 metre ladder to the third floor of the tower and get a hose reel to work from the top of the ladder. The candidate had to get their attention, take charge, brief the crew, keep control, correct mistakes and give a quick debrief at the end. Dead easy. The crew had instructions to behave themselves and not argue with the candidate or give him a hard time.

During the summer we practised a bit outside but nobody on the watch had taken any exams for years, so I was a bit in the dark about what was expected. I had no trouble getting the guys to do what was required. Being ex-military and with more confidence than I had a few years previously was a definite help with this one. I was relieved when we received word that we had been picked to be a crew for some other candidates, the week before my exam. It gave me a chance to check that I was doing what the examiners were looking for.

Of course, the other five moaned and groaned about having to go to Hatfield, then spending the morning running around the drill yard for some effing sprogs who had only been in the job five minutes. Come the day, we pulled up in the yard and hung around the back of the fire engine in our clean fire gear, watching for the first guy to come marching over to us.

Everything went just fine for the first two candidates. They took charge, we ran around, pitched ladders, worked up a sweat, all good stuff. Just one more then you can head off back to Garston for lunch, said the examining officer, looking forward to his cup of tea as well.

We noticed his giant helmet first, at least two sizes too large for his body that was short and tubby, like a gnome in leggings. One of our crew asked incredulously, "What the feck is that?"

The poor sod had to put all of his brain power into marching but, as with any physical task, the harder you try the more you stiffen up and begin to fail. He marched like an RAF cook but with this big yellow hat almost coming down over his eyes. The examiner must have heard us begin to snigger because he glared over at us. A bit of tension just made it worse.

Eventually, the lad, having received his briefing, turned to us and fell us in. We all tried to avert our eyes from the Noddy character in front of us. I could hear chortling and stifled giggling from the rest of the crew. We did our best to hold it in, knowing the guy had worked hard to get this far. What a shame his guvnor hadn't taken him on one side and quietly told him that leadership might not be for him. Not everybody has the character to be the boss, that is just how the cookie crumbles. We all have different skills.

We hushed as he opened his mouth to give us our orders. "Slip and pitch the 10.5 millimetre ladder," he squeaked.

Oh dear, we nearly died. He continued telling us what our tasks for the drill were as we sweated, shook, went purple, gasped, spluttered and wanted to just be anywhere else, please stop. When we mounted the fire engine we had little idea what he had told us to do, we had been trying so hard not to laugh out loud. We tried not to imagine four of us holding a ladder 10.5 millimetres long. When he yelled "get to work" we jumped out, pitched the ladder, ran out hoses and squirted some water like confused week three recruits. His comical manner had completely thrown us. For the only time in my career, I saw a length of hose on the ground that went round in a circle and was connected to itself, like a snake swallowing it's tail. He looked down at that one, then just walked away, not knowing what to say. None of us ever admitted to that little cock-up.

We drove back to base in high spirits, still laughing and joking. I had learned a few things for my examination, which the following week I passed with no dramas.

Phil decided that it was time I started driving to incidents, so a short while afterwards I found myself on a one week long HGV3 course with another lad. We spent an interesting four days driving round the countryside and even made it over to Cambridgeshire. I had never travelled so far east and during a pee stop climbed on top of the engine and looked across at the flat countryside. I couldn't believe it. I could see church spires in the far distance, miles away over the dull flat landscape. On the Friday I drove the brigade's driving examiner around for an hour before he gave me a pass, much like my Land Rover test in the military. From then on I drove the big Dennis automatic back to the station from every fire and on any other trips out and about.

Pride comes before a fall, as we know, and I was more than ready for a fall. One morning a few weeks later, I was reversing an old fire engine out of our garage. Being careful to not scrape the passenger's side on the garage door pillar, I knew to watch in the driver's mirror and keep my door close to the wall. I backed out carefully and heard a terrible scrunching and tearing noise from the front left of the cab. The bloody passenger door had swung open as I let out the clutch and was now bent around the front of the cab. Tony and Dell's smiling heads appeared in the gap where a door was meant to be. They couldn't hide their glee.

"You're in the shit now, 'Arry boy," they mocked. They weren't wrong, either.

The Rickmansworth Rat

We met the blokes from the surrounding fire stations when we visited them to do an out duty. This happened when a neighbouring watch had a few of the crew missing, so one of us would be sent over to work a shift with them. It was always interesting to see how different watches carried out their work, to meet the characters and to drill with them. We regularly went down the road to Watford and Rickmansworth or up the motorway to Hemel Hempstead. The out duty was never given a hard time, that would have gone down badly with their home station.

Rickmansworth was the home of the rebels, miscreants and ne'er do wells. Any fireman that committed some sort of offence would find themselves being posted there, a backwater with very few shouts. Senior officers only went there very occasionally. Often the rebels in an organisation are the cleverest guys working for it. Mavericks that don't move up the ranks because they can see through all of the nonsense. Herts decided to keep them all in one place, where they couldn't contaminate the rest of us. The crews at Ricky loved being there. Their working life really was like a boys club that paid quite well. Mornings consisted of a bit of cleaning, maintenance and training but only if the weather was conducive. Then a drive around the pleasant little town for some shopping. A tasty lunch, followed by a net or two of volleyball, then a rest before going home. On a nice summer evening they had an arrangement to visit a local private school with an outdoor swimming pool. Once or twice they received fire calls from control when they were all swimming up and down in their cossies. The flap to get dressed and on the road would have been worth watching.

One Saturday I drove across to Ricky in the station van with my firegear and my bedding in the back. I had only met the watch at incidents so was expecting the usual pisstaking that new lads usually receive. They turned out to be a bunch of gentlemen who's main aim was to find out any gossip from Garston. They also asked all about my life's journey so far. Anything to pass the time. They certainly didn't plan to drill in the yard because the station officer was on leave that evening. Over our delicious evening meal they proudly told me the tale of the famous Rickmansworth Rat.

The fire station sat back from a busy roundabout with flower beds, grass and a footpath between the station and the roundabout. Pedestrians walked past the fire station to get to and from the shops. The administration office was at the very front of the building looking out at the footpath. One night, for some untold reason, a fireman took his fishing rod to work, maybe to fix it or show it to somebody. By the end of the evening they had invented a new entertaining way to pass their downtime. They made a rat out of some old grey material and attached a realistic tail to the back end. The rat was then tied to the fishing line and cast out across to the grass on the other side of the footpath. Next came the fun part. When a pedestrian came toddling along they carefully reeled the rat in, just in front of them, causing the startled walker to jump, scream or run off. This gave the boys many hours of harmless fun.

The station officer was a particular aficionado of this bizarre sport so his watch decided to turn the tables on him. One Saturday evening when he was fishing, hoping that someone returning from the pub would stagger along, they carried out their cunning plan. One of the crew nipped out of the back of the building and donned a long wig, an old hat and a very long coat. So attired, he resembled a doddery old tramp. He entered stage left at the far end of the footpath and began his slow, ungainly walk, eventually coming into everyone's view. The lads, who were all in on the ruse, egged the officer on, "get this old bastard, Guv," etc.

Like a true professional, he slowly reeled the rat towards the oncoming tramp, timing it expertly so the old guy almost trod on it. What the fireman in disguise actually did was, very theatrically, feign having a heart attack seconds after he was surprised by the rat. The boys told me with pride that he took ages to finally hit the deck.

Meanwhile, back in the building the station officer was having the panic of his life.

"Call an ambulance, quick, hide that effin fishing rod, get out there someone and help him, feckin' hell!"

After a couple of minutes the tramp miraculously came back to life, walked up to the front office, pulled off his wig, grinned from ear to ear and said "Got you there, Guvnor." That was the end of the Rickmansworth Rat.

Never Satisfied

About this time, Jeanette's company moved into a bigger laboratory in Marlow, Bucks. We felt confident that our jobs had security so we started searching for a house to buy. We settled on a brick built semi in Bourne End about four miles from her workplace but twenty odd from mine, down the A40 and the dual-carriageway that was soon to become the M25. The further from Watford the less traffic there was and the countryside improved as the traffic lessened. I received a grant from the Council of nearly £10,000 to renovate the house to modern livable standards and tore into the work immediately. I was a complete novice and couldn't even hang wallpaper properly so I learnt a great deal in the renovation process.

Our new neighbour was a landscape gardener and I worked with him when he needed a hand. It really tested my endurance. If he had to collect a tool from his van he would run to collect it and back again, before carrying on the job. No loitering around as time was money. I also became the handyman at the laboratory, putting up shelves, etc and generally helping out. They also used me as their delivery boy when important documents had to go up to London to the big oil companies headquarters. I had caught the work ethic of the older chaps on my watch, hardly ever having a day off. I was running as often as I could as well, even doing laps of the drill yard on a quiet Saturday afternoon to use up my excess of energy.

My trusty old Marina was booked in for an MOT at the local garage. When I dropped back in there later in the day to pick it up, I received a bombshell. The chassis was rusted right through and about to collapse. They wouldn't let me drive it away, not that I wanted to when I saw the huge corroded hole. To find a decent second-hand car took weeks and money was very tight. The big problem though, was my shifts starting in two days time. Luckily, my brother lived not far away and lent me his beautiful new racing bike for the week. On the first morning back at work, I left home at 6am with my clothes in a rucksack and headed up the road. I hadn't cycled for a couple of years but I was young and fit and the sun was out. I joined the dual-carriageway at Chorleywood and powered along the hard shoulder the ten miles to the fire station. Easy. A quick shower and I was on parade as fresh as a daisy. My legs tightened up a bit during the day but getting home was ok, at least it was with the wind. The next morning was good too, the homeward journey slightly slower than the evening before. I now had really tight leg muscles from two days of cycling but still had four twenty milers to go. I could hardly walk on my last night shift and came in for plenty of good humoured abuse from the gang. Leaving work at 9am after the last shift, I looked at the dual-carriageway in dismay. I almost wished the cops would stop me and ask what the hell I thought I was doing cycling down the hard shoulder of such a busy main road. Two days later I bought an Austin Maxi from my uncle's Toyota garage in Oxford. It was a very dated design of car but anything was better than making that ride again.

The watch had the task of checking about a thousand fire hydrants on our patch. On a dry afternoon we would wander round a few streets lifting the lids, cleaning out the pits and squirting a few gallons of water down the gutter to check everything was in order. Most of the old guys knew where every hydrant was on their station ground, very useful information when you are called to a fire. As we walked around we talked, took the mickey and told stories to entertain each other. Being the new boy, I had to do the dirty work. On one such afternoon we came across a yellow hydrant pit right in front of an old VW camper van. I took out the sharp aluminium opening tool, shaped like a two feet long chisel and put the pointy end under the lid, ready to lift it up. As I tried to flip the lid up, the tool slipped and I rammed it with force right through the front of the VW. The watch, except Phil, nearly died on the spot. He went white and called me a "stupid f'ing c**t."

An old bloke in overalls jumped out of the back of the van and wandered over to see what the noise had been caused by. I was trying to ease the bar out of the hole in his van without making it bigger. He looked down at the damage. I looked up and couldn't keep a straight face.

"Never mind," he said as he smiled, "it's full of holes that I'm filling anyway." Phew, I got away with that one.

Two evening later we received a shout to another VW camper van that had T-boned a lorry at a junction. The driver was in a bad way and he had to cut him out very carefully. Driving a vehicle without an engine in front for protection, didn't seem a very good idea to me after that incident. Shortly after that one, we found ourselves racing up the M1 to a report of an overturned car with the driver trapped inside. On arrival we found a Dell Boy three wheeler that had driven down a slip road heading onto the motorway. Somehow he had managed to roll the thing down the slip road embankment. The driver had followed the old idea of keeping a heavy bag of cement in the back to help stabilise the thing in side winds. Unfortunately for him, as he rolled over, the bag split open and by the time we arrived to cut him out he was completely covered in the stuff. The last we saw of him was a grey man on a stretcher who looked like a statue with two white staring eyeballs looking up, clutching his packet of fags as he was loaded into the ambulance. "Don't let him get wet," someone said, "he will set rock hard."

A few weeks later, on a particularly foggy morning we headed back to the same area having been called to a major RTA. As we drove on to the motorway we had to slow right down, because the visibility dropped to about fifty yards. After a few hairy miles we came to the back of the traffic and eased our way along the hard shoulder, blasting cars out of our way with the horns and some choice abuse out of the windows. We talked about likely scenarios as we approached. The plan was to extinguish any fires first, then split up and check every vehicle for casualties. If they were unconscious, not breathing, or bleeding badly we would stay and try to sort them out. If trapped but ok we were to reassure the occupants then move on. I would have to work on my own which was an exciting thought, I wanted the chance to use my initiative, rather than be watched and told what to do all the time.

The police car that we followed down the hard shoulder was side swiped by some clown deciding to gain an advantage by nipping down the inside without checking his mirror. The copper didn't stop, he knew the job was more urgent and that the driver couldn't escape. He would be dealt with later.

We put out the only small fire very quickly, then set to work on the casualties. Only a couple had serious injuries and a few needed helping out of their vehicles. Luckily, it was so foggy that none of them had been travelling very fast when the pile up began. I thoroughly enjoyed helping people, checking their injuries and making decisions about what to do next without my every move being monitored. The police told us later that there had been about one hundred vehicles involved, a nightmare for them to sort out but we were back home by lunchtime.

Roger, the leading fireman, was an expert knot tier. He thoroughly enjoyed showing me how to use various old fashioned but very useful knots. The new drill book showed fewer of them than the previous edition, so he tried to keep the old knowledge alive by passing his skills on to me. I learnt several different bowlines, self-rescue knots and knots to use for lifting different loads off the ground. Even how to coil and throw a rope properly. Useful skills in many situations.

The watch also had expertise in taking vehicles apart using the different tools kept on the emergency tender. When the older guys started their service, all they had was hacksaws, hammers and crowbars. Now that they had hand operated hydraulic rams and electric saws they could do far more, much quicker but they still used to hand tools on occasion when nothing else worked. One of the most useful tools was a builders disc cutter with a petrol engine and a fearsome metal blade that could take the roof off of a car in a minute or two, with a huge shower of sparks. It was often the first tool we grabbed and used at an incident. We regularly mucked about cutting up old bangers in the drillyard to practise our skills and pass on ideas to each other. I noticed that the car mechanics and tradesmen found this stuff second nature, whilst the firemen from other walks of life generally stood back and let them get on with it.

We had the chance to demonstrate all of these skills one evening when a call came in to an RTA in the middle of Watford. We came across two cars horribly smashed up with the driver of one badly injured and trapped in what was left of his vehicle. Using the big disc cutter we had the roof off and away in a moment. The casualty was ashen faced and in a great deal of pain. Phil sat reassuring him, as we cut the car body away to get closer to his feet that were trapped by the foot pedals. We sighed with relief when the very capable ambulance crew turned up and began their assessment of him. Phil wanted to get him out of there and away to hospital but they weren't happy with that. Their diagnosis had found that he was sitting in the car with a broken femur. The sharp end of the bone was very close to his femoral artery. If we moved him and the artery was punctured, he would bleed out internally in a couple of minutes. So we sat with him for an hour, as a surgical team from a big London hospital was scrambled to join us. On arrival, they set up for emergency surgery, if necessary, at the roadside. We then, very carefully, lifted him out and away from the wreck. The artery thankfully held and he was whisked away for surgery at the local hospital as the crash team packed up. We headed home for a very late burnt dinner. Interesting times, that showed there really was something to learn at every incident, as we had been told.

Later that night, over a pint of beer for the old guys, and a lemonade and bag of dry roasted peanuts for me, I was told the tale of the new boy on the watch who was there before me but didn't last long. He had an attitude that rubbed them up the wrong way. Too cocky and a bit on the lazy side. He was also a very heavy sleeper. After a few weeks on the watch, he made the mistake of telling the guys that he was worried that he might miss calls in the night if he was asleep. He foolishly told them that he slept through anything, even a great big bell ringing just above his bed! They quietly noted this and planned how to cut him down to size a bit.

One night the following week they all said goodnight to each other, then one at a time made off to their pits. A couple of hours later, the sub officer crept very quietly into the dormitory and, one at a time, woke all the guys, except the newbie. They tiptoed out of the room and met up in the appliance bay. The station officer was grinning from ear to ear, he was as big a kid as anyone else. They very carefully opened the front doors and pushed the fire out into the carpark, without making a sound. Once there, they all jumped in and dressed in their fire gear. At a nod from Phil in the officers seat, the driver started the engine and drove round to the drillyard at the back. The crew jumped out and began making a hell of a racket, pretending they had just come back from a fire and were all full of adrenaline. One of them went to the dormitory and woke the stunned new guy with a "what the fuck happened to you, you lazy sod, get upstairs now, the gaffer wants to see you". As he hastened upstairs he could see the rest of the watch, all dressed in yellow leggings putting the engine away and looking serious. Phil played his part well and gave him a firm talking to. Danny stood in the corner of the office playing the part of bodyguard but made sure he didn't catch Phil's eye in case one of them smirked. The new boy left the office much chastened, realising he wasn't quite the bee's knees after all. He transferred away shortly after, unable to blend in with the team of seasoned old boys.

Most young men who joined the Service in the 1970s and 80s were still the breed who completed their apprenticeships. They started a job but then decided it wasn't fulfilling enough for them, so applied to join the Service for a bit of excitement. Their trade training was often very useful in their new career. Most of our work involved taking buildings and vehicles apart, or using tools to break things. Mechanics, builders, welders and plumbers found all this stuff second nature. These guys had a working man's natural strength, gained by many hours of manual work. They didn't mind getting filthy dirty either. If they played a sport, which guaranteed they came with a degree of fitness and enjoyed physical exercise, so much the better. About a quarter of recruits also came from the military, like myself. We had generally proven to be good workers, accepted discipline and, importantly, knew a very good thing when we saw it. Life as a fireman was so much cushier (and better paid) than being a soldier or in the Royal Navy. So we didn't moan about our lot, even when things went wrong and we found ourselves, cold, wet and hungry, fighting a hayshed fire in the middle of the night. We knew that tomorrow we could go home to our warm comfy beds. Not to a wet sleeping bag under a tarpaulin for a couple of hours, before going on stag again at first light. The watch was surprised then, when Phil announced that our new recruit to replace Dave and due to arrive soon, was a graduate. It was almost unknown for such well educated guys to join the brigade in those days.

Neil arrived at the beginning of the next shift, becoming an ally and a friend straight away. It was good to have a pal of the same age at work, who was intelligent, keen and fit. It was obvious to all of us that he was going to go a long way in the service. The boring maintenance and cleaning jobs that we carried out every morning became much less tedious as the pair of us had a similar sense of humour. Monty Python sketches could be heard being recited and laughed about as we checked and oiled the equipment. * *I am pleased to note that Neil is one of a small handful of guys, from all the hundreds I have known over the years, that I am still in contact with.*

I passed my sub-officer's qualification without too much difficulty and began to think about the last one of the five, the station officers exam. The final two days of exams had ended many an ambitious fireman's progress. There was a huge scope of subjects that had to be memorised and a knowledge of chemistry and hydraulics was also necessary to gain a pass. I began the task of distilling all of the information held in the fifteen manuals into note form. Once that was done, I cut my notes down to memorable phrases, rhymes, pictures and easily remembered lists. I was determined to pass with my first attempt, hoping to finally put my O level fiasco behind me.

Everything in the workplace was going well. I was a member of a modern, well-equipped brigade with plenty of promotion on offer. My watch, especially now Neil had joined us, was a good blend of experience and youth. Most shifts were spent laughing and enjoying ourselves whilst we worked. The old heads loved passing on their skills and we attended enough incidents to keep things interesting. Our guvnor, Phil, reached the age of fifty five and decided to retire leaving the door open to me having a spell as a temporary leading fireman. Partly because nobody else was interested in taking the job.

As ever with me, when all seemed tip-top, there was a problem looming on the horizon.

I wasn't a Hertfordshire lad, I missed the sea and I hated being on the edge of London, with all the traffic, the pollution, the noise, the masses of people. When the weather warmed up a bit, by about April, the air always felt humid and oppressive. Living so far inland when I was used to walking down the end of the road to the sea on a hot day, troubled me constantly. The Thames passed through the village where I lived, so I often swam there in the summer but even when I was cooling off in the water, boats chugged past all the time coughing out diesel fumes. The mountains and wild country that I loved was several hours drive away, inaccessible except for holidays. Developers had bought all the farmland around my village and sat on it just waiting for planning permission. My journey to work, which was just about manageable, was bound to become much slower when the dual-carriageway I travelled on was incorporated as part of the new M25. When the London Orbital motorway was finally opened it was bound to suck in traffic and businesses from the rest of the UK, making it even busier in my neck of the woods.

All I wanted was a tidy little house in the countryside with a bit of land, peace and quiet, with a job in the fire brigade not too far from home. Surely that wasn't too much to ask?

One of the historical oddities about UK fire brigades is that firemen could quite easily move between them. The qualifications and training courses were all the same, often run nationally, in fact. Most fire stations had a couple of blokes working in them who had transferred from afar. Scots and Welsh accents could be heard from Cornwall to Kent. Sometimes firemen moved to be closer to elderly parents, or just to get away from their home town because they were bored with it. It was quite easy to move to somewhere a bit shabby, whilst transfers to lovely seaside towns occurred rarely. If a brigade had a couple of vacancies but didn't want to run a full recruit training course, they would happily take a couple of trained and experienced men from elsewhere. It was all a bit swings and roundabouts and benefited everyone. When senior officer's vacancies arose, they usually would be advertised across the UK. Candidates travelled all over the country looking to move up a rank in a new brigade. This was a double-edged sword, if a total duffer was trying to get promotion by moving elsewhere, his chief would sometimes write him a fantastic reference to get shot of him.

I decided to write to all of the fire brigades around Britain's coastline, except the industrial ones like Cleveland, and to a few of the prettier inland places like Derbyshire. I had to exclude the one I really wanted, Dorset, because that was the only one my wife refused to countenance. A warning of things to come, that in my youthful naivety I failed to recognise. I suspect Dorset would have given me the move I wanted, as I was a local boy with a good reason to want the transfer, knew the area well and had passed all of my exams so far.

As it was, I wrote seventeen letters, to places as far flung as Grampian and Highlands and Islands and left things in the lap of the gods. I had to tell Herts of my intentions and, not surprisingly they disapproved and tried to talk me out of going. I was a temporary leading fireman after less than three years service and was destined for a good career, why on earth would I want to move elsewhere, I was asked? My colleagues couldn't understand why I had applied to parts of Scotland and Wales, "where it rains all the effing time and they don't like the English either."

After a couple of weeks in my new temporary rank I was allowed to be in charge of the emergency tender, attending RTAs. This was pretty nerve-wracking the first time, although I was always given a driver who was vastly experienced and would hopefully keep me right. On my first turn out we belted down the M1 horns blaring and lights flashing to the incident. I looked across and asked, "what do you think we should do?"

The driver turned to me and said, "Eff knows, you're the boss!"

That off the cuff remark made me realise it wasn't a game anymore, this was serious stuff and if I wanted to progress I needed to show some leadership, take responsibility and stop mucking about so much. To achieve the management level I wanted to eventually be at, I shouldn't be sitting around waiting to be noticed. I needed to be running through the gears. Pushing on. Making a name for myself.

I reasoned that any brigade I moved to, would be fairly similar to Hertfordshire in their working practises and culture, so promotion would be based on merit and performance. What innocence.

I received a few negative replies from brigades and began to feel a bit despondent about my chances of transferring.

Going Back in Time.

Then, one summer's day, it came. A vacancy had arisen in the UK's smallest fire brigade, Dumfries and Galloway, in south-west Scotland. I knew about the area because my wife and I had driven through the region on our way to a lovely wedding on Strangford loch in Ireland the year before. We had also taken the train along the northern coast from Stranraer to Glasgow on the way home from a caving holiday two years previously, when we marvelled at the views. The countryside was virtually empty. Mostly green hilly farmland with a few lochs and rugged low peaks. The sea bordered two sides of the region. The only full-time fire station was Dumfries, on the Solway Firth. Not too far from the Lake District for a day out walking, I noted. I never felt that living in Scotland would be a problem for me, my grandfather had moved the other way, so I had Scottish ancestry and I had spent over five years in the Highland Gunners without any trouble. I promptly rang the brigade and asked if I could come and pay them a preliminary visit.

A couple of weeks later Jeanette and I found ourselves in the orange Maxi bombing up the M6 over Shap Summit, then slowly through Gretna Green and finally turning left for Dumfries. It was a beautiful warm summer day and we were full of optimism about a new life. During our week's reconnaissance we explored the beaches, hills and the pretty, quiet market towns. I visited the fire station and was introduced to a divisional officer who looked and dressed like the headmaster from Whacko! After a brief chat he took me to have a few words with the firemaster. Very casual, I had never met the chief fire officer in Herts in three years. We talked for a while about my reasons for wanting to move, my experiences and my ambitions for higher rank. He offered me a job on the spot, subject to a good reference. I wasn't required to take a medical, even. I couldn't think of a good reason to turn his offer down so, with a handshake, I agreed and launched myself into a huge adventure in a different fire brigade, with new colleagues and a big, wild country to explore.

A few weeks later, after a leaving party at Garston fire station, I found myself on the train heading north. I had with me my treader, my rucksack and a case full of clothes. Jeanette was staying behind to complete our house sale to a developer, who was buying all of the long gardens in our road, then filling the plot with cramped little houses. I had found myself comfortable lodgings with a very friendly lady, whose main aim seemed to be to double my weight with giant helpings of Scottish food.

My preliminary visit to my new watch was very odd. The station officer wasn't impressed with an English lad coming, so when he showed me round he spoke in the accent his home village would have used a hundred years ago. I hardly understood a word he said all evening. Never mind, things were bound to improve. Unfortunately, I didn't find the guys to be in quite the same mould as my previous bunch. Strangely, I was no more an outsider than several of the lads on the eighteen man watch. Little groups kept themselves to themselves within the team, whilst several of the blokes appeared to not really get on with anyone. There was the little ruling clique, the gamblers, the sporty lads, the masons, the group from one town who thought the lads from another town to be below them. And there was the Catholic.

Another big difference that I noted was that tradesmen didn't fill the ranks, so working with heavy cutting equipment and mechanical tools was not second nature to these guys, with a few exceptions. The brigade employed quite a few lads who could pass the entrance exam but had never done an apprenticeship, so they started their training with a very low skill level. Us ex-forces lads hardly had a look in, either, there were only about five of us out of one hundred full-timers.

Because it was a one whole time station brigade, with sixteen retained stations, in a sparsely populated area, fires and RTA's were few and far between. So it took a long time to gain useful knowledge. I found that the retained firemen, who mostly worked as tradesmen in their local community, had just as much experience and fire fighting skills as the wholetime lads. Sometimes more.

I was issued with a firefighting uniform on my first shift. My modern Nomex tunic was put away and a Korky the Cat donkey jacket was given to me, two sizes too big. That was all they had. And a pair of bin men's rubber gloves, instead of the comfortable close fitting leather ones that I was used to. I decided to keep wearing my Herts tunic which I received abuse for but it wasn't safe to wear a tunic that had sleeves longer than my arms!

A breathing apparatus wearing exercise was organised on my behalf, to check that I knew how to operate it. The boss also wanted to see if I could search buildings properly. That was a bit of a cheek but I had to go along with it. During the exercise, the station officer kept appearing out of the smoke to see that I used the correct procedures. My only problem was working out what my teammate was trying to say to me. Hearing was difficult enough when your oppo spoke through a mask but when his accent and yours differed greatly it became almost impossible sometimes.

I quickly learnt what "yer ken" and many other local phrases meant. When it was my turn to do the watch's food shopping I was sent for the messages. On the day I had to drive to Stranraer fire station to deliver some kit I was told it would be best to take my piece with me. Blimey, it was like being back in the army. Later, I realised a piece was a packed lunch not a handgun. That was a relief.

On my second day shift the watch had arranged an RTA drill, where two old bangers from the scrappy had been dropped off for us to cut up in the drillyard. After the guys had spent a long time using some old fashioned and underpowered tools to cut the roof off, I told the watch during the debrief that in Herts we used a powerful petrol driven disc cutter that did the job in a few seconds. I said that we used it every week up and down the M1 with no problems whatsoever. It was a wonderful piece of kit, simple and reliable, I told them.

I couldn't believe my ears when I was mocked by the officer in charge and told not to be so stupid. His sidekicks amongst the group joined in, openly laughing at my comment. They said quite adamantly that you couldn't use such a tool to cut open cars as the sparks would set them on fire. Being one against about fourteen, I shrugged and shut up. I didn't bother making any suggestions again for several years, even though the brigade was obviously light years behind the more forward thinking ones in the country, as regards equipment and rescue techniques.

On my days off I cycled around the estate agents in town, looking for houses that had just come onto the market. My plan was to buy somewhere within ten miles of work so I could cycle in for my shifts. Jeanette would then have the car for her job, whatever that may turn out to be. If I wasn't searching for a new home, I was out running along the coast or walking around Dumfries, getting to know the roads and buildings. On wet days or during the evenings, I studied for my upcoming station officer's exam.

Nothing suitable was for sale locally, so one sunny day I caught the bus out to Castle Douglas, about twenty miles away. I sauntered down the high street of the pleasant little market town and found the estate agent at the bottom of the hill. The first house I saw in the window looked just perfect, so I went inside to ask for details. Ten minutes later I found myself marching out of town the four miles to the village of Crossmichael, where the pretty house was situated.

The dwelling was as lovely as the brochure had shown and in a truly beautiful location. About four hundred yards from the village and near one end of a twelve mile long loch. On the other side was a quiet road then rough farmland slowly becoming open rough fell. I loved the feel of the place straight away. The owner was expecting me and she welcomed me in for a cup of tea and a look around. Her husband was a big man, a farmer, sadly riddled with arthritis, who painfully helped out on his brother's farm just across the road. They wanted to move into another farm a short distance away, to double the amount of land they could work together. We hit it off straight away, the only problem with the property was that the flat roof on the extended kitchen leaked badly. The rain in Galloway could be really heavy for weeks on end and the walls ran with water on those occasions. A new kitchen roof was all that was needed.

I visited again a few days later to discuss a price acceptable to both parties. I opened with a figure that I could afford and the old guy smiled. Offer £1,000 more and we can shake on it here and now he said. That would save us the bother of closed bids and solicitors becoming involved. I agreed, we shook hands and the sale was done. Included in the deal was first pick from the litter that his Border Collie was soon to produce. His daughter came in the room at this point and complained about him selling to the English but he cut her short and told her not to be stupid.

Back in Bourne End the house sale was completed in early December, so I caught the train down south, hired a self-drive removals lorry and brought our possessions back up along with the two cats. By this time I had made a few friends on the watch and they very cheerfully came along to help unpack our stuff into the house. We had made it.

Christmas Eve was spent in the village pub, The Thistle, famous for it's two hundred whiskeys. The locals welcomed us warmly and early on Christmas day we staggered back down the hill to our lovely new home.

A few weeks later, I sat in a technical college classroom with a group of other hopefuls from work, to sit the station officer's exam. Some of the lads showed up every year with almost no hope of passing as they did little or no preparation. They were relying on this year being the easy year that was often spoken about. Evidently, in Scotland, there was a shortage of suitably qualified sub. officers to fill the rank above, as the exam took a lot of work and preparation. Very few were willing to commit to it. The lads, therefore, reckoned that sometime they would have to have an easy year to let a few more become qualified. (They were proved right and a couple of years later they almost all passed, much to everyone's total amazement).

Personally, I was feeling very confident because I had put so much work into my studies. I had taken copious notes, then taken notes of the notes and ended up with a few sheets of vital lists that I knew off by heart. My head was full of little rhythms and stories that I had made up to help me remember the information I needed to know. My O level misery still rankled with me. Passing the five fire brigade exams without failure had become a very big deal for me. Failure was not an option.

Divisional Officer Whacko began handing out the first of four question papers for the exam. When he arrived at my desk he looked down hard at me and said, "You might have passed your sub's exam in England but you'll never pass your station officer's exam in Scotland."

Charming. Nothing like a bit of encouragement. The hydraulics and chemistry questions troubled me for a while but by the time I left the room at the end of the second day of exams I knew I had passed.

A month later I turned up at work for a night shift and felt the air of excitement as I walked into the appliance bay. I was informed that four lads had passed the exam, three of them had been told but one more had yet to be revealed. A few of the guys on my shift remained hopeful that it was them. When we finished our roll call a few minutes later, I was handed a note from the Firemaster congratulating me on my result. Passed, much to the disgust of a few others. I was absolutely delighted that I had managed to get through all of the necessary exams in three and a half years. I hoped that I could now work my way up the ranks, start earning a decent wage and have the chance to use my brain a bit more, rather than just doing the mundane work I was ordered to do.

Making a Go of Things

Our leaking kitchen was a major problem, with water running down the wall when it rained. I had employed a local part-time builder to put a pitched roof over the old flat one but he hadn't rendered the outside wall because I said that I would do it to save money. It couldn't be that hard, surely? Three times I mixed the cement then climbed the homemade scaffolding, having worked out how to apply the grey sloppy mix. And three times the rain clouds came and washed it straight back off of the lightweight blocks. Eventually I managed to get some to stick long enough for it to dry. I kept climbing back up and slapping some more on, over the next few days. There was twice as much on the ground as on the house. By the time I had finished it looked terrible, like I had just chucked it at the wall blindfolded, from beneath, but at least it kept the water out.

By this time, mid spring 1986, we had settled into the house and I wondered when my wife would start looking for a job. Dumfries had several large factories all with laboratories. The forestry industry was huge in Galloway and many interesting opportunities were out there for someone with her qualifications and experience. I was shocked, therefore, when she decided to set up a small garden nursery, selling plants from home. We only had the plants that grew in the garden, our greenhouse was tiny and she was no gardener.

I had bought a house that incurred more expense than my meagre fire brigade pay. I was back in the financial mire. If I had known of my wife's intention to not find proper work, but to rely on me making enough money for both of us, I would never have left Hertfordshire.

We lived in an era where the mortgage rate changed from month to month. When the chancellor announced a rate change upwards that meant our mortgage payment went up immediately, sometimes by a hundred pounds or more. Some months, any part-time I earned was wiped out in one go, by a short statement from the government.

Working on the side had been respected in my last brigade, only the lazy didn't have a second income. Being on the edge of London, with it's huge population, meant there was plenty of opportunity too. Up in Galloway it was very different. The firemaster frowned on us earning a bit extra and permission had to be sought. His network of cronies extended through the brigade from top to bottom so anyone doing a bit on the side was usually seen and gossiped about.

There was none of the respectful lights out at 11pm to get a good sleep, either. Those that played golf or watched daytime telly on their days off, would come into the dormitory at all hours of the night, turning lights on and talking loudly. The part-timers workers who were all tucked up, cursed them as they tossed and turned, trying to get a bit of kip.

I found a bit of work with two local farmers. One had me picking carrots. Pull them in the morning, cut the green stalk off and bag them in the afternoon. £1.70 a sack. Soul destroying, backbreaking misery. The other one paid me to do tasks like putting in new gate posts on his hill farm. Slightly better but the weather was almost always damp and drizzly up on the hills, which caused me, my boots and all the tools to be covered in glutinous, sticky mud.

A slightly more pleasant way of earning some cash arrived in the form of a new neighbour. Katie had just moved into and had extended the old farmhouse just along the railway track from us. Her huge new garden was once a set of dairy buildings that her builder had knocked down and covered in earth. My job was general dogsbody, garden worker and digger up of rocks and slabs of old outbuildings. She knew I was very much in need of the work and gave me as many hours as my back could cope with.

I ran a few miles as often as I could and during the spring and summer evenings would nip across the field to the loch and go for a skinny dip. Often there was a little mist over the reeds and maybe a Buzzard circling overhead. I usually swam past the headland and over to the little sailing club by the village before returning home, my aching muscles eased and loosened a little.

The sport of triathlon was devised in the late 1970s by three highly competitive Kiwi naval officers, a runner, a swimmer and a cyclist, who came up with a novel event to find out who was the fittest amongst them. Within ten years the sport had caught on across the world as an exciting new way for athletes to compete against one another. Cheshire fire brigade hosted the first UK firemen's national triathlon in Chester and I was on the start line with several hundred others, from all over the country. A fleet of buses transported us all from the fire station across the town in our swimming cossies. Someone said we looked like a day out for rejected Chippendales as we sat on the bus with pedestrians gawping in at us, whilst we waited at traffic lights.

The swim was one mile down the river Dee right through the centre of the lovely Roman town. The chief officer hauled the swimmers out one by one up a ladder at the far end. The race continued with the cycle and the run across the Duke of Westminster's huge estate. I came a respectable 44th and drove home elated. I had heard that our village pub was organising a local triathlon and I started training for that.

Keeping fit and healthy helped me cope with the increasingly unfriendly atmosphere at work and the problems at home. Once again, I was reminded that training hard to build strength and fitness breeds the confidence and willpower to overcome life's many obstacles. Exercise and a good diet, without too much drinking, helped keep me optimistic about the future. Endorphins are a very powerful antidepressant.

Back at work again, I spent several weeks getting to grips with the brigade's ancient turntable ladder. The ladder came in three extending sections, controlled by hydraulics and wires. The chassis was longer and wider than a fire engine by some distance and, as a shortarse, I found driving it rather awkward as my feet left the pedals every time the vehicle hit a little bump. Aiming the tip of the ladder at a window and resting it gently on the sill over one hundred feet away was quite an art and required a good eye. An older lad called Lee, one of the `favoured ones`, had been learning how to operate the turntable at the same time as me. He was, by some margin, the laziest fireman I have ever come across. Lee put far more effort into avoiding work than he would have used up just getting stuck in and doing the job.

The day arrived when the examining officer from headquarters took the pair of us and two firemen, to act as gophers, to a local church for our practical exam. Lee went first. He sited the ladder, put the stabilising legs down on hard ground then pitched the ladder onto a castellated part of the roof. The examiner, an old friend of Lee`s, smiled and told him to pack up. He had passed with flying colours.

The two gophers, pals of mine, one a builder and one a chippy, remarked happily that we should be back home for tea break as that only took ten minutes. Into the hot seat I went and pitched to the same place on the roof.

"Ok," said the officer, "now move the ladder to that window round the corner."

I lowered the ladder and moved the platform into a better position, then extended it. I gently rested the head of the ladder, bang dead centre of the cill. Surely he would be happy with that? But no. "Not bad," now pitch it to the top of that dormer window."

My pals looked dismayed, their sausage baps would be going cold by now. Up went the ladder, once again a reasonable pitch. He still wasn't satisfied.

"Bring it down laddie," he grunted, disappointed that I knew just how to operate the ladder.

I will f******g laddie you, I thought.

To our amazement he then asked me to pitch it back to the same place using the manual pumping equipment, only ever used in an emergency when the hydraulics failed. I had only taken a cursory look at the operation because nobody was ever asked to demonstrate its use. My pals shook their heads and even Lee was embarrassed at how I was being treated, compared to him. We pumped and sweated and finally the ladder hit the spot and I glared at the officer. Anymore, you miserable bastard? I was tested for nearly two hours. Once we had brought the ladder back down he grudgingly let me know that I had done ok and had passed. I am sure that when he ate lunch with his fellow officers later on, he would have told them with satisfaction that I barely scraped a pass.

A few weeks later I ran for three hours and forty four minutes, whilst competing in the Newton Stewart marathon. Amazingly, even a tiny town in the middle of the Galloway hills managed to host a long distance race every year that attracted hundreds of enthusiastic entrants. After I had finished the race, I grabbed a quick shower before heading off to my night shift. I had managed to wangle things so that I would be the turntable ladder driver. My reasoning being that it never went anywhere at night, so I could get some much needed rest. Inevitably, I suppose, at about four in the morning, after I had stiffened up nicely, the tannoy called both pumps and the TTL to an alarm sounding at the hospital. Dear me, I could hardly get out of my pit, let alone run down the stairs or slide down the famous fireman's pole. I staggered down the staircase and just about made it to the vehicle, every step an agony for my swollen knees. The climb up to the cab looked impossibly high with my lactic acid stiffened legs. After much complaining they bent just far enough for me to pull myself up by my arms and off we went, sirens wailing, to yet another false alarm, burnt toast.

Lift Him up by the Oxters

I was now the only fireman in the station who was qualified to the rank of station officer, a requirement in Dumfries at the time to gain your first promotion. So I was the next in line whether they liked it or not. I was therefore sent on a leading fireman's course at the Scottish Fire Service Training School, in preparation for a vacancy becoming available.

The SFSTS was where all Scottish fire service recruits went for their initial training. Beautifully situated in the lovely golfing village of Gullane, to the east of Edinburgh, just down the road from Muirfield. The building was an old golfing hotel, converted many years ago to house up to one hundred and twenty recruits at a time. The school also ran courses in other essential firefighting skills for experienced firemen. In the huge drill yard stood three towers, usually with the cold wind blowing off the North Sea whipping around the tops, for ladder pitching. Behind the drill yard stood a very effective fire house where temperatures often reached up to two hundred degrees centigrade which gave the firemen an incredibly realistic and difficult building to train inside.

Discipline was rigorously enforced, the instructors always had to be called sir. Recruits stood up when an instructor entered the room. About two thirds of training time was spent doing practical work, the remainder being in the lecture room. Evenings saw recruits studying, cleaning and ironing their kit. On Friday mornings they had an inspection by the commandant. On that day almost everybody, including any instructors that were drinkers, stood with terrible hangovers, swaying and staggering in ragged open order in the yard as the commie strutted past. Thursday evening was the traditional night for getting pissed in the village's three pubs and most recruits had more than earnt a beer by then.

When I arrived there on the first Monday morning of my course, I had the disadvantage of not spending fourteen weeks at Gullane doing my recruit training, like the other twenty lads on the course had. They knew the layout of the fire house and where the trapdoors and exits were. I had never seen the building before. In Hertfordshire there was a far smaller building to use for BA training, this one was like a big two storey factory.

We spent the first morning in the lecture room being briefed. I was, straight away, extremely impressed by the instructor's bearing and knowledge. Leading firemen apply to become an instructor at the school and, if accepted, serve for two years there. Part of the contract is the promise of promotion to the next rank when they return to their own brigade.

The aim of our course was to teach us some management skills and also to weed out those who couldn't lecture or control a fire house exercise. Some of my fellow trainees didn't want to be there and wasted their time, getting drunk every night and being surly. The rest of us gave it our all and picked up as much of the knowledge being passed on as we could.

One afternoon we sat in the video conference room where a huge old video camera had been set up. The game was that the senior instructor handed us each in turn, a bag from which we put our hand in and selected an article. Once we pulled something out, we had thirty seconds to gather our thoughts, before delivering a two minute talk about the item to the camera. I pulled out a little cardboard parcel label which gave me plenty to ramble on about. One bright spark from Glasgow pulled out a Tune, a small cough sweet. He unwrapped it, popped it into his mouth and stared into the camera for the two minutes, sucking it quietly but not saying a word. The rest of us were in stitches. Somehow, I don't think he wanted to be there!

Before we planned and then ran our own fire house exercises, the school set up one for us to partake in. They said it would blow away the cobwebs and remind us what sort of temperatures and workrate we could stand.

The firehouse was a concrete building, built like a factory with partitions, internal ship's ladders and a room at one end with a big metal crib bolted to the floor. In that crib went an endless supply of pallets which provided the heat and flames. Smoke generators could also be used to make it more claustrophobic. It was pitch dark inside anyway, in the rooms away from the roaring fire. Instructors, who ghosted around in blacked out gear, enjoyed hosing water above the fire to increase the humidity and therefore the fatigue and suffering of those carrying out the exercise.

I was paired up with a Glaswegian lad. We entered the building on the top floor, wearing BA, carrying a hose reel and a coil of rope. Immediately, we felt the heat from the fire and began searching the room we had entered. Once we had groped our way around the walls of the room we checked the middle for casualties then moved on to the next one. We were both experienced firemen so we hardly needed to communicate, a mumbled "ok?" was usually enough.

Through the door it was even hotter, like a furnace. Our plastic leggings burnt our legs if we stretched them tightly over our thighs by bending down. We checked our gauges by the light of a torch, goodo, plenty of air left. A facemask appeared out of the murk under a black helmet, looked at us and moved away, an instructor keeping an eye on us. We found our target, a ship's ladder going down to the ground floor. At the hatch it was searing hot, the heat from the fire came up through it like a chimney. My partner quickly climbed down, then kicked the ladder and stood back. My signal to come on down. At the bottom our hose reel became badly snagged up for a couple of minutes. That damned facemask appeared again watching how we dealt with it. We moved on, by now soaking wet right through to our vests and feeling the effects of the heat and humidity. Thankfully, whilst doing our foot sweeps across the floor we bumped against a dummy, finally we could now turn around and head out, away from the heat. Another gauge check, then, between us, we picked up the stiff canvas body, about 50 or 60 kg in weight, all arms and stiff legs. One in front of the other we shuffled back to the ladder. This was seriously hard work. We found the metal ladder and held a conflab. I was to tie a bowline around the chest of the dummy, my mucker was to climb up first, then haul aloft whilst I lifted from below. All in the dark at about one hundred and fifty degree centigrade. As I started tying I knew the facemask would come leering back into view, haha, there it was, right on cue, checking my knot tying ability. No problems there, being a Sea Scout paid off eventually. I sat the dummy at the bottom of the ladder then yelled "haul aloft." My partner began pulling on the rope as I started lifting from below. He didn't have the strength left to lift the dummy and thought I must be resting, so he yelled down to me, "lift him up by the oxters."

What the f**k are his oxters, I wondered? I was doing my best to lift the dummy already but struggling to get a grip on the stiff canvas in my bin men's gloves. Eventually, with much sweating and gasping for air, we stood him up. Very slowly, I climbed the ladder with the dummy on my shoulder whilst matey hauled away. At the top we groaned and puffed, our air nearly gone, our whistles about to sound a ten minute warning. We whipped off the rope and staggered to the exit, just about keeping the body off the floor, with his head safe from banging on the walls. As we left the building the first whistle peeped. Just in time.

We saw several other teams who had exited the building before us. They sat against the building or lay on the ground, soaking wet with sweat, completely exhausted. Some were drinking saline solution to help revive them. At these times, it is interesting to see who is most knackered.

It is not helpful, when wearing breathing apparatus in a fire situation, to be built like a bodybuilder or a prop forward. The big lads generally use up their air much quicker than the racing snakes.In fires, I sometimes saw them make their way to the part of a building where the search or firefighting operations were taking place, only to have to then turn around and head straight back out before their whistle blew. They had used all their air up just getting to the job. They often struggle, too, when climbing internal ladders and crawling through confined spaces. Team members must have enough physical strength to rescue their partner if he is injured inside the building. So that is another disadvantage for the big lads, they are much more difficult to extricate from a building if they go down. The best build for a breathing apparatus wearer is that of a mountaineer. Strong but lithe. The big lads powerful come into their own in other areas. Pitching ladders, carrying pumps and equipment, knocking things down and using heavy rescue equipment.

After we had collected our tallies from the control and taken a long drink of saline I asked my new pal what oxters were? He looked at me with a confused expression on his red, sweaty and smudged with smoke, fizzog.

"Oxters are under your arms, you English numpty."

"Oh, I see," I answered, annoyed by his attitude, "so you meant me to lift him by the armpits. What the f**k do you think I was lifting him by, his ears?"

The days flew in, those of us who put the work in had a fun time, the end of course piss up came all too soon for me. I loved my morning run along the beach. Somedays I dived into the freezing water and dashed back to my room soaking wet. All good bracing stuff, wonderful for my morale and the cold waves set me up for the day.

A Cunning Plan

When I heard that the instructors received one hundred pounds per week trainers allowance plus petrol money, a cunning plan began to form in my mind. I enjoyed teaching, the school was very well run, the senior staff and instructors were mostly good guys. This could be the path to my next rank and an end to part-time work on rainy Galloway hillsides. I left on the final Friday afternoon wondering if I could get back to the school again.

My plan came to fruition. A year after my two weeks at Gullane, I applied for a post there and was called in for an interview. The tape of me giving a two minute talk on my previous course was dusted down and viewed by the selection panel. Thank god I didn't just suck on a Tune. I gave a lecture to them about a piece of fire brigade equipment and answered a host of questions about my reason for wanting to be an instructor. I omitted to mention that I really needed the money. A short while later I began a very enjoyable two year stint as an instructor, with some of the best lads I ever had the privilege to work and play with. I spent the most pleasant time of my fire brigade career, passing on the skills and knowledge I had been taught, or picked up along the way. Some of those techniques and disciplines came from my earliest days in uniform, the cubs and sea scouts, where I learnt to tie knots and had my first taste of uniformed discipline. From the CCF, where I began to learn what endurance was and how to dig deep and keep going, when all I wanted to do was to pack in and go home. And, of course, from 19 Regiment, where I found out how to carry on whatever the weather, however tired and hungry I was, to get the job done. The military had been where I finally grew into a man with confidence, humour and a bit of steel.

It was a very satisfying feeling to become one of the best. The breathing apparatus instructor in the black fire gear, completely at home in the smoke, heat and fire. I was finally in top gear.

However, there was one more major incident in my life to be faced before I could start enjoying those halcyon days as an instructor. Because, a couple of months after the leading fireman's course came the long night that the firemen, police, military and civilian helpers who attended, will never forget. Next on my agenda was the cold, frosty night of 21st December, 1988 and the terrible tragedy of the last flight of Clipper, Maid of the Seas.

Printed in Great Britain
by Amazon